Through the
Rainbow Canyon

"Rhyolite Walls of Meadow Valley Canyon at Carson's Ranch." Plate VIa of "Descriptive Geology of Nevada South of the Fortieth Parallel and Adjacent Portions of California", J.E. Spurr, U.S. Geological Survey Bulletin 208, 1903. The ranch became the Elliott ranch. This 2000-foot cliff is west of the house; in the winter, the sun comes up late and goes down early.

Through the Rainbow Canyon

WALTER R. AVERETT

GRAND JUNCTION, COLORADO 81503
1995

© 1995 by Walter R. Averett
Published by Walter R. Averett
Grand Junction, CO 81503
Published in the United States of America
All rights reserved.

ISBN 0-87062-237-4
Library of Congress Catalog Card No. 95-094459

Also written and published by Walter R. Averett: Directory of Southern
Nevada Place Names, Las Vegas, Nev., 1956, and Rev. Ed., 1962, reprint-
ed 1963

Text is composed in Palatino type, page format designed by Kitty
Nicholason, Pyramid Printing, Grand Junction. Printed by Pyramid
Printing, Grand Junction. Bound by Mountain States Bindery, Salt Lake City.

Photos from the collection of Walter R. Averett unless otherwise credited.
Ink drawings by Walter R. Averett. Harold Bryant cartoon of wild horses
courtesy of Walker D. Wyman.

FRONTISPIECE:
"Rhyolite Walls of Meadow Valley Canyon at Carson's Ranch." Plate VIa
of "Descriptive Geology of Nevada South of the Fortieth Parallel and
Adjacent Portions of California", J.E. Spurr, U.S. Geological Survey
Bulletin 208, 1903. The ranch became the Elliott ranch. This 2000-foot cliff
is west of the house; in the winter, the sun comes up late and goes down
early.

TITLE PAGE:
Rock fence between Tunnel 5 and Elgin. Rocks are intercepted by wires
on angled crossarms or they landed behind the woven-wire fence; either
way, a broken wire caused a red block to be thrown in both directions to
warn that rocks might be on the track.

CONTENTS

ILLUSTRATIONS

PREFACE

Since the late 1950s I have been writing and rewriting a manuscript of some local history of southern Nevada, concentrating on the Rainbow Canyon, that part of the Meadow Valley Wash I knew in the 1930s and 1940s. The time is from about 1875 to 1945, with some updating into the 1990s.

Information for this book was drawn from personal interviews and letters, from a variety of published sources, from the Deed Records of the Lincoln County Recorder's Office, from files in the office of the U.S. Bureau of Land Management in Caliente, and from headstones in the Caliente and Bullionville cemeteries. The interpretations are mine unless specifically stated otherwise. If I have reservations about something I have heard or read, I express my concern when I pass it along. If I know of more than one version of an event or episode, I include the alternates.

This book is intended to be informal and readable, so I have not used a rigorously formal style when I cite references. Books are indicated briefly in the text, usually by citing the author's name, with the full identification in the Bibliography. Newspaper sources are mostly identified in the text.

Access to some of these sources was possible only through the assistance of other people. Some of the people who deserve special mention are Yuriko Setzer and Leslie Boucher, of the Lincoln County Recorder's office; Allison Cowgill and Annie Kelley of the Nevada State Library and Archive in Carson City; the Reference and Interlibrary Loan departments of Mesa County Public Library in Grand Junction; Trent Shaskan and Shawn Smith, of the BLM in Caliente; Lorell Bleak, Principal of Lincoln County High School; Dr. D. Don Francom, Lincoln County School District, Panaca; Wilma Bankston, who led me to Alice and Loren Rucker; and Alice Rucker, who found out where I could obtain microfilms of Nevada newspapers.

In the 1950s I spent a lot of time in the Clark County Recorder's office in Las Vegas, reading old newspapers from Las Vegas and Searchlight. In the 1960s I worked in the library of the Colorado School of Mines, Golden, searching through back issues of mining magazines. In 1993 and 1994 I mined the microfilm reels of Caliente, Pioche, and Las Vegas newspapers that were obtained on Interlibrary Loan from the Nevada State Library. I followed those veins in their dips, angles, and spurs, and sometimes I opened up a bonanza. That was fun!

All the talk of places where things happened would, in my opinion, be nothing but a jumble of confused information without a map to show where these places are (or were). These were my two most important groups of maps: (1) The 72-minute sheets (scale 1:24,000) of the U.S. Geological Survey, especially the Caliente, Carp, Elgin, Elgin NE, Ella Mountain, Leith, Lyman Crossing, and Vigo sheets. (2) The 1:100,000-scale Surface Management Status maps of the U.S. Bureau of Land Management, especially the Caliente, Nev.-Utah, and the Clover Mts., Nev.-Utah sheets. From them, I have prepared two maps to show the general lay of the land and the specific locations of some of the places or features.

As people dig deeper into the relationships between human activity and the environment, greater and greater amounts of detail about commonplace activities are needed. The study of the way in which groups of people think of their environment and adapt to it is called "ethnoecology". Such a study goes far beyond the limits of a manuscript such as this, but if the study were ever performed for this area, this information would contribute to it.

Someone recently asked me why I pursue these stories to such a level of detail and with such concern for making them accurate and complete. My answer was that, first, I am interested in knowing more about the times and places where I lived, and second, some people are still alive who have this kind of information, and if we don't set the record straight, who will? Will anybody care? Yes.

And now, what's left to be done? Plenty. This book does not exhaust the subject of the Meadow Valley Wash. We need to know about the ranches between Carp and Moapa, and this book touches only fleetingly on the Meadow Valley Wash north of Caliente, and not much more is said about Clover Creek Canyon; we need the history of Caliente, Panaca (including Lincoln County High School), Delamar, Bullionville and Pioche and associated mining areas, and the Fay-Stateline mining area. This is my invitation to you to take it from here.

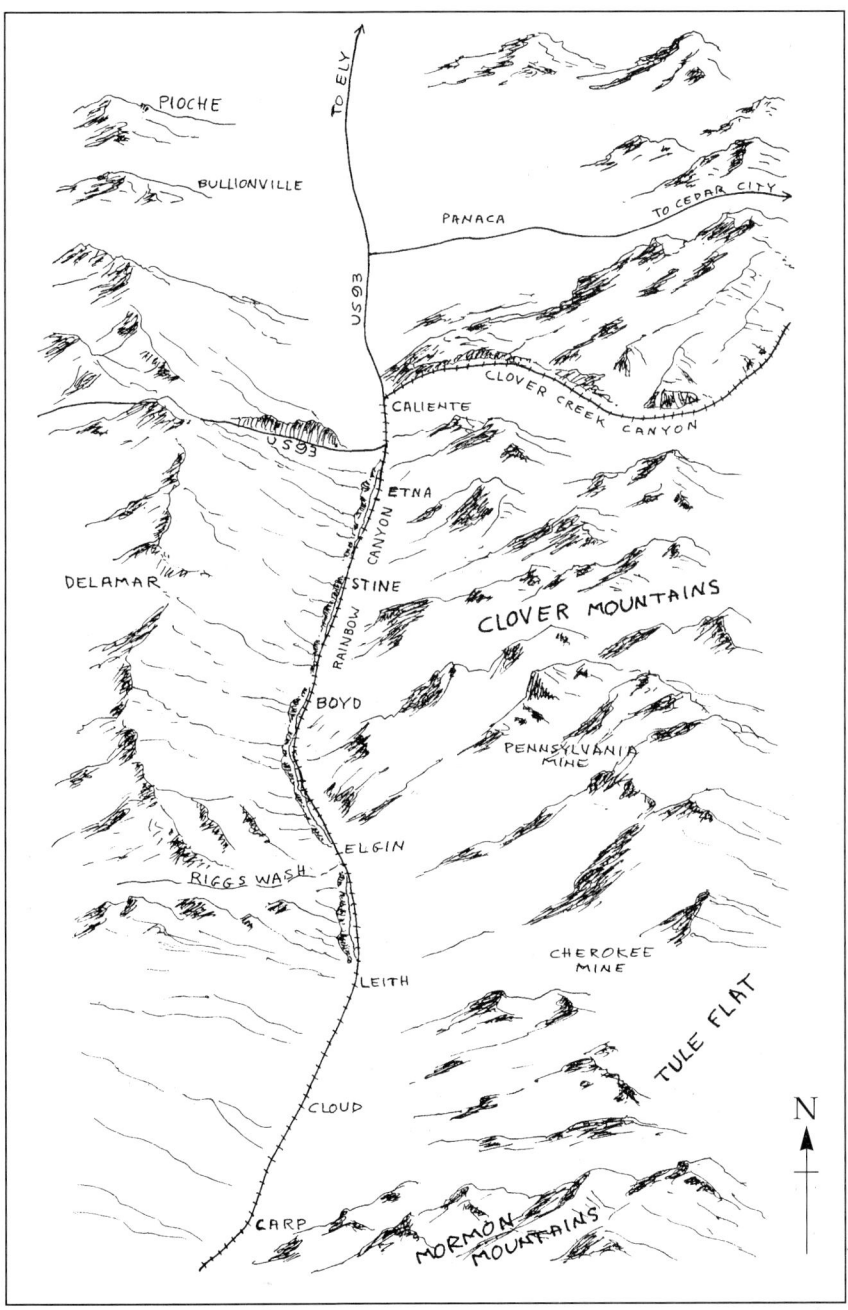

PIOCHE

BULLIONVILLE

TO ELY

PANACA

TO CEDAR CITY

US 93

CALIENTE

CLOVER CREEK CANYON

US 93

ETNA

STINE

DELAMAR

RAINBOW CANYON

CLOVER MOUNTAINS

BOYD

PENNSYLVANIA MINE

ELGIN

RIGGS WASH

CHEROKEE MINE

LEITH

TULE FLAT

CLOUD

N

CARP

MORMON MOUNTAINS

General features of the Rainbow Canyon country

NOT TO SCALE   WRA 2-95

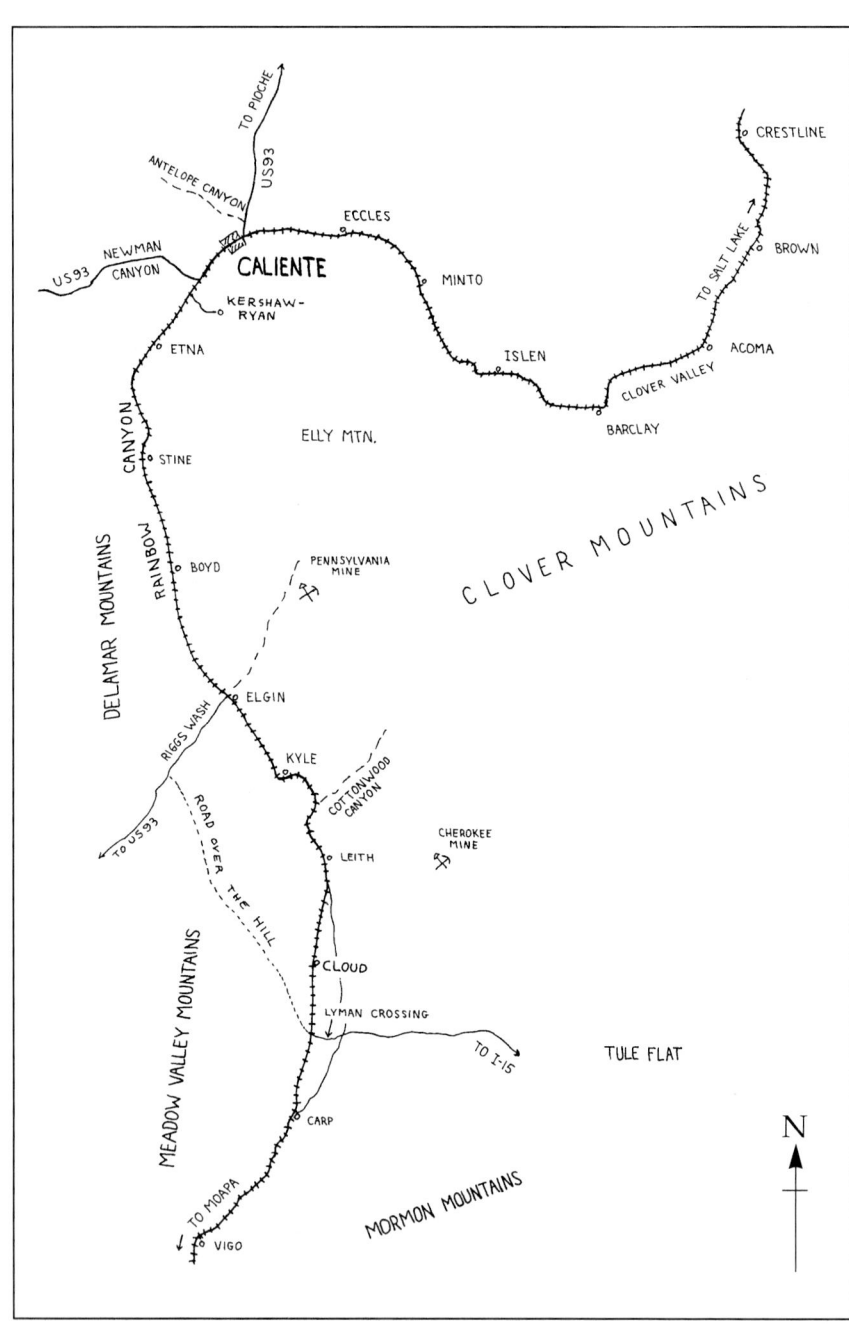

Locator map, Rainbow Canyon area

NOT TO SCALE   WRA 2-95

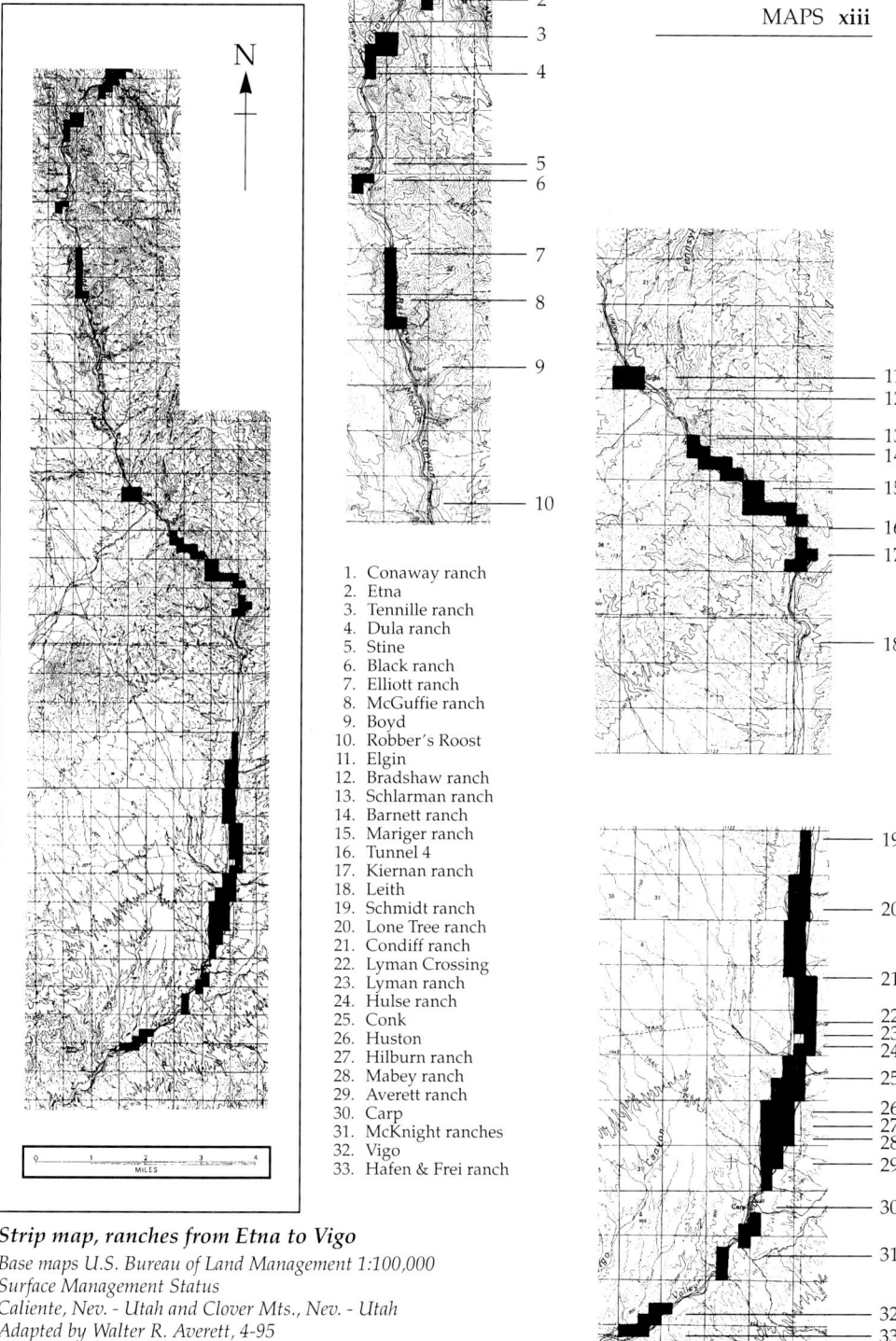

1. Conaway ranch
2. Etna
3. Tennille ranch
4. Dula ranch
5. Stine
6. Black ranch
7. Elliott ranch
8. McGuffie ranch
9. Boyd
10. Robber's Roost
11. Elgin
12. Bradshaw ranch
13. Schlarman ranch
14. Barnett ranch
15. Mariger ranch
16. Tunnel 4
17. Kiernan ranch
18. Leith
19. Schmidt ranch
20. Lone Tree ranch
21. Condiff ranch
22. Lyman Crossing
23. Lyman ranch
24. Hulse ranch
25. Conk
26. Huston
27. Hilburn ranch
28. Mabey ranch
29. Averett ranch
30. Carp
31. McKnight ranches
32. Vigo
33. Hafen & Frei ranch

Strip map, ranches from Etna to Vigo
Base maps U.S. Bureau of Land Management 1:100,000
Surface Management Status
Caliente, Nev. - Utah and Clover Mts., Nev. - Utah
Adapted by Walter R. Averett, 4-95

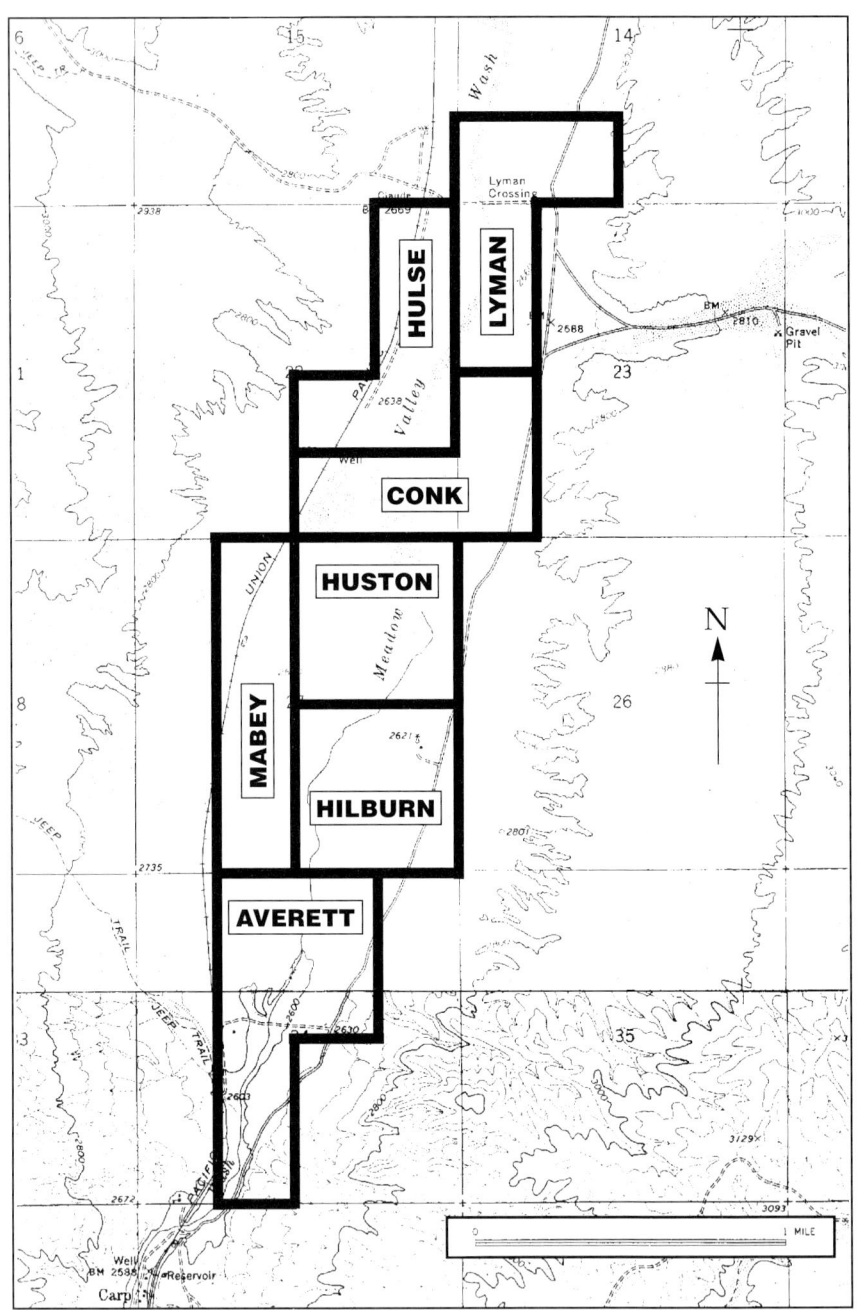

Ranches between Carp and Lyman Crossing

Base maps U.S. Geological Survey 7.5 Minute Quadrangles
Carp, Nevada, and Lyman Crossing, Nevada   Additions by Walter R. Averett, 4-95

CHAPTER 1

DOWN THE CANYON
TO CARP

THE SETTING

If you stand at the right place on the flank of the Wilson Creek Range, north-east of Pioche, you will be at the head of the Meadow Valley Wash. To reach the other end, you must go southward through wide valleys and narrow canyons, finally arriving at the valley of the Muddy River at Glendale. (A note about terminology: The drainage is from north to south, and when I refer to one place as "above" or "below" another, I mean north or south, respectively; Elgin is below Caliente and above Carp.)

The Meadow Valley Wash, in the most general sense, starts where the Wilson Creek Range breaks away into Ursine Valley; it runs south through Condor Canyon, the Meadow Valley (the valley in which Panaca is situated), the Rainbow Canyon, and finally into the Muddy River. In this book, it will mean the valleys and canyons between Caliente and Rox unless otherwise stated.

A very simplified geologic summary of the terrain between Caliente and Carp is as follows, drawn mainly from Tschantz and Pampeyan.

South and southeast of Caliente, about 600 feet of volcanic rocks (interbedded tuffaceous rocks and thin rhyolite flows, and welded tuffs) rest on a reddish or pink rhyolite. The uppermost unit is a dark-gray rhyolitic welded tuff. (Tuff is composed mostly of volcanic ash and

> In Pleistocene time, a lake, now called Lake Carpenter, filled the present Lake Valley, which runs from the area of the Geyser ranch south to near Pioche, so in a sense Lake Valley is the upper end of the Meadow Valley Wash. The two major drainages of Lincoln County are the White River and Pahranagat Valley system in the western half and the Meadow Valley Wash system in the eastern half.

dust that may have been hot enough to fuse into hard rock, as in the dark cliffs below Caliente, or that may have remained as fairly soft rock, as in the crumbly white rocks along the road at Stine and in Rock Springs Canyon. Don't confuse tuff with tufa, which is a calcium carbonate sedimentary deposit; those white rocks at Stine are often called tufa, but they are not.

Rhyolite consists of visible crystals of quartz or feldspar in a glassy matrix.)

The colorful rocks between Caliente and Boyd are various young volcanic rocks. Near Boyd, they give way to welded tuffs of darker color; they might have come from vents near Boyd. From there to Elgin, the deep, narrow canyon (sometimes called Palisade Canyon) is cut in dark welded tuffs that are technically called "ignimbrite", meaning they are the result of ash-flows, including some that were swift-moving incandescent clouds of ash and heavier fragments.

A bed of multiple thin basalts overlies some of the tuffs. As many as six basalt flows are visible north of Leith. The canyon opens out fairly rapidly just north of Leith, and from there past Carp, the hills consist of Tertiary and Quaternary gravels. (The Tertiary Period was from 65 million to 2 or 3 million years ago; the Quaternary Period is everything since then.)

M.S. Duffield, *Engineering and Mining Journal*, Jan. 28, 1904, described a trip along the line of the San Pedro, Los Angeles & Salt Lake Railroad (abbreviated here SPLA&SL), then under construction down the canyon south of Caliente. He said, in part:

Cliffs between Caliente and Kershaw-Ryan State Park. These cliffs and ledges are welded rhyolitic tuff.

After leaving Kalientes, in Lincoln County, Nevada, the country becomes an arid region of the worst kind. The roadbed is already graded some 40 miles below Kalientes. When the building of the railroad through to Los Angeles was contemplated, the Meadow Valley Wash, which affords the only practicable gradient from the high Utah plateau to the desert regions of western California, became the all-important route . . . .

The Meadow Valley Wash is the first long dry riverbed that is encountered along the southern edge of the Great Basin. The word 'wash' is unknown in those parts of Oregon and Idaho

Cliffs near Leith. Mojave Desert plant association in foreground. Multiple basalt flows in this area.

lying within the great plateau, and in northern Utah and Nevada; but in Lincoln County, Nevada, and in Washington County, Utah, the term is heard everywhere. These 'washes' are the infallible signs of the breaking down of the Basin plateau . . . The Meadow Valley Range on the west and the Mormon range on the east represent a gradual drawing together of approximately parallel ridges. Thus the slight moisture which the climate affords is confined, and the result is that at intervals, where the deposits are not too thick, there is running water. From Kalientes to Bamberger, where the new power-plant for the De La Mar Mines has been installed, there is a perennial supply of water. Not far below Bamberger the water disappears entirely, only reappearing at three places the entire length of the wash, and then affording scarcely enough to support a small ranch at each place.

The valley itself is narrow, often a box-canyon with high lava bluffs; but occasionally it widens out into small basins flanked by rolling gravel foot-hills. On either side, above the lower trap rocks, are two high mountain ranges, the Meadow Valley and the Mormon mountains.

The railroad mentioned by Duffield, now the Union Pacific, comes in from Utah through Clover Creek Canyon, joining the Meadow Valley Wash at Caliente. The Meadow Valley north of Caliente is a wide valley, but just above Caliente it pinches down to a narrows, and below Caliente the Meadow Valley Wash becomes the deep, narrow Rainbow Canyon. Sometimes the sheer walls rise 2000 feet, and the canyon may be only a few hundred feet wide there. The canyon belongs to the creek; the railroad and the road have to fit in where they can.

Just above Leith the canyon opens out into a wide, sandy valley between alluvial hills. This valley was once known as Long Valley. It extends southward about 10 miles, becoming a canyon again at Carp. From Carp to Rox, the canyon was

Cliffs between the Elliott ranch and Stine.

shown on old maps as Mormon Canyon, probably because it swings around the west end of the Mormon Mountains. The entire canyon, from Caliente to Rox, has been called Rainbow Canyon, although the most colorful and rugged part is the section between Caliente and Elgin.

The Meadow Valley Wash is a tributary of the Muddy River, and some maps label it the Muddy River. For those of us who lived there, the creek didn't have a name. The creek is mostly perennial from its source down through Caliente (where it is joined by Clover Creek) and on down to about Leith. There the creek disappears into the alluvium of the valley floor; it is then an ephemeral stream. It does not flow again at the surface until near the upper end of our old ranch. There it becomes perennial, and it is mostly perennial until it joins the main channel of the Muddy River near Moapa.

Most of the water in the Muddy River comes by way of Pahranagat Valley and big springs not far from Moapa. That's why I'm surprised to see our creek called the Muddy River, or called a river at all.

The common stories had almost all the well-known early travelers passing through the Meadow Valley Wash—-Jedediah Smith, Father Escalante (we never heard Father Dominguez mentioned), and Father Garces are examples. Evidently the Dominguez-Escalante expedition missed the Meadow Valley Wash by quite a bit. Jedediah Smith might have followed the Meadow Valley Wash or Beaver Dam Wash to the Virgin River, but the Meadow Valley Wash seems to be the least likely route. Fur trappers are said to have trapped beaver on the Muddy River, so they probably did follow the Meadow Valley Wash. And Father Garces? Impossible.

Brad Stuart told me in the 1950s that many years previously, John and Rube Bradshaw were at or near the Big Field at the Elliott ranch, and they found two skeletons that had been exposed by a washout. Some U.S. Army buttons were with the skeletons. Brad said some men of the Mormon Battalion came through this area, and seven of them started up the Meadow Valley Wash but never did reach Salt Lake City. He surmised the skeletons to have been the remains of two of the men.

The Bradshaws also found skeletons at Elgin with Civil War buttons and a canteen. If men of the Mormon Battalion came through the Meadow Valley Wash, it was soon after their expedition in 1847, so this would be two different findings.

NAMES

The names of railroad sidings provide convenient references for location of mines, ranches, and other features. The sidings were spaced at intervals of about 5 miles; down the canyon from Caliente, the siding names most commonly used after about 1910 were Etna, Stine, Boyd, Elgin, Kyle, Leith, Cloud (formerly Rapelje or St. George), Carp, Vigo, Galt, Hoya, Rox, Farrier (formerly Guelph), Acton, and Moapa. Some of the sidings were discontinued after about 1950.

Where did those names come from? What is "Carp" doing out in the middle of the desert? Moapa is Piute for "water valley", but what about the rest? Galt is a railroad city in Canada, named for John Galt, a Scottish novelist. Vigo was a Spanish seaport that was captured and burned by Sir Francis Drake; Vigo County, Indiana, and a street in Vincennes, Indiana, are named for Col. Francis Vigo. Leith is the Scottish seaport at which Mary Queen of Scots arrived from France in 1561. Guelph is a city in Ontario, Canada, but the name originated in medieval Germany. Who picked these names to be used in remote southern Nevada, and why?

Consider Rapelje (or Rappelje), for example. My parents pronounced it "rappel-jay", and when I was a boy, it was one of those exotic names, such as Pioche, Paso Robles, San Berdoo, and Chevrolet, whose significance I neither questioned nor asked to be explained.

Rapelje still meant nothing to me until, in my fiddle-footed days, I came to rest in Vicksburg, Mississippi. I read that one Isaac Rappelje held a land grant at Vicksburg in the 1790s. According to the "Encyclopedia Americana", Sarah Rapelje, born in 1625 in Fort Orange, New Netherland, was the "first-born Christian daughter" in New Netherland. And now I have a highway map that shows a Rapelje in Stillwater County, Montana.

Some names change with time, or they were not correctly shown in the first place. The January 1906 timetable of the SPLA&SL shows St. George at the place that was later Cloud siding. However, I have read that Leith and Carp were each called St. George.

Some maps show "Uen" instead of Lien; do you think somebody's handwriting wasn't legible? Is that what is known in common language as carelessness? Also, Iceberg Canyon of the Colorado River (between Gregg Basin and Grand Wash) is shown as Keberg Canyon on some maps; same problem?

This is the sequence of sidings listed in the 1906 timetable, from Las Vegas through Modena, Utah, with the distances in miles from Los Angeles:

Las Vegas 334	Rox 398	Eccles 463
Stewart 339	Hoya 403	Minto 468
Valley 343	Galt 408	Islen. 473
Dike. 347	Vigo. 413	Barclay 476
Apex 352	Carp 418	Acoma. 482
Garnett 358	St. George. 423	Brown 487
Dry Lake. 363	Leith 428	Crestline 491
Crystal 369	Kyle. 433	Lien, Nev. 495
Ute. 374	Elgin 438	Uvada, Utah. . . 499
Byron. 378	Boyd 443	Tomas 503
Moapa. 383	Cana 448	Modena. 507
Acton. 388	Etna. 453	
Guelph 393	Caliente. 457	

Some of the elevations were Las Vegas 2026 feet; Moapa 1664; Carp, 2484; Elgin 3445; Caliente 4407; Crestline 5971.

The immediate area of Stine siding, 10 miles south of Caliente, has had a profusion of names. On Oct. 29, 1892, long before any railroad was there, Kershaw post office was established. (Samuel Kershaw had moved his family into present Kershaw Canyon, about 4 miles south of Caliente, in 1870.) Kershaw post office was on the east side of the canyon, and the original railroad was built there.

When Bamberger-Delamar Mining Company put in their pumping plant to supply water to Delamar, the plant was built in the bottom of the wash, near Kershaw. The original siding on the railroad was named Bamberger, for Simon Bamberger, who was a principal in the Delamar company and who later became Governor of Utah; Stine was the name of the pumping plant. The siding had been named or renamed Cana by 1906, although Kershaw post office was renamed Stine on Dec. 30, 1904. (Marcus Stine, of International Pump Co., was a vice-president of Bamberger-Delamar.)

Old Stine, 1994. Photo by Dot Rowe.

Harry Bennett, an old-time engineer on the railroad, told me that the first time he went to Caliente after the 1910 flood, the railroad had been located from the east side to its present route on the west side of the valley, and the siding was named Stine.

Just below Tunnel 7, between the road and the railroad, the walls of a building and some concrete rubble under the trees are what's left of Stine community. Stine had a section gang until the early 1930s, and it was a busy place during railroad construction.

SETTLEMENTS AND RANCHES

Permanent settlement by white men apparently started when Phil Klingensmith arrived in about 1857 (Denton, 1945) and started a ranch at Dutch Flat, on Clover Creek above present Caliente. He had been involved in the Mountain Meadows Massacre in September 1857, and he took refuge for some time in the area of the present Cherokee Mine after the U.S. authorities began their investigation in 1859.

Jim Ryan, as a small boy, milked cows for the Culverwells for 50 cents a day; with that money, he bought his first heifer (see Mathews). I was told he started punching cows for William Culverwell for $10 and a heifer a month; when he had a hundred head of cattle, he quit his job and homesteaded the ranch that was later known as the Newman ranch, above Caliente. In 1886 he bought the Lewis Sharp ranch below Caliente, and it passed to his son-in-law, Preston "Pres" Duffin. Willard Smith told of seeing a check to Ryan for $106,000 for one shipment of cattle. The house on the Ryan ranch was built in 1872; it burned in June 1932.

After about 1870, the settlers of the Moapa Valley hauled produce and salt through the Meadow Valley Wash to the new mining camp at Pioche and later to Delamar. Ranches were established in the 1870s by Jackman at present Caliente, Samuel and Amity Kershaw 3 miles south of Caliente, Aunt Maggie Shedden near present Stine, and John Kiernan at present Kyle. Ben Padgett had a ranch near present Elgin that Jim Bradshaw bought in 1880. Bradshaw had crossed the plains in 1863. In White Pine camp, he entered a partnership with Joe Conaway, who established the Conaway ranch in 1876.

The Kershaws settled in a side canyon. They planted an orchard and had a fine garden. The ranch passed through various hands; Jim Ryan was the last private owner. The Ryans donated it to Lincoln County in 1934 as a recreation area. It is now known as Kershaw-Ryan State Park. The Civilian Conservation Corps did a lot of the development of the park. Floods in recent years washed out the road and made the park inaccessible until the road was reopened in 1994.

The Conaway ranch was next down the canyon from the Ryan (Duffin) ranch. The Conaways lived at Bullionville, and when the smelter was shut

Cliffs in Kershaw-Ryan State Park.

down in 1876, they bought the Ferguson ranch (previously owned by James Applewhite), in the Meadow Valley Wash.

Joe and Emma Conaway's son John was born at the ranch on May 19, 1890. He attended school at the Red Rock school (later the site of Etna) a mile from the ranch house, and he took over management of the ranch when his father died. He married Viola D. Kiernan on June 25, 1918; she was a daughter of John Kiernan, who had the Kiernan ranch, below Elgin. John Conaway was a successful rancher and a good and respected citizen. He died on January 12, 1950.

Destruction of property by fire was a risk everyone faced, and the Conaway ranch had its share. On July 27, 1938, John Conaway's daughter, Geneve, discovered fire in the bunkhouse. Flying sparks ignited haystacks, barns, and corrals; with the help of three boys who were riding past on bicycles, the fire was kept away from other buildings. When the Caliente fire department arrived, their pumper enabled them to put out the fire.

Harry Keats tried to develop a small plot of ground in a little cove near the Etna bridge, where he had a small house, but the lack of water was apparently a problem he could not overcome. His brother Walter was a railroad car repairman.

Etna had a section gang, homes, and a school in the 1940s, but by 1994 all the buildings were gone.

The next ranch was started by J.E. "Jake" Colburn. A half interest was sold in 1901 by his heirs to a relative, John Pippin, from Warren County, Kentucky. The Pippin ranch was bought by George Warren, who sold it to Thomas C. Tennille about 1916; we knew it as the Tennille ranch.

Colburn had a race-track and a saloon on his ranch, and gambling at the saloon led to trouble. Clarence Leavitt, who carried the mail down the canyon, owed Colburn a gambling debt. One day when Leavitt rode into the

> *Joseph Conaway: Born Zanesville, Ohio, July 16, 1840, died Oct. 31, 1914. He married Emma Ferguson at Bullionville Feb. 25, 1874; she died Nov. 11, 1933. She was a daughter of Mr. & Mrs. John Ferguson, of Ganesboro, Tenn., and niece of Mr. & Mrs. C.R. Carden. The Conaway children were John H., Dana R. "Daney", Emma, Nevada, Margaret, and Lydia.*

yard, Colburn came out and grabbed the horse's bridle, with results as described in the following story, quoted from the *Pioche Weekly Record* of Feb. 16, 1893:

> *Last night about nine o'clock Dr. Campbell was hastily summoned to attend Jake Colburn at his ranch in Meadow Valley Wash, whom, the messenger stated had been shot that afternoon by one Clarence Leavitt.*
>
> *The doctor went down and returned at four o'clock this afternoon, having left Colburn at his ranch at nine o'clock this morning in a dying condition. Realizing that he could not live, Colburn made a statement of the occurrence which entirely exonerates Leavitt from all blame in the shooting. It appears that Leavitt, who is a half breed Indian boy, just turned twenty-one, owed Colburn a gambling debt of $40, due since the recent races at Panaca. Owing to the horse case tried at Panaca last Monday, referred to elsewhere in this issue, and to a slight jealousy, Colburn entertained hard feelings toward Leavitt, and yesterday afternoon about four o'clock as Leavitt, together with Rufe Pippin and Will Colburn, an adopted son, passed Colburn's house, going down the Wash, Colburn ran out and holding Leavitt's horse by the bridle, demanded that he at once pay that $40. Leavitt said he could not, when Colburn demanded that he come into the house and give his promissory note for the amount. Leavitt refused point blank to do this, when Colburn, whipping a colt's revolver from his hip pocket said, "you little black s__ of a _____, I'll make you sign it." At sight of the gun, Leavitt slid quickly from his horse to the ground, at which Colburn fired at him twice, both shots missing the intended mark. Leavitt ran around his horse, and with a single action Smith & Wesson 32 calibre pistol, fired at Colburn, the shot taking effect in the stomach. He then fired a second time, the shot breaking the Ulne bone of Colburn's right arm. During this time Colburn was snapping his pistol, the shots missing fire. In his statement Colburn said he only intended to frighten the boy when he drew his gun, and had no idea that he, in turn was armed, and shot at him when he slid so quickly from his horse, supposing then, that he might have a weapon, which supposition the sequel proved to be true.*
>
> *Leavitt was adopted when a child by the Leavitt family now at Bunkerville this county, and is a good ranch hand, and worked for Colburn all Summer it is said, and until a short time ago. He came to town with Dr. Campbell and is now in charge of the Sheriff awaiting the result of the occurrence, and should it prove fatal, which at this writing is fully expected, will be given a hearing before the proper authorities in order that the facts may be placed on record.*

On Feb. 23, the paper reported that Leavitt had been discharged from custody on the 22nd on the basis of Colburn's dying statement.

The Tennille ranch was owned by Buck Tennille when I lived in the Meadow Valley Wash. When I visited Mrs. Susan Atkinson in Caliente in the mid-1950s and got a lot of information about various ranches, I asked her about the Tennille ranch; she said she didn't know that name, because she had only returned to Caliente a short time before, after having left the area about 50 years earlier. The Tennille ranch was established while she was gone.

> *Etna Cave is about half-way up the cliffs beyond Etna bridge. The cliff face has red-orange pictographs with figures and geometric designs. S.M. Wheeler and the Civilian Conservation Corps excavated the cave in the late 1930s, obtaining hundreds of artifacts that reveal 5,000 years of occupation.*

The Pippins had two sons, Rufus "Rufe" and Tom, and a daughter, Belle; she married Thomas Edward "Ed" Dula on May 29, 1894. Ed Dula was born on June 10, 1862, in Wilkesboro, North Carolina. He walked across the country to the Colorado mining camps and then to Delamar at age 25; he was a registered voter in Delamar Precinct in 1894. From there he came to the Meadow Valley Wash and started his ranch, which we knew as the Dula ranch; the patent is dated June 28, 1919. The ranch is across the creek from the Tennille ranch, just below Tunnel 9.

Ed was later a deputy sheriff under Charles Culverwell and Buck Tennille, he was constable of Caliente in the 1930s and 1940s, and he owned the Taylor Mine. He was Caliente's eldest citizen when he died on May 29, 1952.

The 1910 flood did quite a lot of damage to the Dula ranch. Bill Acklin says his mother, Lena Dula Acklin, told him of seeing the water coming closer and closer to the house, and they loaded everything in wagons to be ready to leave. The water had cut 3 feet under the house before the crest of the flood passed. Their orchard, in the middle of the present channel, was washed away.

Emmett Meyers was leasing the Dula ranch when the dwelling and three other houses burned on June 15, 1935. An ad in the *Caliente Herald* on Aug. 22 said the ranch was for sale. Sam Wengert bought it in 1937.

A few miles beyond, at Stine, was the Acklin ranch, started by John Acklin, who was from Florence, Alabama. His parents had moved to Minersville, Utah, in about 1875. He sold it to Parley

> *James Buchanan "Buck" Tennille was born Nov. 7, 1889, and died April 26, 1972. He was a son of Thomas Conley and Nannie Cobb Tennille, from Gonzales County, Texas. They came to Nevada in 1898 and to Lincoln County about 1916. They died in 1925 and 1927, respectively. They had five sons (George, Oliver, Thomas, Richard, and James B.) and three daughters.*

Black, who sold it to Sam Wengert in 1937; Sam sold it to the Meadow Valley Scattered Settlers Project in 1940. Parley had an orchard and a garden, and he sold fruit and vegetables in Caliente.

The site of the Delamar pumping and power plant is in the bottom of the wash, opposite the lower end of the Black ranch. The pipelines and the power line to Delamar ran up Rock Springs Canyon. We were told that a road was built through Rock Springs Canyon, but Frank Pace told me that the main road (which he helped survey) from the Meadow Valley Wash to Delamar went up Taylor Mine Canyon (Easter Mine Canyon). The steep jump-offs made it difficult to get a horse up Rock Springs Canyon in the 1940s, and a road seems impossible.

Margaret "Aunt Maggie" Shedden had a ranch in the 1870s. She sold it to C.R. "Cap" Carden in 1889, identifying it as the "Barter" ranch. Susan Atkinson, who lived at the Pennsylvania Mine about 1890, knew the ranch as the Carden ranch. Cap Carden sold the ranch to Samuel V. "Sam" Carson in 1898; he said it was "in the Meadow Valley Wash about 30 miles southerly from Panaca and known as the Red Rock ranch". It passed to Carson's heirs, and L.L. (Lazille) Carson sold it to I.L. "Ike" Elliott in 1916. It was identified then as the ranch known as the Cap Carden ranch, "about a mile in a southerly direction from what was formerly known as the 'Bamberger Power Plant' said Power Plant being formerly owned and operated by the Bamberger Gold Mines Company".

Sam Wengert bought it in about 1940. Wengert and my father, C.L. Averett, went into partnership in 1939, and the ranch became the base for the partnership. We moved to the Elliott ranch, as we called it, in 1941. (Old-timers knew it then as the Carson ranch.) The partnership sold it in 1944

> *Cap Carden arrived in Pioche from Kentucky in 1870. After he sold his ranch to Aunt Maggie, he moved to Caliente. He owned the Cosmopolitan Saloon and was involved in other businesses and mining. He died on Jan. 22, 1908, at the age of 78.*

to Carl and Rachel Ballow (pronounced "blue"). They were later divorced, and Rachel married Carl's brother, John. The Ballow ranch, as it is now known, was sold by John Ballow in 1992.

Ike Elliott thought the remote location would be a good place for a still, so he set one up. Supposedly the still was never found. However, in the 1940s the wreckage of another still could be seen in Whiskey Spring Canyon, which drains west into the Meadow Valley Wash opposite the ranch buildings. I have heard the comment, "Ike made good whiskey".

We were told that one dreary day a car got stuck in one of the creek crossings in front of Ike's house. He got his team and pulled the car out. Everybody was wet and cold, so he invited them to the house to get warm. He played the hospitable host and offered them a drink; they were Prohibition agents, and Ike went to prison.

According to Ike Elliott's obituary on June 20, 1940, he was born in Arlington Heights, Texas, 70 years earlier, and he had lived in Globe, Arizona. About 1915 he moved to Nevada "where he acquired a fruit and cattle ranch a few miles west of Caliente", and he lived there until his death.

The McGuffie ranch was next down the canyon, reportedly established in the 1870s; it adjoined the Carson ranch. A.H. Norris sold 160 acres unsurveyed, "joining Carsons Ranch in the Meadow Valley Wash . . . formerly known as the Clark Reed ranch" to Eleanor McGuffie in 1916. (Clark Reed's wife Eva was formerly Eva Carson.) The homestead patent was issued to Joseph McGuffie in 1930. Agnes Horn, Josephine McGuffie, Joseph McGuffie, James McGuffie, William McGuffie, Eleanor McGuffie Damron, and Henrie McGuffie sold it to

Aunt Maggie's sister, Mrs. Henley (remembered now as Grandma Henley), was Mrs. John Pippin's mother and lived on the Colburn ranch. She was a midwife; Jim Bradshaw says she delivered some of his aunts and uncles.

Joseph William McGuffie in 1938; Joseph William and Josephine McGuffie sold it to the Meadow Valley Scattered Settlers Project in 1941.

The ranch had a nice orchard, typical for ranches in that part of the Meadow Valley Wash, and a two-story house with a small stained-glass window in the upper story. The house was torn down in the early 1940s. I remember the stained-glass window and the orchard.

On May 11, 1923, the *Pioche Record* ran Joseph McGuffie's obituary. He "died suddenly at his ranch below Caliente last Friday" at age 76. He was born in England in February 1847, came to America in 1849, and settled in Utah in 1850. (At 3 years old, he was evidently a precocious child.) He lived in or worked from Hiko for a number of years. In 1870 he married Eleanor Halsall, a native of the Isle of Man. (She died in late 1922.) They had five children: James McGuffie, Pierce McGuffie, Mrs. Belle Latimer, Mrs. C.A. Horn (of Delamar), and J.W. McGuffie (of Elgin). Joe and Eleanor moved to Pahranagat Valley in 1870, then to Delamar when its boom started, then to the Meadow Valley Wash.

J.W. McGuffie was a registered voter at Elgin in 1928 and 1930. J.W., Josephine, and Henry McGuffie were registered in Caliente precinct in 1932. The *Caliente Herald* occasionally refers to Bill McGuffie, and it often refers to J.W. McGuffie. J.W. "Bill" McGuffie was Joseph McGuffie's son, and Henry was Bill's stepson. Minnie was Bill's daughter.

I have a bill of sale executed by Wm. McGuffey to my father, September 1934, for stock and range rights; I will spell the name "McGuffie" in this book, because I have not found "McGuffey" anywhere except on that bill of sale.

According to my notes, George and Belle McGuffie lived on the ranch, but I cannot find those names anywhere else; my notes must have been wrong. However, Don Bradshaw agrees that we knew the last name as McGuffie. I wonder if the "Belle" was Belle Latimer.

Here's another of the problems with the correct form of names. When I looked at the lists of registered voters in the *Caliente Herald*, I found Mrs. Rachael Schlarman, Mrs. Rachel Schlarman, Rachael Schlarman, Rachel Schlarman, Rachael Ballow, and Rachel Ballow. What's a body to believe? The only thing I know for sure is that I have an agreement dated Aug. 24, 1944, signed by C.L. Averett, Rachel Ballow, and S.B. Wengert. (Mrs. Joe Schlarman was the mother of Rachel Schlarman Ballow.)

As I worked through the newspapers and saw the many garbled versions of names, I concluded that in the hurry to get the paper out, neither the editor nor the Linotype operator seemed to have done much proofreading. Names in lists of registered voters, legal notices, and lists of jury members, which should have been right, were not. Look at the variations of one name in different news stories in the *Lincoln County Record*: Archie William "Walt" Huston, at Carp, was identified as Walter Hueston, Hewston, Hewetson, and Tuston.

Down the canyon 3.4 miles beyond the Elliott ranch, Grapevine Canyon comes in from the east (from the left as you go down the canyon). Some of the cliff faces have petroglyphs incised into the rock and red pictographs painted on them. Visitors are asked not to outline the figures in chalk; it used to be a common practice, but chalk speeds up erosion that damages the figures.

Next down the canyon, about 2.5 miles from Grapevine Canyon, was Robber's Roost. This area was an extensive swamp before the 1910 flood, and the ranch was known as the Swamp Ranch or, according to Mathews, Tulley swamp. When J.W. Bradshaw came to Lincoln County, he lived at the ranch or its future site in 1879-1880, then he moved to the present site of Elgin, as noted later. On Feb. 17, 1900, John and Maggie Harty conveyed to John Pippin the property in the Meadow Valley Wash "known as the Swamp Ranch situated about 5 miles south of Cap Carden ranch, which is now owned by Sam Carson". (Maggie Harty was a Pippin. John Harty was a registered voter in the

Railroad bridge just west of Boyd. Grapevine Canyon visible in center distance.

Grapevine Canyon, just west of Boyd; the canyon comes in from the left.

Meadow Valley Wash Precinct in 1894, and in 1897 his ranch was in the Meadow Valley school district.) John Pippin conveyed it to Clair Carson on May 28, 1901.

Why was it called Robber's Roost? We heard various stories, including the following; I consider the possibility that all of them are true.

■ *Bullion from Delamar was cast into 500-lb spheres to discourage the attention of thieves, but somebody did get away with one or more spheres, according to this story. The thieves got as far as the ranch before they were caught. Lewis Bradshaw says Charlie Culverwell told him that the thieves holed up in the rocks, and it would have been suicide to try to take them by force. They had been quite a while without food, so after a while the posse cooked a batch of bacon, and the smell of that bacon was too much; the thieves gave themselves up. I can relate to that.*

■ *Jewish peddlers used to come through with goods to sell, and one was beaten and robbed there. I don't have the details, but according to the* Pioche Weekly Record, *Feb. 22, 1900, in the short article "The Wash Robbery", John Hartey and Rufus Pippin were bound over to the Grand Jury for action on the charge of robbery. The article says, "John Lewis, who was also held failed to furnish bonds and will be jailed. Some of the stolen goods, principally ladies and childrens wear, were found by Sheriff Johnson on Lewis's premises in the Wash. Lewis says the articles were given him by the Hartey's, the night after the robbery that he might secrete them. The Hartey's in turn seek to throw the blame of the whole affair upon Lewis." On Jan. 25, 1901, the paper says that Rufus Pippin had been pardoned from "his term of 1 year for*

larceny". The peddler had said he did not see Pippin among the people who robbed him.
■ *Butch Cassidy and members of his Wild Bunch used to stop there on their way through. Now it's your turn; can you top those stories?*

This item is from the *Caliente Herald*, April 2, 1931: "V.H. and Lee Phillips have recently taken over the Half Way Service Station and Rest Rooms in Meadow Valley Wash, the station was formerly known as 'Robber's Roost'." The road down the canyon from Caliente to Elgin and Carp and on across Tule Flat to the Arrowhead Trail (U.S. Highway 91) on Mormon Mesa had been developed as a service to the many ranchers and railroad people in the Wash. People hoped, and even believed, that the route that finally became U.S. 93 would go that way, and a service station at Robber's Roost would have had a lot of business; but the highway went through Pahranagat Valley instead.

The idea of a road down the canyon wasn't new; according to the *Lincoln County Record*, Aug. 20, 1925, automobiles were frequently seen going down the Meadow Valley Wash to reach Las Vegas, making the trip from Caliente "easily" in 7 hours. They must have been going on down the canyon from Carp to Rox to Moapa, which wasn't a lot of fun; I question the "easily" part.

On May 11, 1933, the *Herald* said the County Commissioners had approved completion "of the highway, at Robber's Roost, on the Rainbow Canyon Route". They had also agreed to "open and maintain the road from Elgin to Reppelje on the same route" (the road that we knew as the road over the summit or the road over the hill).

Later in the year, the Civil Works Administration sent a crew to improve the road from Caliente to Elgin and the road over the hill to Carp. The article in the Herald said they would eliminate "a number" of creek crossings near Robber's Roost.

Just past Robber's Roost is Tunnel 5. A boulder near the west portal of Tunnel 5 has petroglyphs that include bighorn mountain sheep. The railroad crosses the creek there on a steel bridge, and the road goes up onto the grade that was built by the Oregon Short Line during the early days when both railroads were trying to secure the right to build the railroad through this deep, narrow canyon, also called the Black Narrows (Denton, 1957). The creek bed below the OSL Grade has abundant coyote willows, where beaver dams are found. However, tamarisk is taking over, as it is in many other places down the canyon. Deer, cattle, and beaver will eat willows, but tamarisk doesn't do them much good.

From Robber's Roost, the next spot down the canyon I knew by name was Crow Corral, just above Elgin. It was a relic of George Crow's days running wild horses; some of it is still visible in 1994.

George Edwin Crow was a registered voter at Elgin in 1930 through 1938. He was born near Barclay in 1870 and died in Caliente on Nov. 6, 1955.

Bighorn mountain sheep petroglyphs at Tunnel 5, Oct. 1994.

George's father, "Button" Crow, started the ranch in 1913 on which George received a homestead patent in 1918. Later it became the Barnett ranch. An item in the *Caliente News*, Dec. 2, 1920, referred to the Barnett-Farrier ranch; the Farrier name is a mystery to me, so far.

When the railroad was under construction, saloons were not allowed close to the construction area, and a State law or a county regulation prohibited a saloon within a mile of the railroad. Saloons were set up in tents ("rag dumps"), just beyond the mile limit. One rag dump was in the canyon just below Crow Corral.

Ben Padgett started a ranch at the site of the future Elgin that was bought by J.W. Bradshaw in 1880; it became the Bradshaw ranch. His sons John B. and Reuben Joseph "Rube" Bradshaw lived at Elgin. They were cattle ranchers and they also had interests in mining, especially in the Pennsylvania district. (See the Elgin chapter for more about Elgin and the Bradshaws.)

Ben Padgett died on Jan. 11, 1901. The *Lincoln County Record* that day said he was about 75 years old, he was from Georgia or South Carolina, and he had lived in Lincoln County for 25 years.

Joe Schlarman's ranch was beyond the Bradshaw ranch, on the west side of the canyon. Albert Barnett's ranch (originally the Crow ranch) was on the east side, just beyond the Schlarman ranch. Next, above Tunnel 4, was the ranch of Vivian K. "Viv" and Etta Mariger. The Kiernan ranch, started by John Kiernan in 1876, was between Tunnel 4 and Cottonwood Canyon.

The Kiernan ranch was sold to Parley Henrie, and it became known as the Henrie ranch. Henrie also owned the Schmidt ranch and the Lone Tree ranch. Dave Brundy married Parley and Ethel Henrie's daughter Dagmar, and they lived on the Henrie ranch in the early 1930s.

John Perkins said he hauled supplies through there while the railroad was under construction, and the Caldwells had a ranch between the Kiernan ranch and Elgin. On Sept. 18, 1903, the *Lincoln County Record* listed the railroad construction camp at Caldwell's ranch; during rebuilding after the 1910 flood, Caldwell's ranch was described as being 16 miles below Caliente. According to the Union Pacific track diagrams, that would be halfway between Elgin and Boyd, an unlikely (if not impossible) place for a ranch. I consider the "16 miles" to be incorrect.

Charlie Dimmick and Sam Beal had their ranch in Cottonwood Canyon, which comes in from the east, above Leith. The Carp chapter of this book has more information about them.

Leith was a siding where a section gang was stationed for many years. Some of the abandoned houses still stand in 1994. On the hill above the railroad, part of the word LEITH in white letters is still visible.

The Schmidt ranch was several miles beyond the Henrie ranch; Gustave "Gus" Schmidt lived there in the late 1920s, but he had left by about 1930. My mother told me that Schmidt and another man sneaked out behind the pumphouse at Carp one night and stole some coal from a car that was spotted on the spur. My father saw them, and he made them pull up to the railroad grade between the pumper's house and the depot and unload the coal. They had shoved it back under some lumber that was in the wagon, and they had to crawl under to get it. She said people stood around, horrified, saying "Don't you know they'll get a gun and kill you?" My father replied, "But not until after they've unloaded that coal."

Ruins of Leith, 1994. Photo by Dot Rowe.

Someone built a large, white house on the Schmidt ranch in the 1940s, said to be comparable with the best house in Caliente. It's gone now.

The Lone Tree ranch, below the Schmidt ranch, was named for a big, lone cottonwood tree that grew near the ranch buildings. (I'm told that some years ago, a plane crashed into that tree.) My mother said a Clark family from Cedar City lived on the Lone Tree ranch in about 1930, and they tried to raise goats. The venture failed, and they moved to Las Vegas.

The ranch is said to have been the site of a settlement run by Lyman Woods, of Barclay. Some people say the settlement was active in the 1860s; John Richard and Fay Perkins said it was at the Lone Tree ranch after the railroad came through, and Fay said he saw it when about 10 families lived there; and some people say it wasn't there at all, it was near Barclay, in the Clover Valley. Ves Hulse said the foundations of the settlement were on the Foreman ranch, which he said was later owned by Parley Henrie and called the Lone Tree ranch. He said Lyman Woods was in charge. The ranch had an orchard and a vineyard, but a string of dry years caused the settlement to fail.

Joe Foreman ran a ditch down from near Leith to bring irrigation water to the Lone Tree ranch from the creek. Parts of the ditch are still visible where rock walls took it around the points of hills. Old-timers say the water never ran in the ditch, because Bradshaw and Kiernan wouldn't let Foreman have any water. From what I remember of the ditch, I can't believe it would carry water that far.

According to Edwards, Clover Valley was settled by Mormons in 1863, but the settlers left the valley in 1866 because of trouble with the Indians. Lyman Woods and Taylor R. Bird reoccupied the valley on May 18, 1869. If Woods ran the settlement at the Lone Tree, he must have made lots of trips between there and Clover Valley.

Jim Bradshaw says Foreman built his ditch and applied for the right to divert water into it, but the application was contested and rejected. Until 1910, the beneficial user of water obtained the right to it; Kiernan and Bradshaw thus had prior right. Foreman had thought that because the water had not been filed on, it was there to be claimed.

The next ranch belonged to Walter Condiff, a telegraph operator at Carp. Melvin Bunker said his father, Hector Bunker, started the ranch. Hector and Mina Bunker conveyed it to Walter A. and Louise Condiff in 1926.

Some years ago, Don Bradshaw traded land for 420 acres, a little north of Lyman Crossing; the 420 acres included the Condiff ranch. He obtained the Shoebox Well and drilled another, and from those he irrigated the ground and grew fine crops of barley and alfalfa. He called it Carp Flat. He sold it, and with the money he started an apple orchard at Elgin.

Bert and Marguerite Lyman's ranch was next, where the topographic maps now show Lyman Crossing. Lyman received two homestead patents, one in 1926 and one in 1933. The family returned to Logandale in 1933. From my earliest memory, it was the Dimmick ranch, because Charlie Dimmick bought it in 1934. Charlie sold it to Sam Wengert in 1943, and Sam sold it to John Morrison in 1950.

Morrison lived in our old house, even though it was on public land. He was shot and fatally wounded by his stepson, Darrell "Smoky" Collins, in the house, on Sept. 7, 1949; the Coroner's Jury ruled it was justifiable homicide. John's widow, Otelia, inherited the property. Later she married Stewart Henrie, and they sold the property to Kevin "Oley" Olson, of Panaca.

Daniel Sylvester "Ves" Hulse received a patent in 1926 on a homestead adjoining Lyman's on the west. Mr. Hulse built a house on his ranch in August 1933. He sold his ranch to Sam Beal in 1937, Sam sold it to Sam Wengert in 1943, and Wengert sold it to John Morrison in 1950.

Walter Barham Conk, the signal maintainer at Carp, homesteaded next to the Hulse ranch; his homestead patent is dated 1924. Archie William "Walt" Huston homesteaded adjoining the Conk ranch on the south; the homestead patent was issued to Pearl Huston, dated 1930. John, Sy, and Oliver Fitchett had a dugout and a cabin across the road east of the Conk ranch. They are said to have made whiskey during Prohibition.

Adjoining the Conk ranch on the south was the homestead of Albert Lee "Roy" Hilburn, the patent dated 1926. Maybe his middle name was Leroy, because my parents used to talk about Roy Hilburn, and according to the Caliente paper, Roy Hilburn was an inspector on the primary election board at Carp in 1930.

Clarence Mabey homesteaded to the west of the Huston and Hilburn ranches; the homestead patent is dated 1920. (I don't know who filed first, so maybe they were east of him.) Mabey had left by 1924; his children returned later for a while and raised garden produce for sale, without much success.

Fred Montgomery, of Las Vegas, bought the Hilburn ranch, and later he bought the Huston and Mabey ranches. He sold the block of 480 acres to Sam Wengert in 1943, and Wengert sold the property to John Morrison in 1950. The 1920 Census lists Archie Huston, Hector Bunker, Walter B. Conk, and Clarence Mabey in Elgin precinct, which evidently included Carp.

My father's ranch, said to have been the last homestead filed in that area, extended south from the Mabey and Hilburn ranches. From the north end of our ranch (or the "upper end", as we called it), the valley pinches down fairly rapidly to a canyon past the lower end of our ranch. Carp is just inside the canyon. Our ranch was a homestead and a desert entry. The desert entry application was dated 1929, and the patent was dated 1939; that gives some idea of the time that might elapse between filing and obtaining title. The homestead patent was dated 1936, and I believe the application date would have been 1924 or 1925. We sold our ranch to the Meadow Valley Scattered Settlers Project in 1940 (see the description of the project in the Carp chapter).

Where the canyon opens up about a mile below Carp, Matt Reese had a homestead that Tom Henrie recalls was started by Nate Foreman. Nate sold his ranch to Wright McKnight; Wright's son, Preston "Pres" McKnight, filed an adjoining homestead. Aaron "Bill" Stiver lived on Pres McKnight's ranch from the late 1930s until he went to jail in April 1941 on a morals charge involving his daughter, Velda. Frank Hardy had the next homestead; Dan Turnbaugh lived there in the late 1930s.

Arthur L. Gifford received a homestead patent in 1925 for property down the canyon from Carp. Gifford was listed by the *Caliente News* as a telegraph operator at Carp in 1920 and 1921. Later he was a dispatcher for the railroad at Las Vegas. I think his homestead became the Frank Hardy property.

Tyson Lionel "Lee" Bean, an uncle of the Fitchett brothers, had the next homestead, at Vigo. (Bean was also said to have been a moonshiner; they seem to have been common.) His homestead patent was dated 1927. He sold his ranch to Hafen & Frei Brothers, of Santa Clara, Utah. They came into Lincoln County when they bought out Charlie Dimmick after World War I. They ran cattle on Tule Flat and north into the Clover Mountains. Albert Lee Hilburn filed on an 80-acre desert entry but gave it up, and Viv Frei filed a desert entry that partly overlapped it and that became part of the Hafen & Frei ranch. My father filed on a desert entry adjoining the Hilburn entry and later sold it to Viv Frei.

The last ranches on this list include those of Frank Wilson, at Rox, and the Huntsmans just beyond. The Huntsman ranch had a stage station at Cane Springs. I just know these ranches by name, so I don't have anything to say about them, and I don't know how many others were between Rox and Moapa. The canyon between Vigo and Rox has been known as Huntsman Canyon.

THE ELLIOTT RANCH

By about 1940, Sam Wengert, an engineer on the Union Pacific, had bought the Elliott ranch and was buying other ranches in the Meadow Valley Wash. Sam and my father set up a partnership, even though Dad told me "A partnership's a poor ship to sail in". After we sold our ranch at Carp, we moved to the Elliott ranch.

We rented a boxcar from the railroad as an immigrant car, consigned to us at Boyd siding. We loaded our furniture, household goods, farm equipment, tools, implements, and two milk cows. On June 16, 1941, we left Carp and drove to the Elliott ranch and began what was, for me, a new life. We made many trips to Carp afterward, but we didn't live there again.

The partnership leased from the Government the Black and McGuffie ranches and our old ranch and the Conk ranch at Carp. (See the description of the Meadow Valley Scattered Settlers Project in the "Carp" chapter for information about the Government purchase of these ranches.) The Elliott ranch became our home and the base of operations for the partnership.

The ranch had several structures: the main house (a three-room frame house with a lean-to that contained the kitchen and a screened porch); the "schoolhouse", a one-room building with a cellar; an open barn; a chicken house made of stone; a tool shed; and various corrals. (These buildings were gone long before 1994; the house burned in the 1950s.)

I got the scare of my life in that tool shed. It was a small structure with slat floors and an overhead shelf. We were cleaning out the shed, and as I pulled an apple box from the overhead shelf, some dynamite caps fell through the bottom of the box and bounced around on the floor at my feet and then dropped through the spaces in the slat floor. They were either too old to detonate or else I was lucky.

Elliott ranch, 1943. Ranch house barely visible in trees at left. Big Field across railroad to left, Bean Patch right of railroad at the curve. Grapevine Field in right distance. View down the canyon (toward Elgin).

We put my bed in the schoolhouse one summer, but I was always uneasy there. Spiders make me spooky, and the place was full of spiders, including black widows. Awakening in the night to find a daddy long-legs crawling on my face produces an immediate visceral reaction, even though he doesn't really answer to the generic name of "spider".

Sam Carson's sons were said to have lost heavily on racehorses at tracks such as the one at Colburn's. The usual story was that Sam committed suicide in the cellar of the schoolhouse, reportedly because of financial problems brought on by the losses on the horses. We were told Sam went into the cellar, put the muzzle of a shotgun to his head, and pulled the trigger. That story didn't do anything to reassure me. Frank Pace told me that while he was surveying up the canyon, Sam Carson hanged himself in the barn. Did I worry about that cellar for nothing?

According to the *Lincoln County Record* on Aug. 1, 1902, someone had called from Delamar to say that Sam Carson had shot himself in the shoulder and died. Whether it was an intentional injury was not known. (From the Carson ranch, the closest telephone was at Delamar, connecting with Pioche.)

The house, corrals, and orchard were in a cove where a small canyon comes down from cliffs that stand at least 1000 feet above the valley floor. In the winter, the sun comes up in midmorning and goes down in early afternoon. We called the canyon "Spring Canyon", because a spring in it was the only source of drinking water except the creek. The water had been piped down to the house; the remnants of the pipeline were visible when we lived there. We hauled our drinking water 12 miles from Caliente.

A trail goes up that canyon and to the top of the cliffs, where Elliott grazed his cattle on the high mesa. McGuffie also took his cattle up to graze on the mesa.

The Elliott ranch had an old, neglected orchard when we got there. It had apples, peaches, pears, plums, cherries, and apricots; Ike Elliott sold fruit in Caliente. We pruned the orchard, and it was soon back in good shape. It was irrigated by water that was diverted from the creek through a ditch, then through a culvert under the railroad grade and out into the orchard.

The railroad crosses the creek on a steel bridge at the east side of the cove, where a spur ridge comes down from the east and forces the creek to make a dogleg to the west. The county road followed the creek, with one crossing jut above and one just below the bridge.

The 30-acre main field, the Big Field, was beyond that spur ridge and east of the railroad. It was irrigated from a ditch that left the creek at the end of a partly-sunken abutment at the west end of the bridge, went by flume across a low area, and went to the field through a culvert under the railroad grade. (That made two places where irrigation water went through a culvert under the railroad.)

Just beyond the flume, west of the railroad grade, was a 7-acre field called the Bean Patch. It was fenced along the west side, next to the road, by barbed wire that was strung on a row of ancient cottonwoods; the bark of the trees had grown over the wires. (That row of trees was removed in the 1950s or '60s because they restricted the visibility on the road.)

Much of the Rainbow Canyon is characterized by groves of cottonwoods. These trees may live to be 100 years old. The

> *Hadley and others mention that in Arizona, the pioneers usually had a small cultivated area, an orchard, an irrigation ditch, pens for domestic animals, a corral, and a house. They could have been describing the ranches here, too.*

thick, dark green leaves rustle and clatter against each other in the breezes of summer, then they turn gold in autumn, then they fall to the ground and yield a rather spicy odor as they decompose. Just the thought of that fragrance takes me back!

The other field, called the Grapevine Field, was smaller than the Big Field. It was west of the creek, approximately opposite the lower part of the Big Field. We raised alfalfa in the Big Field; I don't remember what grew in the Grapevine Field and the Bean Patch, except that we raised neither grapes nor beans. The names were apparently from Ike Elliott's days on the ranch.

Two weeds were troublesome though not cause for great dismay: bindweed, which we knew as wild morning-glory, and gourds. We did have a weed around the house that was cause for dismay; someone had planted horehound, and it had spread everywhere, becoming a pernicious weed. Our New Rockford cotton socks and the tails of the dogs were matted with horehound seed capsules. On farmsteads on Bonito Creek, Arizona, horehound had become a weed (see Hadley and others).

Bridge at the Elliott ranch, 1972. Second truss span has been replaced by a plate girder bridge.

Gourds are large, spreading plants that are easy to see but difficult to kill. The large, fleshy root must be dug out completely, because any scrap of the root will develop a new plant. The root can be pulped in water and used as soap if you can stand the rank odor.

Gophers were troublesome. We diverted water from the ditch to the Big Field by building a dirt dam in the ditch, then letting the water flow down to it. When that part of the field was watered, we built another dam farther down, dug the last one out, and let the water go to the new dam. Sometimes a gopher would burrow into a dam and cause it to wash out, or perhaps it would burrow around a dam, with the same result. The gopher's fan-shaped mound is distinctive. The gopher's tunnel gives protection, but it also give access to roots and underground stems of plants.

Before long, we started using canvas barriers in place of dirt dams. We fastened a sheet of heavy canvas between two 2x4s that were longer than the ditch was wide, and with the 2x4s across the empty ditch, the canvas sagged down to the bottom and extended upstream a few feet. We piled some dirt on that part of the canvas to keep water from getting underneath, and when we released the upstream barrier, the water surged down and was held just as if a dirt dam had been there.

Hollyhocks had been planted around the house, and by the time we got there, they grew everywhere. We liked them, and we liked the huge lilac that grew near the house. A vineyard had existed there, but only a few grapevines were left in 1941. A thicket of currants was left from the old days.

Sagebrush, "purple sage", the state flower of Nevada, is common from here northward. The plant thrives in good soil, especially when it is adequately watered. Sometimes the main trunk of a bush is several inches diameter, and the plants appear to be able to live 200 years or so.

Velvety galls are often found on sagebrush; one type of gall is produced by the larvae of plant midges. The most common gall occurs at the ends of small branches. It is a round ball of modified leaves in clusters; the gall is green the first year, but then it turns dark.

Indian paintbrush, a beautiful flower of the sagebrush country, is parasitic or semi-parasitic on sagebrush and other shrubs. Paintbrush takes water and minerals from the host plant but it makes its own chlorophyll and most of its sugars. Dodder, by comparison, is parasitic; it takes all its nutrients from the host plant and does not make any chlorophyll.

Sagebrush has various uses, including this one that I have not read about: My wife and I stopped at a rest area near Duchesne, Utah, in 1991, and we saw a man and woman apparently picking the flower heads from sagebrush. The woman said they use the flower heads to make a bug-repellent smoke. Put them in a coffee can so they can't burn very well, set them on fire, and the smoke will drive away mosquitoes and other pests.

Another plant, a broom rape, is parasitic on sagebrush and other plants. The flowers develop while the stems are under ground, and they open as soon as the heads get above ground. The plant may be purplish or yellowish, and it may have a few or many flowers. It is not abundant, but because it is inconspicuous, it isn't often seen.

While we lived at the Elliott ranch, we made many trips to Carp, and during the school year, my sister and I made the round trip to Caliente every day until the winter weather got bad and we began staying in our house at Caliente. One thing we had to learn was the nature of every creek crossing between Elgin and Etna (the last crossing before Caliente).

My notes list these crossings, starting at Elgin and working up the canyon: Elgin, Crow Corral, below the OSL Grade, at Tunnel 5, above Robber's Roost, at Boyd, two at the Elliott ranch, two at Tennille's ranch, and one at Etna. The one at Crow Corral was always treacherous; I don't recall ever crossing it without stopping first to size up the tracks where other cars had crossed (or tried to cross), the depth of the water, changes in the sand bars, and the general nature of the crossing. The two in front of our house at the Elliott ranch were ordinarily pretty good, but the upper one of the two could be mean.

> *Sagebrush is in the genus* Artemisia, *in the aster family. The Greek goddess Artemis was a daughter of Zeus and the twin sister of Apollo. Chiron, the Centaur, was known for his wisdom and his skill in surgery; she delivered a medicinal plant to him, and he named it artemisia.*

The crossings were usually passable, but as was the case with the other crossings, some element of risk was always involved. (In the 1950s, Don Bradshaw ruined a new car in one of the crossings, and he decided to run for County Commissioner and do something about the crossings. He ran, and he won, and he took care of the crossings.)

The crossings at Buck Tennille's ranch were variable. We got our Chevrolet truck down to the rear axles once in the lower crossing, and we were about worn out trying to dig out, when Tom Tennille came along on horseback. He tied a rope to the saddle horn and looped it over the bumper and took a pull, and when my father gave the engine just a little power, we walked right out!

Sometimes these crossings were problems for us, but Tom Pippin and his family had more trouble than we ever thought of. The *Caliente Herald*, on April 18, 1929, looking back 20 years, said they got into quicksand in the Meadow Valley Wash (location not specified) and were almost drowned. The sheriff happened to be there, and he helped rescue them and their team, but their wagon and all their possessions were lost. And I thought we had been really stuck a time or two!

THE SCHOOLHOUSE

Nobody I talked to knew why the schoolhouse at the Elliott ranch had that name. Maybe it was a school in the days when travel to school in Caliente or

Elgin was not reasonable...or maybe it was a school before Caliente or Elgin existed. But there is an interesting story. Don Bradshaw says in alternate years in perhaps 1900-1905, his grandmother Bradshaw took her children to the McGuffie ranch, camped in a tent there for the school year, and sent the children to school at the Carson ranch; then the Carson family went to Elgin and camped the next year and the children went to school there.

The Elliott ranch was in the Bullionville school district, and we were told the Bullionville school was at Etna. John Conaway went to Red Rock school, about a mile from their ranch, which is the distance to Etna. The early newspapers list Red Rock school through 1920, and Bullionville school for the same and later years, and no Etna school through 1925, at least. When Cap Carden sold his ranch to Sam Carson in 1898, it was known as the Red Rock ranch, according to the deed. Perhaps Red Rock school was at the ranch at that time and was moved to Etna after 1900, leaving the building at the ranch. On March 17, 1927, the *Lincoln County Record* said that Bullionville school had a new school bus "which leaves Stine for Etna" with five children, so I presume the Red Rock district had been absorbed into the Bullionville district.

Where did children at Stine attend school in the early years? Evidently Stine had no school of its own; the *Caliente Progress*, Oct. 29, 1904, lists polling places for the election, and the polling place for Pump Station Precinct (at later Stine) was "at the power house"; many precincts listed the schoolhouse as the polling place.

The *Pioche Weekly Record* on Feb. 22, 1890, listed these school districts in Lincoln County (which then included present Clark County): Pioche, Bullionville, Panaca, Clover Valley, Virgin, Eagle Valley, Ash Springs, Pahranagat, Spring Valley, Bunkerville, Lake Valley, and Bristol. New voting precincts established that year included Meadow Valley Wash, with the schoolhouse as the polling place; Jake Colburn, C.R. Carden, and John Pippin were the election inspectors. Bullionville precinct was established in 1892, with the schoolhouse as the polling place; Samuel Kershaw, John Pippin, and John Kiernan were the election judges. The Meadow Valley Wash school closed for the year on March 3, 1893. The list of school districts on March 1, 1894, included Bullionville and Dutch Flat, but nothing about a Meadow Valley Wash district. Smith Brothers (who lived at Dutch Flat) petitioned in July 1895 for a school district at Dutch Flat, but not enough children lived there; in November they petitioned for a Meadow Valley Wash school district, and the petition was approved. On Jan. 30, 1896, the school districts included Bullionville and Meadow Valley Wash.

On Aug. 5, 1897, a petition was presented to the County Commissioners for "the formation of a new school district in Meadow Valley Wash, to embrace the ranches of John Hartey, James Bradshaw and John Kiernan". Action was deferred while they determined whether there were enough children in the proposed district. The polling place for the 1898 election was the schoolhouse; the election inspectors were John Kiernan, James Ryan, and C.M. Swindler, and the clerks were William Culverwell and Joe Conaway. The school districts in 1899 and 1901 included Bullionville, Cottonwood, Dutch Flat, and Meadow Valley Wash. These were some teachers listed in news items in the *De Lamar Lode*: Violette McCarthy at Bullionville in 1896-97 and at Dutch Flat in 1899-1900; Margaret A. Conaway at Bullionville in 1897-98 and 1899-1900; and Josie Kiernan at Dutch Flat in 1898-99 and at Cottonwood in 1899-1900.

The *Lincoln County Record* reported on Sept. 5, 1902, that John H. Kiernan and James Bradshaw, trustees of Cottonwood School District, petitioned for a new school district in the Meadow Valley Wash. On July 28, 1905, the districts included Cottonwood, Meadow Valley, and Red Rock. On Feb. 12, 1919, the districts included Red Rock, Kiernan, and Carp. On June 30, 1920, James Bradshaw and Parley Henrie were listed in Kiernan School District, and I.L. Elliott and J.W. McGuffie were in the Red Rock district. On Feb. 14, 1925, the school districts included Bullionville, Kiernan, Henrie, and Carp.

I still don't know what school, if any, was at the Carson ranch, nor when.

Joshua tree

Deed.

Margaret Shedden.
To
C. R. Carden

Know all men by these presents that I Margaret Sheddon of Meadow Valley Wash. Lincoln County & the State of Nevada. in consideration of the sum of Four hundred ($400) Dollars). to me in hand paid by C. R. Carden. of Meadow Valley Wash. Lincoln County, & State of Nevada. the receipt whereof I do hereby acknowledge. have bargained, sold quitclaimed. & by these presents do bargain, sell & quitclaim unto the said C. R. Carden. & to his heirs & assigns forever. all my right, title, interest, & demand. both at law & in equity. & as well in possession as in expectancy. of. in & to all that certain farm or piece of land situate in Meadow Valley Wash. Lincoln Co. State of Nevada. and known as "Barter" ranch. with all & singular. the hereditaments & appurtenances thereunto belonging. March 20th 09.

Witness! Joseph Conway.   Mrs. Margaret Shedden
                                      her + mark

State of Nevada }
County of Lincoln } ss.

On this 3d day of June A.D. one thousand eight hundred and eighty nine. before me John Shier

CHAPTER 2

CALIENTE
THE ROSE CITY OF THE SILVER STATE

Charming Caliente is at the bottom of a narrow crooked side canyon. Its very wide main street is bisected by rails of the Union Pacific, for which it is a division point. Before the highway turns onto this main street it passes a long row of comfortable company houses, painted the familiar bright yellow, behind neat fences and very tall poplars. The stores, of cement block painted white or grey, have the air of prosperity inseparable from a community that has long had a steady source of moderate income. Conspicuous in the center of the main street, by the station, is the solid hotel owned by the railroad company.   —NEVADA, A GUIDE TO THE SILVER STATE

HOW IT ALL BEGAN

According to Denton (1945), in about 1857 Phil Klingensmith started a ranch at Dutch Flat, on Clover Creek just above Caliente (the Dave Barnes ranch in the 1940s). Brooks (1962) gives some information about Klingensmith. He was a Bishop in the Mormon church in Cedar City, and he was involved in the Mountain Meadows Massacre. He was released from the office in July 1859 and went into hiding in the mining camps of Nevada. He made an affidavit in 1871 in Pioche regarding the massacre. He was reportedly found dead in Sonora, Mexico, in 1881.

In some documents cited by Brooks, he was listed as P.K. Smith, and evidently in Nevada he changed his name to Phil K. Smith. He had twin sons, Phil and John Smith, born in Cedar City in 1859. Phil and John lived on the ranch at Dutch Flat. The *Pioche Weekly Record*, Jan. 20, 1898, says they had bought the Vietti sawmill south of Delamar and would move it to "a timber patch east of Meadow Valley Wash in the vicinity of Pennsylvania district where a million or two feet of timber can be got out".

Denton (1945) says the next ranch in the area was started by Ike and Dow Barton; it later became the Yoacham ranch. Caliente is on the site of perhaps the next oldest ranch, started in the early 1870s by a man named Jackman. (A vague story is told about a Jackman partner who disappeared while supposedly on a trip but whose body was found in a well at the ranch.) Jackman sold his ranch to Miller and Hopkins. William Culverwell obtained part interest in the ranch by 1874. His brother, Charles Culverwell I, obtained the rest by 1879; Charles Jr. was Charlie Culverwell to us.

Denton says, "The old ranch house was located in the grove of native cottonwoods on the rise of ground south of U.P. tracks and west of the present Spring Street". (A commemorative plaque at the site of the Culverwell ranch was dedicated in July 1969.)

Charles Culverwell owned the hot springs, and by late 1901 he was operating the Culverwell Hotel there. The hotel had hot baths, a blacksmith shop, and a livery stable. He was called the "City Mayor".

The reason for a hotel was the construction of the railroad, described in the chapter "The Salt Lake Route". The San Pedro, Los Angeles & Salt Lake Railroad (SPLA&SL) and the Oregon Short Line (OSL) were jockeying for control of the canyons and the right to build and operate a railroad.

HOW CALIENTE GREW

The valley had wide, green meadows and some boggy areas at that time. The Culverwells sold land to the SPLA&SL, a town was platted, and lots were sold in 1901; Thomas McCaffrey bought a lot on Nov. 30, 1901, where Dr. J. Wesley Smith built the Smith Hotel, known as the Cornelius Hotel after Charles Cornelius took it over in 1931. The *De Lamar Lode*, July 2, 1901, reported that the OSL intended to build a new station. The paper said, "The First Citizen of the place will be P.B. McKeon, who is building a store and will move from Uvada with the change of the terminus".

Denton (1945) says the P.B. McKeen Forwarding Company, of Milford, started the first store in a box car. The next store was Ed Clark's. He had been

Cornelius Hotel; Company Row to the right.

operating a forward-
ing company out of
Uvada while it was
the end of track, and
he moved to
Caliente with the
railroad.

Known at first
as Culverwell's
Ranch, the site was
next called Clover
Junction, because it
was the junction of
Clover Creek and
the Meadow Valley

Caliente yard after the 1910 flood. Original depot left center.
View south, probably from top of coaling station. Photo from
T.C. Himstreet.

Wash. The name officially became Calientes in July 1901, then it became
Caliente in 1903.

"Caliente" is Spanish for warm, hot, or heated; there are hot springs at
Caliente. In a letter in the *Caliente Herald* on Aug. 25, 1949, Thomas Dixon
passed along the story he had heard that an assistant engineer of the SPLA&SL
named Caliente during the survey for the terminal.

Of course, we don't use the Spanish pronunciation. We are not alone in
our ability to garble foreign or otherwise unfamiliar words. (That's how the
Purgatoire River in Colorado became the Picketwire.) In Spanish, "caliente" is
pronounced (approximately) as kahl-yen'-tay. We call it callie-antee, often
shortened to callie-ant.

The number of employees of the railroad had increased so much that in
1905 the construction of Company Row began. House #12 was built first, then
6 more in 1907 and 6 in 1908. Construction continued until 24 had been built.

The first railroad doctor according to Denton (1945) was Dr. Quick, followed by Dr. Hosmer. The railroad had fitted out the "old depot building" as a
hospital, according to the *Caliente Herald* on March 11, 1926, and it was ready to
open. Dr. Clyde W. Countryman was in charge.

Ed Clark was appointed Postmaster when Caliente post office was established on Aug. 3, 1901; J. Lester "Less" Denton became Postmaster in 1912, and
he held the position until he retired in 1942. Clark moved to Las Vegas and
became a prominent merchant and banker.

A small building in Kershaw Canyon was used as a school in 1883. School
moved to a building near the hot springs, called the Bath House school, in
1901. A rock schoolhouse was built on Culverwell Street in late 1906, when
enrollment had reached 60 pupils in all grades. A frame building was added,

and the two buildings served until 1926. The middle section of the Caliente Elementary School that we knew was built then, and the wings were added a few years later.

1907 VIGNETTES

The town was a busy place in 1907, and Charles W. Patterson, the editor of the *Caliente Lode-Express*, brought out a booster edition on June 29. Here is a summary of what was happening, based mainly on that issue of the paper.

He said, "The townsite of Caliente is so-called from several hot springs having a temperature of 95 degrees and is situated at the junction of Clover and Meadow valleys. . . . Originally the land was owned by the Culverwells and was called – before the advent of the railroad – Culverwell's Ranch. . . .

"The Hot Springs here would make a fame for Caliente as a health resort second to none, and it is only a short time before a large sanitarium will be built here by the owners, the Culverwells.

"It is in the center of a rich agricultural section, the soil is a rich black loam, water is plentiful and all the products of the temperate zone may be successfully produced here. . . .

"Most all kinds of business houses are represented. The San Pedro, Los Angeles & Salt Lake Railroad Company are doing an immense business here and recently increased the forces at this point.

"They have shops and a roundhouse here as well as a material yard, and recently established an oil storage tank with a capacity of 720,000 gallons, and put new oil burning engines into commission here to facilitate the handling of the increased traffic. Six years ago Caliente consisted of a ranch house, a grading camp and 26 tent saloons."

Because Caliente was the connecting point to mining camps in the area, large amounts of freight were being handled, and new Concord coaches had been put on the stage lines to accommodate travelers. He said that by 8:00 pm, all the hotels had posted the signs "Rooms All Taken".

The "oldest pioneer in this part of the state of Nevada" was Capt. C.R. Carden, a native of Kentucky, who came to Pioche in 1876. The area that became Caliente had "but a few farmers cutting hay" at that time. In 1907 he purchased a corner building known as the Cosmopolitan Saloon. He had other lots in town and a ranch "about a mile north of here", and he was interested in

The Caliente Homemakers' Club was established in 1918 for civic improvement purposes. Denton (1945) says the club started the first library when they received 100 or more books from the Red Cross in Reno that had been returned from use overseas in World War I. The club was disbanded in 1928, and by then they had built up to about 300 volumes. The books were turned over to the P.T.A. library in the Caliente grade school.

"several mining enterprises".

C.P. Christenson came to Caliente in 1903 and built a large store building for the general merchandise trade. "Everything and anything to be found in a first-class general store can be found at Mr. Christenson's place, his stock of goods is comprised of only the best that money can buy. . . ." He also had two large warehouses.

George C. Collins had arrived 3 years before from Montana and opened the Mint Saloon on Clover Street.

The parents of Charles Culverwell, Jr., "originally owned all of the property on which the town of Caliente is now situated". About 3½ years earlier, he opened a butcher shop, the first one in Caliente. In 1907 his Caliente Meat Market covered 1,000 square feet, and he operated a slaughter house. He intended to plat 160 acres of his ground near the depot into town lots.

Alice Culverwell, his cousin, was "one of the largest owners of real estate here and is also one of our most progressive citizens. Miss Culverwell owns several large tracts of town property, an interest in the hot springs here and a number of nice new cottages." In an ad in the same issue, she offered for sale "choice business and residence lots, also acreage property, smelter sites and mill sites".

Mrs. Eliza Culverwell, widow of William Culverwell, had the Caliente Hotel, "one of the best in town".

Senator James A. Denton, "The Cyclone of Lincoln County", owned the Denton Hotel, Denton Railroad Eating House, Denton Heights, 40 acres platted into lots, a two-story brick building, and several frame buildings. He was born in Iowa in 1849 and became a mail carrier in 1863; he had been "identified with the transportation of the mail in this State for the past 15 years". His chief business was "connected with all stage lines running out of here for a hundred miles".

J.A. Denton's nephew, Less Denton, born in Waterloo, Neb., in 1870, came to Pioche in 1898 and to Caliente by 1903. Less helped with his uncle's stage line, became a lineman in 1904, and was a deputy sheriff in 1907.

Less Denton's brother, Lloyd Cleveland Denton, born in Waterloo, Neb., in 1888, came to Caliente with his mother in 1903 to visit Sen. Denton, and he stayed. He started driving stage for his uncle, then he worked for the Ed Clark Forwarding Co. (In 1914 he joined Lester Burt in the theatre business, which led to his career with the Rex Theatre.)

The Caliente Mercantile Co., "the largest and most prosperous general merchandise store in Lincoln County", was owned by George C. Fetterman. He owned the building that contained his store and was soon to house the Lincoln County Bank. He owned the DeLamar Mercantile Co., and he operated a general freighting business in "all of south-eastern Nevada". Fetterman had owned the gold mines at Caliente (see "Mike's Cave", in Chapter 7 of this book), and he had recently been appointed Postmaster in Caliente. (The next issue of the paper said he had reportedly sold his Caliente businesses because of poor health and would move to Southern California.)

Mrs. Edna S. Foster came from Waterloo, Canada, to Delamar in 1892 and opened a mercantile store. She sold the store in 1904 and moved to Caliente to open another one. Her husband was an undertaker and also had a lumber yard.

Miss Mabel Gregor was principal and Miss Issabella Smith was assistant principal of the Caliente school.

Dental care was provided by Dr. J.F. Irvine, who came from Salt Lake City in 1904.

W.H. Liston was a year old when his father moved to Nevada and developed the Liston ranch, a 200-acre property 2 miles northwest of town. W.H. Liston had opened a butcher shop that developed into the Blue Front Meat Market and grocery store that opened in 1906. He expected to build residences on several of his lots, and he intended to build an ice plant during the summer.

Frank R. McNamee, "one of the brightest attorneys in the state", had "spacious apartments" in the Lincoln County Bank building. He had a large practice, and he was chief counsel for the San Pedro, Los Angeles & Salt Lake Railroad in Nevada.

W.P. Murray, M.D., came to Caliente in 1905 and developed a private practice. He soon became resident surgeon for the railroad.

W.C. "Billy" Noble operated a saloon and restaurant ("open day and night"), and he had mining interests.

A.H. Norris had the North Side Saloon (north of the tracks), with "Fine Wines, Liquors and Cigars...Lodging's in Connection".

Hans Olsen came from Sweden to Delamar in about 1895 and started a saloon. He moved to Caliente in 1904 and put up a large building in which he opened a saloon. He owned "much of the choicest real estate", and he had built "one of the finest residences in this section". He had a 330-acre ranch 9 miles from Caliente. He joined C.W. Patterson in applying for a franchise "for the construction, maintenance and operation of an underground pipeline for the conveyance of water from a point approximately one and one-half miles easterly of the town of Caliente, to said town, to enable said applicants and give them the right to supply the town of Caliente with water. . ."

Hyrum Rice, born in Utah in 1862, had been in the mercantile business in Panaca and Caliente. He had recently disposed of those interests, but he still owned property in both places. He had a beautiful home in Panaca.

George K. Riding, who had lived 18 years in Lincoln County, had operated the Square Deal Grocery Co. for about 18 months. His ad in the paper said

"Moapa Vegetables received on Tuesdays, Thursdays and Saturdays... Royal Baking Co.'s Bread Fresh every day...California fruits of all kinds received every day...Fresh fish every Friday".

John Shier was proprietor of the Caliente Drug Store in Caliente and a drug store in Delamar.

W.H. Underhill, a native of New York, started a saloon in a tent in 1902, then he expanded to the recent erection of "a modern business house with heavy plate glass front. His saloon has the appointments of a metropolitan resort . . ."

George V. Warren, who arrived in 1904, owned the Caliente Saloon, with appointments that were "equal to any in cities of the first class". He owned a large opera house, and he was ready to build a business block. (After a fire in 1918 burned most of the business district, Denton and Burt moved their theatre to the old Warren Hall on Spring Street.)

The Arizona Club, "Headquarters for Sporting Fraternities", opened for business in 1906. A new stone building was to be erected to take the place of the present quarters. (When Denton and Burt started their theatre in 1914, they moved into the former Arizona Bar.)

The Lincoln County Bank was organized on March 9, 1906, and it opened for business on June 1. The bank was making expenses within 3 months after opening its doors. The president was Homer G. Taber, of Los Angeles, and George Fetterman ("one of the ablest and best known attorneys in Nevada") was vice president. (The bank closed in 1914.)

Phil Smith (son of Philip Klingensmith) was elected sheriff of Lincoln County in 1906. Several stories in the *Pioche Weekly Record* in 1907 and 1908 concern Phil and his twin brother, John. On the evening of Dec. 21, 1907, an unknown man had confronted John near Phil's house on Spring Street and fired at him, wounding him in the body. John was taken to Salt Lake City, where he died of complications on Jan. 29, 1908, at Holy Cross Hospital. Sheriff Phil Smith was accused of having killed John, and the Feb. 8 newspaper said he was held to answer before the Grand Jury. The headline on March 21 was "Phil K. Smith Is Acquitted". The details are not given, but the article does say everyone in the courtroom applauded when the verdict was read. He resigned as sheriff in July. He died in Huntington Beach, Calif., in 1928.

NEWSPAPERS

A newspaper was started in 1904; Lingenfelter and Gash give this sequence of Caliente newspapers: The *Caliente Progress* began in early October, 1904, to support J.A. Denton's campaign for reelection to the state assembly. He was defeated, and in January 1905 a new owner resumed publication as the *Caliente Express*. It lasted until June 1906, when the Lincoln County Publishing Co.

bought it out, closed the Caliente operation, and combined it with the *De Lamar Lode* as the *Caliente Lode-Express*. That paper was discontinued in December 1908. The printing plant at Caliente was purchased by Robert Graham, and he began publishing the *Caliente Prospector* in March 1909. He sold out in 1912, and after further changes of owners, the paper went out of business in February 1913.

NOTICE - Notice is hereby given that the shooting of fireworks must not be indulged in on the Fourth of July within the town limits of Caliente. Merchants are warned against selling any kind of fireworks to children. By order of Phil K. Smith, Sheriff of Lincoln County, Nevada, June 29, 1907.

A glimpse behind the scenes is contained in this paragraph from the *Caliente Lode-Express*, June 29, 1907: "The plant of the *Lode-Express* consists of an old army press and several handfulls of type, both of which came to Nevada in the year '01. . . . The plant is made up from odds and ends of more than one office and considerable of the material came to this country via Cape Horn in the early days. Occasionaly we find several letters missing to the font and therefore are compelled to get along any old way."

In May 1920, E. Charles D. Marriage began publishing the *Caliente News*. He had a running fight with the *Pioche Record*, and in June 1925 the Pioche Record Publishing Co. bought him out and closed the paper. E.C.D. Marriage was back in 1928, establishing the *Caliente Herald* on Jan. 12, 1928. He was appointed State Librarian in 1935, but he continued his ownership until selling out to David and Edna Williams in 1946. They sold it in about 1956, and Francis L. Peters, editor of the *Pioche Record*, bought it and published it in Pioche until he suspended it on May 30, 1968, and merged it with the *Pioche Record* to become the *Lincoln County Record*. (The *Pioche Record* had been previously published as the *Pioche Weekly Record*, the *Pioche Record*, and the *Lincoln County Record*, depending on the whim of the owner.)

CALIENTE PUBLIC UTILITIES

J.A. Denton bought about 40 acres of land south of town (later known as Denton Heights) in 1902-1905, according to Denton (1945), and he drilled a well that supplied enough water for the Denton Hotel. He installed a windmill to pump water to a 5000-gallon tank on the hill. The hotel burned in 1907, and he realized that a better water system was needed. He decided he could extend service to businesses on Clover Street and across the tracks to the corner of Front and Spring Streets.

His windmill couldn't keep up with demand, and he got a gas engine and it also was inadequate. He was a friend of Sen. William Clark, owner of the railroad, and about 1910 the railroad began supplying water to the city.

Negotiations with the railroad to furnish electricity started in about 1917, but after a major fire in 1918, the interest in electricity waned and nothing was done. The 1921 session of the Legislature provided for creation of the Caliente Public Utilities, and construction of a power plant started. The Public Utilities plant was supplying electricity after 1924, but the cost was so great that in about 1927 the railroad agreed to furnish water and electricity, to extend the water mains, and to put in a sewage treatment plant. (The *Caliente Herald* said on Feb. 5, 1931, that the railroad was to take over the power system of the Public Utilities.)

The Caliente Public Utilities was reorganized in 1937. In November, electricity became available from the Hoover Dam power system through the Lincoln County Power District.

THE CITY OF CALIENTE

The railroad was the biggest economic basis for Caliente, with mining, agriculture, and stock raising also playing a part. Completion of the Pioche Branch of the railroad (officially the Caliente & Pioche) in 1907 made Caliente the railroad connection for the Pioche mines. Growth is obvious from the articles in the newspapers, until the Depression affected railroad employment.

Pioche Branch train at Caliente, 1911.
C.J. Himstreet, Engineer. Photo from
T.C. Himstreet.

Engine 3411 with train at Caliente,
Feb. 23, 1907. C.J. Himstreet,
Engineer. Photo from T.C. Himstreet.

With the coming of World War II and the surge in railroad business, Caliente saw some prosperous years. The city grew so much that incorporation was sought. The *Caliente Herald* for May 11, 1944, reported that the first City Council had been elected: Thomas E. Dixon was mayor and Hyrum "Hy" Thompson, Walter A. Ray, and Jack E. Ellison were the councilmen. The council appointed the following officers: Philip J. Dolan clerk, Press W. Duffin, Jr., treasurer, and Evan H. Edwards, police judge. On June 1, the paper said the Certificate of Incorporation as a third class city had been received, effective May 27, 1944.

Tom Dixon had a fine rose garden, and roses grew so well in Caliente that it was called the Rose City.

When the railroad converted from steam to diesel, the steam engine servicing facilities were no longer needed, and demolition began. The round-house and the water tank survived until Feb. 1970, and their removal completed the job.

However, the depot still survived. A frame depot burned in 1922, and the mission-style depot was built. It was later expanded to include the Union Pacific Hotel, and it was still there in 1970. The *Lincoln County Record* for March 30, 1972, reported that the railroad had deeded the depot to the City of Caliente in December and leased the grounds to the city. The building had various uses, including the City Hall. A restoration project was undertaken in 1972, and improvements have continued since then. Caliente is the closest thing to a home town I have, and that fine old building is a link from now to those pleasant years in Caliente.

> *Thomas C. Himstreet was born in Denver in 1894, moved to Caliente in 1905, and started work for the railroad in 1909. His father, C.J. Himstreet, was an engineer whose assignments included the Pioche run. The family lived in #11 on Company Row. Tommy was in continuous service on the railroad from June 9, 1910. He was Road Foreman of Engines from 1937 to 1944. In 1962 he was No. 1 on the engineer's seniority list and was the oldest man between Caliente and Los Angeles.*

What do I mean by that last sentence? What's my connection with Caliente? It's like this: The Averett family moved from Carp to the Elliott ranch in June, 1941. I began high school at Panaca, and my sister, Mary Louise, entered the 6th grade in Caliente Elementary School. My father knew the weather would be chancy at times to drive from the ranch to Caliente during the winter, so he rented a place from Paul Mears, then he bought the George Cram house at 275 Osborne St. We lived in Caliente during the winter and commuted the rest of the time. We sold our interest in the ranch in 1944 and moved to Caliente to stay.

Caliente depot, 1994. Built in 1922. One of three surviving mission style depots on the Union Pacific; now the Caliente City Hall.

Clover Street, Caliente. J.C. Penney store left, Rex Theatre center.

I worked in Darryl Mayhew's service station, while we lived there, and I was a projectionist at the Rex Theatre. My father was appointed Superintendent of Streets and Parks in the new city administration. My sister started high school in September 1944, and I graduated in 1945 and went on to the University of Nevada, where I got a degree in chemistry. I have not lived in Caliente since then. The city discontinued the position my father had held, and he became manager of the Kopenite operation of the A.J. Mackie perlite property on the west side of Delamar Flat. My sister went to the University of Nevada for the 1948-49 year; she got married and did not return to college. Much later, she studied for Holy Orders and became an Episcopal priest. My parents lived in Caliente until my father died in 1950, and then my mother stayed there until I moved her to Rifle, Colorado, in 1952. We moved from Rifle to Las Vegas, and I went on to work in other places in later years. My mother died in 1966. They are both buried in the Veteran's section of the Caliente cemetery. And that is my connection with Caliente.

This brief chapter barely hints at the story of Caliente, a story that deserves a book of its own. In case there is any doubt, I will say I liked being a small-town boy, and I liked Caliente being that town. When I was in college, one of the instructors called me "Caliente". I had a photo in which I had a beard and wore a Colt six-shooter, and someone said, "There's the Caliente Kid". Right on!

Lincoln County High School Band at Caliente.

Ads from Caliente newspaper.

CHAPTER 3

ELGIN

THE RAINBOW'S END

A bout half-way between Caliente and Carp, the deep, narrow canyon gives way to an open area that accommodates nice ranchland, and that's where Elgin is. Don and Barbara Bradshaw have developed a fine apple orchard on the Bradshaw ranch, and they picked the felicitous name "End of the Rainbow Canyon". The canyon continues on past Kyle, with deep, narrow segments alternating with open areas that have ranches, but in the absence of a legal definition of the end of the Rainbow Canyon, Elgin is as good a place as any to say, "This is where it ends".

When I showed a draft of the manuscript to Jim Bradshaw, he said, "You have a Carp section, but nothing about Elgin". My reply was, "I don't have the information for that". But things change, and now I do, and here it is. When I got to the *Pioche Record* for 1922 and 1923, I found Elgin Personals and Elgin Notes, and now I can give Elgin some of the recognition it deserves. I quote extensively from the newspaper.

Most of the time, the personals or local notes in the newspapers don't give the name of the person who wrote them (except for "Caliente All The Time", in the *Caliente Herald*, by J.M.R., who was Hazel B. Denton). These Elgin notes don't list the author, but Jim and Don Bradshaw and I are convinced they had to have been written by Etta Mariger. My folks referred to her as Maryetta Mariger; in the lists of registered voters, she was always listed as Etta M. Mariger; in the 1920 Census, she was Marrietta Mariger. Jim Bradshaw knew her as Etta, and he says she was his father's school teacher in 1900. She was known as a historian of the area, but I got seriously interested in this project too late to benefit from her knowledge.

May 26, 1922, Elgin Personals:

"The local school has been brought to a successful close by Mrs. Etta Mariger, the following pupils being graduated: Hazel Bradshaw and William Schlarman." (When I graduated at Carp in 1941, I was the only pupil in the

8th grade, and I think the entire enrollment was six or seven that year, and it was probably never more than 10 or 12.

"Since the first of May school has been held in the fine new schoolhouse just completed by Rube Bradshaw as contractor and William Allison as carpenter. It is modern in every way, and certainly does credit to Elgin."

"A Sunday School is being organized, and great interest is being shown. An average attendance of twenty or so is looked for by Mrs. Chas. Andrews, Supt.

"Lee L. Dixon and wife returned Monday, the 15th, from a short stay in Los Angeles and vicinity. Mr. Dixon drove his light speedster out from Los Angeles, accompanied by Stewart Henrie. They drove through Cajon Pass, where they hit the storm experienced here a few weeks ago. They continued on to Las Vegas, then via Moapa, and Coyote Holes, cutting through the range to Elgin. Mr. Dixon has the distinction of driving the first car through the canyon from Coyote Holes to Elgin. Mrs. Dixon returned by train."

Lee Dixon must have gone north from Moapa past Coyote Spring, up Kane Springs Wash, easterly out of Kane Springs Wash to the head of Riggs Wash, then down Riggs Wash to Elgin. That route is now a shortcut between Caliente and Las Vegas, bypassing Oak Springs Summit (Delamar Summit, as we knew it) and the Pahranagat Valley.

"Lawrence Rowe has just finished his house on a five acre piece of alfalfa a quarter mile west of the station, and he is gradually equipping an up-to-date chicken ranch. He just received three hundred thoroughbred Plymouth Rock chicks from a Los Angeles hatchery, and is putting up runs, etc. Mr. Rowe expects to return to his duties with the Union Pacific as relief operator about the first of June, leaving his wife and family permanently located here." Lawrence Rowe, a telegraph operator at Elgin, married Mary Bradshaw. His alfalfa patch was on ground that was in about the center of the Bradshaw apple orchard now.

John Bradshaw and his family left Joplin, Missouri, to come West, and John died of cholera in Cheyenne. His son James Webster "Jim" Bradshaw, born in Teabo, Mo., continued on to Nevada in 1864, ending up in Lincoln County. James W. Bradshaw was born in 1845 and died in 1929. He married Jane Crowe in 1886; she was born in 1867 and died in 1948. Their children who survived to adulthood were Jane, John B., Reuben Joseph, Mary, Ida, and Hazel. Three young children were buried in the cemetery in the railroad cut at a curve toward Caliente from Elgin, just over the hill from the Bradshaw home. Two babies of other families are also buried there.

On our ranch at Carp, we raised chickens for the market in Las Vegas. We received boxes of baby chicks, usually Rhode Island Red or Buff Minorca, by Special Handling mail from Spiegel's, in Chicago. We had home-made incubators where the chicks got their start.

Schoolhouse at Elgin, 1994. Road at the top of the hill beyond the school is the road to the Pennsylvania. Photo from Don Bradshaw.

"Operator Blankenship relieved Mr. Lee Dixon on his recent two weeks lay off, leaving here for Rox, to relieve Operator C.E. Kendrick at that place."

"The Utah Construction Company has spurred out their drag line at Kyle. They will do extensive strengthening of the retaining wall at that place. "

"Mr. H.M. Reece, formerly maintainer here, and now located at Pomona, Cal., advises us that he will make us a visit sometime during June. Mr. Reece was well known in Caliente, and had many friends throughout Lincoln County."

"The Bradshaw ranch is putting in a considerable patch of watermelons for shipping this year. However, close inquiry fails to divulge the location of said patch. We understand that Elgin watermelons cannot be beat."

"Rube Bradshaw has his new five-room bungalow virtually completed. It is to be modern in every way, with stucco exterior, and will make him a fine comfortable home." The house was at the north end of Elgin community ("east", in railroad terminology).

"The lawns and gardens being put in by various company employees will add very much to the creditable appearance of Company Row." Don Bradshaw says Company Row or Company Road was between the houses and the railroad, west of the crossing. A nice white border fence enclosed spacious lawns with an underground sprinkler system.

"John Bradshaw lost a valuable Percheron draught stallion a few days ago, it being run down by a train during the night. Mr. Bradshaw brought the animal from Leamington, Utah, and they feel the loss very keenly. The horse has been very much admired locally, and was a family pet." He rode the horse from Leamington and drove three head of milk cows.

Elgin Personals, Aug. 4, 1922:

"Mrs. W.B. Conk, of Carp, wife of the signal maintainer at that point, has been visiting with her daughter Mrs. Lee Dixon, of Elgin for a few days. Her small son is an extremely precocious child in every way, we think, not five months old and weighs nineteen pounds, and is the owner of two brand new teeth. Ranch life must agree with him. Mr. Conk has recently moved onto his ranch a mile east of Carp, and they have one of the nicest ranch houses in this section." Six years later, Walter Conk, Jr., contracted scarlet fever at Carp. His parents took him to Los Angeles, but the *Caliente Herald* of Dec. 13, 1928, reports that he died there.

"Rube Bradshaw is loading a car of alfalfa hay for shipment to local buyers in Caliente. The stormy weather of the past few days is retarding the cutting of the hay, but he states he was fortunate in not having much cut when the storm commenced. The Utah Construction Co. are also taking quite a bit of hay from the Bradshaw ranch."

"The Mariger ranch is the first on the market with sweet corn, which is of very good quality, tender and sweet. They also report that their watermelons are just beginning to ripen."

"The ground under the apple trees at the Elliott ranch is covered with fruit, which Mr. Elliott states is very hard to market, altho of very fine quality. We believe if local growers were better patronized it would result in more fresh goods on the market here. The local ranchers at present have no incentive to raise anything but hay, as this seems to be the only product for which there is any market."

When we moved to the Elliott ranch in 1941, the orchard still had lots of apple trees, plus peaches, pears, plums, apricots, cherries, and crabapples. We enjoyed all of them.

"Bert Barnett is wearing a broad smile these days, occasioned by the arrival of a second son, to be named, we understand, Roland Stanley. He now has a nice family, two boys and two girls. Mother and baby are both doing very nicely, and are being cared for by Dr. Geo. A. Bell, with Mrs. Jas. Bradshaw as nurse."

"J.J. Grandin, erstwhile section foreman at Stine, visited at the McKinnon home Sunday. Mr. Grandin is resigning in order to go out on the Maynard Project as soon as conditions are favorable for winter quarters."

"J.D. Pittman and Ed Huntsman, foremen of Extra Gangs 3 and 4 respectively, it is understood will be moved to Stine the later part of this week, and from that point will complete the work of dressing up track on the ballast raise."

"We understand that Guy Cox, relief section foreman at Rox, Nev., has bid in the position vacated by J.J. Grandin at Stine, and will move his family as soon as relief can be arranged." Stine section was discontinued long ago, but the walls of one building at Stine community are still visible from the road.

"Joe Schlarman is laying the foundation for his new house this week. He intends putting up a very comfortable ranch house on his farm a mile west of Elgin, which has already been developed considerably." Henry J. "Joe" Schlarman and his wife Rachael came to Stine in 1913 and to Elgin in 1914. He was building a house on his ranch in August 1922. He was section foreman, later the Roadmaster.

Stories in the *Lincoln County Record* on Dec. 23 and the *Las Vegas Review-Journal* on Dec. 25, 1926, said that Joe Schlarman was fatally injured on Dec. 20 when his speeder (motor car) was struck by helper engine 6058 at 5:56 pm at milepost 443, about 4 miles east of Elgin. The motor was not running right, and he stopped on a curve about 4 miles east of Elgin to get it going. He was put on Train #25, which was following right behind, but he died on the way to Los Angeles.

Ralph T. Salt was the engineer and R.T. Caulfield was the fireman of the helper. Salt whistled for a crossing and had slowed to 17 miles per hour on the curve, but he didn't see the speeder, and evidently Schlarman didn't hear the whistle or see the signal, which was about 300 feet away.

"Lee Dixon has a half grown coyote running up and down his clothesline, which he says he intends to raise. We will admit it has stopped snapping now, and permits him to pet it. He can pet it, but not for us."

Elgin Notes, April 20, 1923:

"A cloud burst back up in the hills has caused the river to come up quite a bit which means more water for the farmers."

"Miss Hazel Bradshaw arrived today from Bakersfield where she has been attending high school for the past term. Her sister Ida lives there also and reports everything in fine condition there."

"Chas. Dimmick came in to Elgin today from his ranch below Carp on business."

Elgin Notes, June 22, 1923:

"Mr. A. Barnett is up in the hills attending to his big herd of cattle. Miss Bernice Barnett is staying with J.W. Bradshaw while her mother is in Salt Lake City."

"Mr. Tom Casey has been appointed first trick operator at Elgin recently. He will take charge of his new duties in the near future." Tom Casey had bid in the first-trick position at Carp by 1925. I don't remember Tom, but my parents talked a lot about him.

"R.J. Bradshaw has been quite successful in selling International Harvester machinery lately. Go to it Rube." If he was selling machinery, a market existed somewhere. Well, the Meadow Valley Wash had ranches all the way from Caliente to Moapa. He was probably in the right place at the right time. He had a store and the International Harvester agency at Elgin. His store prospered while the tunnels on the railroad were being concreted.

Don Bradshaw says, "He started with a tie shed. Men came from around the area nightly to play poker. R.J. didn't play but provided beverages and took a chip from each pot. It continued to grow, so he built the store, which had a Delco light plant for keeping meats, etc. He had fresh bread daily from train service and carried meat, fresh fruits, vegetables, all store goods, clothing, and a couple of 'one-arm bandits'. He expanded further and sold International Harvester products and carried parts for them. One night when I was small, there was an electrical short in the Delco system and the store burnt to the ground. The folks had no insurance, so it was quite a loss." According to the *Caliente Herald*, the fire was on June 23, 1932.

"Joe McGuffie spent Sunday in Elgin visiting L.A. Rowe. Mr. and Mrs. L.A. Rowe and Mrs. W.F. Rowe motored to Bill McGuffie's Monday in their Buick six picking cherries and visiting."

"Miss Hazel Bradshaw says she has some awful enemies. One of them hates her as bad as a gourd." Wow! That's pretty bad!

Elgin Notes, June 29, 1923:

"The U.P. Railroad is laying steel at Elgin now, preparing for the heavy traffic rush."

"R.J. Bradshaw says he challenges anyone in the state of Nevada to beat him growing wheat. He has 3 acres 5 feet high and heads on from three to six inches long. Bring on your wheat."

"The radio of Mr. C.D. Smith of Elgin is sure a dandy, we heard concerts and music from Los Angeles last night that was hard to beat."

"Joe McGuffie has been working for J.W. Bradshaw during the past week."

Elgin Notes, Sept. 27, 1923:

"Mr. Stewart Henrie and sister Dagmar visited with Mr. and Mrs. L.A. Rowe Sunday evening, although Stewart managed to stop at J.W. Bradshaw's as Hazel was swinging on the gate waiting for him."

"Buddie Barnett is the proudest boy in Lincoln County. He has just received his new wagon from the *L.A. Examiner* for selling papers. It sure is a beauty. Bud, don't get it muddy." We didn't subscribe to anything but the *Caliente Herald* at Carp; the *Examiner* and the *Salt Lake Tribune* were the other newspapers we were most likely to see.

"R.J. Bradshaw has just purchased a new wagon and you see him every morning going up and down the boulevard showing it off. J.W. Bradshaw has started to bale hay this week." All these years, I didn't know Elgin even had a boulevard!

Elgin Notes, Nov. 23, 1923:

"Hazel Bradshaw spent four hours ironing one dress. It ought to be nice and smooth Hazel."

"Mr. Ike Elliott came down to Elgin Friday after his horse. Some ride Ike but come oftener, we like to see you once in a while."

"Mr. E.F. Davis, employee of the P.F.E. Company at Las Vegas spent Saturday and Sunday in Elgin visiting the Bradshaws." P.F.E. was Pacific Fruit Express, a large fleet of refrigerator cars to move fruit from Southern California to eastern markets. Terminals such as Las Vegas had large icing sheds to ice down the cars of fruit.

"Mr. John Bradshaw, section foreman at Wann for the U.P., spent Sunday and Monday with his father and mother, Mr. and Mrs. J.W. Bradshaw."

"Mrs. P. Henrie and Mrs. Mariger inspected the new addition to the school house Sunday which has just been completed by Gus Schmidt. The addition consists of a kitchenette and bedroom, all built-in features, and will be quite cozy and handy for the teacher in case of bad weather."

Elgin Notes, Nov. 30, 1923:

"R.J. Bradshaw is working for Ryberg Bros. at Kyle . . . . The U.P. is busy now ballasting their road bed from Boyd to Las Vegas . . . . The water tank at Elgin has been out of commission for two days on account of broken valve. . . . Lonesome John spent Saturday in Elgin. He is now employed at Kyle on the Ryberg Construction gang."

"Ryberg Bros. of Salt Lake City have a big contract at Kyle putting in a 1500-foot retaining wall in Dimmick Canyon to check the over flow of water. The work calls for about 3 months work and employing quite a few men."

Dimmick Canyon (Cottonwood Canyon), can carry a lot of water, and the railroad goes right across its mouth. Don Bradshaw says his father, Rube, had "about six teams with Fresno scrapers working for Ryberg at two bits a yard".

When the Delamar mining boom developed, people such as John Kiernan and J.W. Bradshaw had a market for fruit, produce, and wine, if they could get it to Delamar. (For example, the *Lincoln County Record*, June 29, 1900, says, "Kiernan makes tri-weekly trips to Delamar, with fine peaches, & etc".) The distance from present Elgin across the mountains to Willow Spring and then by the existing road to Delamar was about 18 miles. Those two men had a long-standing dislike for each other, and they would not cooperate to build a road. Each one asked the County Commissioners to build a road by his route, but the Commissioners refused to take sides; they said for each one to build a road, and the County would maintain the one that was completed first. Jim Bradshaw won the race.

Kiernan built his road about 3 miles up the wash that is now known as Riggs Wash, then to the right and to Willow Creek. Later the county extended that road on up Riggs Wash, across the summit, and down into Kane Springs Wash. The road connects with U.S. 93, and it has been developed into a graveled road that makes a short-cut between Caliente and Las Vegas, bypassing the road over Oak Springs Summit, across Delamar Flat, and down through Pahranagat Valley.

Bradshaw's road, which was finished first, went up the canyon just below Crow Corral and into Willow Creek. Nothing can be seen now of it.

In 1898, James Bradshaw was awarded a contract to improve or build a road between Carden's ranch and the Moapa Indian Reservation, according to issues of the *Pioche Weekly Record* in July through September. That road appears to have gone down the Meadow Valley Wash.

Elgin was originally situated in the mouth of the canyon, a mile or so north of its present location (east, in railroad terminology). The 1910 flood stranded a passenger train there and washed away most of Elgin. The siding and associated facilities were relocated to their present site as part of the reconstruction after the flood.

In the 1920s, this was the make-up of Elgin, as described by Don Bradshaw, starting at the little cemetery and working south: Just beyond the cemetery was a hill, and the Bradshaw home was beyond the hill. The site of the store was beyond the house, with two residences between them and the railroad. The railroad crossing was next; the road turned left past the Bradshaw house, went straight ahead to the school, or turned right to the rest of Elgin.

The water tower was south of the crossing, and the pumping plant (a hothead engine) was beyond it. Next was the depot, with living quarters for the first-trick operator. The section foreman's house was next in line, followed by the second-trick operator's house opposite a little hill, a low place referred to as a swamp, and two more houses. Company Row ran parallel to the railroad, between it and these houses south of the crossing.

John Kiernan had an orchard and vineyards on his ranch, and during the construction of the railroad, so I am told, he "got rich selling wine at 25 cents a quart". He had several stone cellars for storage of his wine. He sent some bottles of his wine to a World's Fair, and he won a first prize. (He had his problems with his crops; on Sept. 5, 1902, the *Lincoln County Record* reported that the grasshoppers had destroyed his grape and hay crops.)

Kiernan and Scott Allen developed the Cherokee Mine (see the separate description of the Cherokee in Chapter 7), and they sold it for $50,000 and split the money, $25,000 to each. Kiernan invested in property in Salt Lake City, and he sent his wife to buy and take care of the property. I am told he died on Jan.

6, 1904, of a heart attack, while she was gone. He was by himself, and he collapsed in the yard. His pigs ran loose, as was a common practice, and they found his body and chewed on it. (When somebody says, "Oh, he died and the hogs ate him", it might have been true.)

According to the *Lincoln County Record*, Jan. 8, 1904, he died at 5:00 in the afternoon on the previous Wednesday. The article says he "stumbled and fell which started him to vomit-

Looking west at Elgin, 1972. Section foreman's house on left; all railroad buildings were demolished since then.

ing which continued until death came two days later". He was buried at Bullionville, "by the side of his children". He left his wife Philippa and daughter Josephine.

The phrase "by the side of his children" refers to one of those poignant early-day tragedies. Four children are listed on the obelisk; three of them died of diphtheria in July 1892: John H., age 13, on July 1; Lena P., age 3, on July 7; and Lizzie A., age 18, on July 25. Emery A. had died as an infant in 1875.

On Feb. 10, 1898, the *Pioche Weekly Record* had a story about a shooting "at a point some ten miles below John Kiernan's ranch". Bob Bonds and Rufe Pippin were returning from a trip to St. George, and they camped with Ernest Keats, the mail rider. Bonds stayed on the wagon (which means there was a wagon road), and Keats and Pippin were lying on the ground when Bonds shot Pippin in the back of the head. Bonds claimed he intended to shoot a rabbit, but Keats said it was attempted murder. (Pippin recovered from the injury.) John Harty and T.E. Dula went to Delamar and filed a charge of assault with intent to kill, and Bonds was arrested. He was tried in June and convicted.

Hills at Elgin.

CHAPTER 4

CARP

RAILROADING AT CARP

Half a dozen or so houses, a pumping station, a railroad depot and other railroad buildings, and a sidetrack; it isn't much, but it was important to me. I spent the first 13 years of my life there or at our ranch nearby.

Carp's history as a place with a name apparently began with the establishment of a railroad construction camp in about 1903. A rag dump was set up in a dry wash on the east side of the Meadow Valley Wash, not far beyond the west end of the siding. In about 1940, my father showed me the rubbish pile where a tent saloon had been. He said a flash flood came down the normally dry wash, and in his panic to escape the flood, the owner ran the full length of the saloon and didn't even think about a valise full of money by the door. The money vanished with the tent.

In the days of steam locomotives, Carp was important to the railroad because it had a good supply of water and because it was where helper engines coupled to eastbound trains for the long pull to Caliente or beyond. Most eastbound trains stopped at Carp so the engines could take on water.

Carp is situated where the Meadow Valley Wash pinches down to a canyon with conglomerate cliffs full of caves inhabited by monkey-faced owls (barn owls). The hills are Pliocene to Pleistocene fan gravels with conglomerate facies. The floor of the valley from Leith to Carp is Quaternary alluvium - soil, sand, and gravel. The conglomerate strata bring all the water close to the surface at Carp, and the railroad got a good well by digging down 55 feet.

A steam pumping plant, where my father became pumper, was installed. The water was pumped to a reservoir on the cliff. The sedimentary rocks in that area contain gypsum (calcium sulfate), which causes problems when the water is used in the boilers; a soda-lime softening plant to treat the water was installed at Moapa in 1924 and at Caliente in early 1928. The water softener was installed at Carp either just before or just after the one at Caliente. I believe the boiler house was enlarged and the big boiler was installed then. (Pumping plants were located also at Dry Lake, Moapa, Rox, and Elgin.)

The water contains slightly soluble gypsum and soluble calcium bicarbonate. (Calcium carbonate is insoluble, but carbon dioxide in the water converts it to soluble calcium bicarbonate). The problem is that calcium carbonate and calcium sulfate will precipitate as scale on the surface of the boiler tubes and reduce the efficiency of heat transfer from the hot gases to the water.

In the soda-lime process, the raw water is mixed with a slurry of hydrated lime and soda ash (sodium carbonate). The hydrated lime converts the calcium bicarbonate to insoluble calcium carbonate, and the soda ash converts the calcium sulfate to calcium carbonate and soluble sodium sulfate. The treated water is white from the calcium carbonate and the excess hydrated lime, and at Carp

View of Carp from the top of the coal chute, looking west, about 1925. Pumper's house on right, depot beyond. Main line on left, siding in center, oil spur on right.

the mixture was pumped to the top of the tall, cylindrical softener tower that was stacked full of bales of excelsior. The insoluble compounds were filtered out by the excelsior, and the water that came out the bottom was satisfactory for boiler feed-water.

When the bales of excelsior plugged up with accumulated solids, the tower had to be repacked. The old packing would be taken out and discarded, and new bales would be put in. I remember seeing those white bales of used excelsior around the water softener tower and the white powder all around the tower while the work was in progress.

Charles Walsh says the theory of soda-lime softening might be okay, but when he was at Carp, the process didn't work. He says my father never had to clean the lines to the boilers before the softener was installed, but afterward he had a lot of trouble with the lines plugging up. Perhaps that was before the correct operation of the softener was worked out.

The building with the softener feed machinery had a concrete floor that was kept painted and clean, especially when officials were expected. When my father was away once, a relief pumper painted the floor in preparation for inspection, and he painted right over matchsticks, cotton waste, and anything else on the floor.

A four-story coal chute stood astride the sidetrack by the water standpipe that was used to fill the water tanks of locomotives. The locomotives originally burned coal, and later they were converted to oil-burners, then back to coal, then back to oil.

My father took pictures when the coal chute was pulled down in 1928. A winch was anchored to the cliffs by the track, and a cable was run to a bridle that had been put around the top of the coal chute. Workmen cut through the base of each leg on the side away from the winch, made a notch at each cut, and put dynamite in the notches. The winch operator took a pull on the line, the dynamite was set off, and over she went!

The oil tank was the body of a tank car, set on top of a tall structure of timber. The oil (No. 6 boiler fuel) was delivered in tank cars; it drained into a holding reservoir below a spur track, then it was pumped by a steam pump to the elevated tank. It was delivered to the tenders of locomotives through a piece of plumbing we knew as the oil spout.

Helper engines ran light from Caliente to Carp, then they coupled onto the front or were cut into east-bound trains. The engines ran from Caliente down to Leith, turned on the wye, and ran backward the 10 miles to Carp. The railroad finally put in a wye near Carp in about 1943, running it onto our old ranch. The railroad switched to diesels a few years later, and then there were no steam engines to be turned.

One of my earliest memories is of the helper engines waiting near the depot, air pumps occasionally hitting a few licks, and the smell of the steam engine drifting through the air. The engineer and fireman might be waiting in the cab of the engine, or they might be in the depot, visiting with the telegraph operator.

The siding was named Carp, but the post office was Cliffdale

Charles Walsh stayed with us when we lived in the pumper's house at Carp. He told me that he would climb to the top of the coal chute at night to sleep with the benefit of the occasional breeze to relieve the stifling heat.

Wrecking the coal chute at Carp, 1928. Boiler house beyond coal chute. Cable from near top of coal chute pulled it over. Monkey-faced owls live in those conglomerate cliffs.

Boiler house, well, oil tank, and coal chute at Carp, before 1928.
Reservoir on top of cliff at the right.

from its origin on June 7, 1921, to Dec. 1, 1925, when Tom Casey, the first-trick telegraph operator and the postmaster, got the name changed to Carp; the post office was in the depot then. (The day shift at the telegraph office was the "first trick", the night shift was the "second trick", and the graveyard shift was the "third trick".) The post office was discontinued on July 1, 1974, after having been out of operation about a year.

According to Gamett and Paher, the name Carpsdale was assigned on June 29, 1918, but it was rescinded and never used. They list the following post offices from Caliente through Moapa:

Name	Established	Discontinued
Caliente	Aug. 3, 1901	
Carp	Dec. 1, 1925	July 1, 1974
Elgin	March 3, 1913	Dec. 30, 1966
Kershaw	Oct. 29, 1892	Dec. 31, 1904 changed to Stine
Kiernan	Dec. 14, 1908	Jan. 15, 1912
Moapa	July 22, 1889	
Rox	May 20, 1921	Aug. 15, 1949
Stine	Dec. 31, 1904	Oct. 30, 1909

The depot had the railroad telegraph office, the freight office, and the original post office. The railroad telegraph operator was the Western Union operator as well.

Carp had separate houses for the pumper, the first-trick operator, the signal maintainer, and the section foreman. Bunkhouses were provided for the section crew and their families. An ice-house, dug into the railroad grade, made possible the storage of ice in the summer. A small freight-house stood beside the tracks, and it is the subject of the Carp version of a story that is probably told with variations all over the country.

Pumper's house at Carp. Note the Derail switch. Derailed cars would have landed in our bedroom. Depot at far left.

The freight house was on a timber foundation at the edge of the railroad grade, and the timbers began falling apart from dry-rot. The operator sent a telegram to the main office in Omaha, "Foundation under freight house needs attention". What was he to make of the reply, "Feed the lion and notify the livestock department"?

The section gangs, signal maintainer, and various other railroad people traveled on motor cars (which we knew as "speeders"). Railroads provide sidetracks to let trains meet and pass each other, but motor cars don't rate sidetracks. A small motor car can be manhandled off the track and onto the set-off, a little piece of track that is just big enough to hold the motor car. The crew of a large motor car picks it up and puts it on the set-off. We heard about a section foreman at Rox who was the lazy type; he stayed on the motor car while the crew picked it up and set it off the tracks. One day he saw the smoke of an approaching train not far away, and he said, "Just hold 'er boys; this train is a short one".

His name is unknown to me, and I wouldn't repeat it if I knew. But here are some names of railroad employees at Carp during the years 1925-1945:

Thomas L. "Tom" Casey, Edward Sparks, Walter A. Condiff, Arthur L. Britt, Ray "Shorty" Monford, Albert E. Ewing, A.D. Paglia, H.L. Haskell, and E.K. "Ernie" Wright, telegraph operators; Walter B. Conk, Cecil Killam, Charles O. Maxwell, Charles W. Logan, and Leo Desmarias, signal maintainers; Charlie Brainerd, Fred Eddins, John R. Jansen, and Tom Anderson, section foremen; C.L. "Clint" Averett, George T. Ely, Ed Snorf, Leroy Whiting, Andy Bohn, and Ted Spahn, pumpers; and (when needed) John Snorf, foreman of a Water Service gang, and Oliver "Dutch" Schlarman, foreman of a Bridge & Building gang. George Ely had been relief pumper for my father, and he became the regular pumper when my father left the railroad in 1932. I think Andy Bohn replaced George Ely, then Leroy Whiting replaced Andy Bohn in August 1937. Eugene Houck was at either Carp or Leith in the early 1930s; the news items don't make it clear. Tom Casey was second-trick operator at Elgin in 1920.

Charlie Brainerd was the section foreman in 1924. He was replaced by Fred Eddins. My mother said that until then, the railroad had not hired white men for the section gangs (except as foremen); Tim Houck (I think this was Eugene Houck) and Mark Howcroft were perhaps the first two. Eddins was replaced by Tom Anderson by 1930.

Escobar cites a report that until the late 1920s, the union rules had forbidden promotion of Mexicans to section foreman. She comments on the invisibility of Mexicans in the newspaper items of that time, and I realized that in my search of the *Caliente Herald*, I saw few Spanish surnames. The section hands at Carp were mostly Mexican, but I knew very little about them.

Tom Casey lived in the first-trick operator's house, across the tracks from the rest of the houses and maybe a quarter of a mile west (in railroad terminology) from the depot. He had a housekeeper, Mrs. Helen Leisander, and she disturbed the railroad routine for a while.

One of the surreptitious messages on a railroad was the "whisker" sign. A man's length of service was called "whiskers", because the longer he was with the railroad, the more time for whiskers to grow. We referred to railroad people of exalted rank and title as "officials", and officials often had long service with the company,

Mr. & Mrs. Charles Brainerd and son Jack at Carp depot, 1926.

thus lots of whiskers. If you knew some officials were in the area, you could pass that information along by cupping your chin in one hand and moving the hand as if stroking a beard: the whisker sign.

Casey's house was built with an extra bedroom where visiting officials could stay overnight at Carp. For a while, officials were pleased but suspicious to see how well the Book of Rules was being followed when they visited; not many "brownies" (demerits) were issued for infractions of the rules. Finally the secret came out: Mrs. Leisander stood in the front window, giving the whisker sign to engine and train crews as they came by the house.

❖ ❖ ❖ ❖ ❖ ❖ ❖ ❖ ❖ ❖ ❖ ❖ ❖ ❖ ❖ ❖ ❖

My father was a cattleman most of his life, but he was also the pumper at Carp for several years. He had been around steam boilers and engines, and he had studied stationary engineering and diesel engines in night school in Los Angeles. In January 1924 he was running cattle west of Dry Lake, and he often went to Dry Lake at night to visit with Brad Stuart, the day pumper. (Dad told me people thought he was romancing Brad's daughter, but they were wrong.) One evening Brad's relief didn't show up, so Dad and Brad's son, Bob, worked through the night. Dad returned to his riding the

> *While the Howcrofts were at Carp, my father was building a cow-trough at the ranch. Mom said I was confused about the situation; I wasn't sure whether Dad was building a howcroft and Mr. Cowtrough was at Carp or whether it was the other way 'round.*

next day, and when Brad's relief still didn't appear that night, Dad was hired on the spot by Frank Cornelius, General Foreman in the Water Service Department. My mother told me that some of the officials in the Water Service held a grudge against him because he had been hired directly by Cornelius.

Dad's home was Logandale, but he wanted to get away from the terrible summer heat of the Moapa Valley. He said Cornelius helped him look for a chance to bid on a pumper's job where land was available for homesteading, and Carp turned out to be the place. Dad developed the homestead while he worked as pumper at Carp until 1932, when he left the railroad to spend full time at the ranch.

My parents first met at a rodeo in Cedar City. Dad had gone there from Logandale, and he met young Sylvia Willis, and that's how it all began. They were married on Nov. 24, 1924, and she became Sylvia Averett.

My mother was born in Warren, Utah, and she had lived in Warren, Morgan, Parowan, Fillmore, Milford, and Cedar City, but she wasn't prepared for a remote place such as Carp. The siding is in the bottom of a narrow canyon with conglomerate cliffs on both sides. The monkey-faced owls living in caves in the cliffs made the strange surroundings even stranger.

Carp is a spot of green in a wide, stony desert, reliably accessible mainly by train at that time, and my mother knew only that she felt imprisoned between the cliffs. My father had to be away a lot, helping run the pumping plants at Moapa and Dry Lake, and she was lonely, frightened, and depressed.

When Dad realized how she felt, he saddled two horses and they rode out toward the foothills of the Mormon Mountains. Within a mile or so, they were high enough above the valley to have a fine, sweeping view south and west and north. The mountains loomed up south and east; the Meadow Valley Wash was spread out before them; the Clover Mountains were to the north; and that deep, dark, oppressive canyon at Carp was just a slight irregularity in the terrain. My mother said she was never again afraid of the desert.

The pumper's job at Carp included pumping water to the reservoir and oil to the oil tank on its high platform. When work trains were operating out of Carp, or when traffic was heavy, the pumper sometimes had trouble keeping up with demand. For about a year, in perhaps 1928, eastbound trains regularly took on both oil and water at Carp, and many westbound trains took on water. Soon after Dad started work at Carp, a second, larger boiler was installed to increase steam capacity. A small oil-pump had been used, and it could barely keep up, even before the engines were oiling regularly at Carp, so a larger one was installed when so many engines began oiling there; my mother said the larger one never did work right. Sometimes John Pendergast's gang was sent in to help pump oil. They lived in outfit cars that were spotted on a spur at the west end of the siding.

I have a letter from Frank Cornelius, in which he lists the equipment my father had operated. The list doesn't distinguish between Carp, Moapa, and Dry Lake. Between the three of them, the pumping plants included this equipment: Oil-burning 35 hp and 100 hp return tubular Erie Economic boilers (these were at Carp); single displacement piston pump; Fairbanks-Morse duplex pump; triplex pump; 400 cfm Ingersoll-Rand and Laidlaw-Dunn-Gordon air compressors; deep well with steam heads, sucker rods, and air lifts (this must have been at Dry Lake; the water table was 480 feet down); shallow wells with Fairbanks-Morse centrifugal pumps (Carp and Moapa, at least); and lime and soda ash treating plants (certainly includes the one at Carp).

Charles Walsh spent a lot of time around the boiler house (also called the pump house) when he lived with us at Carp, and he was old enough to remember a lot about the equipment. He says the two boilers were embedded in insulating bricks with asbestos mortar. The safety valves were behind the smokestacks. He says the safety valves could be heard all over Carp when they let go, and he was "scared stiff" when he first heard one. A safety valve letting go certainly does get a person's attention.

Water and waste oil from the boiler house ran out into a pond we called the oil sump, where the oil accumulated as a layer on the water. Now and then the pumper would burn the oil sump to get rid of the accumulated oil. I have a vivid memory of the billowing clouds of black smoke, with the red flames shooting up through them.

When I was just old enough to get around on my own and to slip away from the adults, my father was always worried that I might fall into the oil sump. My mother says that once I did get away, and they found my tracks all around the edge of the sump. Dad put a high chicken-wire fence around the pumper's house, with child-proof gates, and he said that even at that, he caught me once just as I was going over the top of the fence.

Charles Walsh reports in "Historic Railroad Well" that the well at Carp was dug by hand, 22 feet diameter and 55 feet deep, and lined with stone. It was round, and the top of the stone wall stuck up 6 feet above the ground. Two Fairbanks-

C.L. Averett in door of boiler house at Carp, Sept. 1928.

Morse pumps were installed on platforms in the well, the upper one just above the water level and the other at the vacuum break point, about 20 feet down. (These were suction pumps, so their useful lift was only about 20 feet.) When the well was shut down, the water would rise to the static level and submerge the lower pump. When pumping began, the water level would go down until the lower pump emerged; then the upper pump would be shut down the lower one would take over.

According to records of the Nevada State Engineer's office, the well was at Milepost 420 (the distance from Los Angeles), and the permit allowed withdrawal of 0.250 cubic feet per second. The priority date for the well was Jan. 1, 1904, and the water was first used in 1905. The well is listed as being 19 feet wide. The water was stored in a reservoir that was 34 x 72.5 feet. The information comes from the Proof of Appropriation of Water for Irrigation, dated Aug. 9, 1912.

My mother remembered that the pump was just barely adequate when the demand for water was heavy, and sometimes a work gang would be stationed there to do various jobs, including assistance with pumping. She said that if a pump needed parts, he would send in an order, and he would usually be told "Speed up the pump", even though it was already running so fast that he was reluctant to go down into the well with it.

Charles Walsh says that after the railroad had converted to diesels and the pumping plant was no longer needed, the equipment was removed, the boiler house was torn down, the masonry wall was pushed over by a bulldozer, and the well was filled.

Until about 1942, sidings such as Carp had a commissary. Gunn Supply Company had the contract to supply the section gangs, and the commissary was operated for Gunn Supply. The men could buy on credit, with paycheck deduction. The commissary at Carp was in the section foreman's house.

The contract with Gunn Supply expired before 1942, and the Dining Car & Hotel Service Department of the railroad (DC&H) took over. The railroad paid a cook to feed the section crews during World War II, using supplies from DC&H.

Railroad supplies, commissary supplies, ice for the ice house, and larger orders of groceries from Los Angeles usually came in on a supply train, a local train that made its way from station to station. Sometimes the supplies would have been dispensed too liberally, and something would run out before the last station was reached; maybe the last few places wouldn't get coal oil, or track spikes, or something. Sometimes an item requisitioned for one place would be mislaid, omitted, or unloaded too soon, and the result could be trouble.

Once when Dad was desperate to receive parts for one of the water pumps, the supply-train supervisor insisted they were not on the train. Dad was sure they had to be, and hostilities were in the air. The problem was that the supervisor hadn't been told they were on the train, and someone found them and came running, shouting, "Stop the fight! Here they are!"

The *Las Vegas Age*, Feb. 22, 1932, had a human-interest story. On Feb. 17, eastbound Train #22, the Pacific Limited, was between Galt and Carp when a baby was born on the train. The parents were on their way from Los Angeles to Ontario, Canada. On Feb. 24, the paper added some more human interest; the father was wanted in Los Angeles for bank robbery, and the publicity enabled the police to intercept the train and arrest him.

PEOPLE, PLACES, AND EVENTS

In about 1926, soon after my father started pumping at Carp, a cloudburst and its flash flood took out the track at Vigo and in several places between Carp and Elgin. Carp was isolated, and a passenger train was stranded there. The passengers could sleep on the train, even in chair cars, but the dining car didn't have supplies for that many people for that long a time.

My mother and Mrs. Brainerd had just received a large order of groceries from Ralph's Grocery, in Los Angeles, and some vegetables were available from Mrs. Casey's garden. Matt Reese had melons and squash in his garden. These were all made available.

The women at Carp and from the train arranged to cook and serve two meals daily in shifts, using the houses of the section foreman, the first-trick operator, the signal maintainer, and the pumper. The younger people ate at our house. As soon as breakfast was finished, preparation of supper began.

My mother served slices of fried summer-squash at one meal. The women in the kitchen were laughing as the men kept calling for more of "that good fish". Then one of them found a piece of "fish" with the seeds still attached.

A motor car loaded with meat and bread came from Caliente, but everything had to be carried around each washout. The food took 2 days and 3 nights to reach Carp. The bread was stale by then, and the train pulled out on the third day, leaving the bread at Carp. But the railroad paid for everything, including the stale bread.

In 1925, the railroad sent a geologist to prepare a report on the area around Carp. He was German, and his name was Dr. J.D. Von Galscale (or something close to that). Because the pumper's house had a spare bedroom, he stayed with us. Charles Walsh remembers him as a stern-looking old man with a grey mustache and goatee and dressed in a grey suit with a coat and vest and a black tie. My mother said he always wiped all the silverware with his napkin before he ate.

I don't know how many times this is claimed to have happened, at how many places, but I'll repeat it and call it true, with the disclaimer "I tell the tale I heard told":

One young operator at Carp ran a trap line to catch coyotes, wildcats, or whatever else he could. One day he discovered a touching sight, a poor little cat, helpless and weak, caught in one of his steel traps. A marvelous idea came to him; why not free it and keep it for a pet?

His actions might further excite the already distraught animal, so with brilliant presence of mind, he took off his coat and held it in front of him, expecting to smother the kitty in the coat and then release the trap. You have already guessed what it was: it was a bobcat. Did you ever try to wrap a coat around a bobcat that has one foot in a steel trap? Don't.

Charlie Dimmick had a ranch in Cottonwood Canyon, and he and Sam Beal lived in a cabin that was built against a cliff. The stovepipe ran clear to the top of the cliff. Charlie had made money ranching and lending money. We thought of Charlie Dimmick and Jim Ryan as the bankers of the area. Charlie's main account was in Walker Brothers Bank in Salt Lake City, and my father said that when a bookkeeping error led to one of Charlie's checks being returned with the notation "No Funds", Charlie blew up. "What do they mean", he demanded, "saying Walker Brothers has no funds?"

After Charlie's death on Nov. 24, 1948, the *Caliente Herald* ran a story on Dec. 9 about his life. He was born on March 26, 1871, near Des Moines, Iowa. About 1873 his father moved the family to Decatur County, Kansas. In 1889 he left home and traveled west. He worked in Colorado, in Salt Lake City, and finally as a cowboy for the Bar Z Cattle Company, near Cane Beds, Arizona. Evidently he made his money there on the Arizona Strip.

About 1910 he bought a ranch "near Elgin and Caliente", then he sold it in 1919 and "retired from active work". The ranch had an orchard and a vineyard. The article says, "Dimmick never lost his active interest in the cattle business and, during his later years, offered help, advice and financial assistance to many people in this vicinity." He had known Zane Grey, and he appears under a different name (as a villain) in one of Grey's books. Charlie is said to have warned Grey not to do that again.

They enclosed the opening of a cave at the foot of a bluff, and that's where they lived. Their stove wouldn't draw with that cliff above it, so they ran a 50-foot stovepipe up the face of the cliff, guyed to the cliff. In the 1950s, I was talking to one of my co-workers about old cars, and he said he had gone with someone to look at an air-cooled Franklin in a shed in a canyon off the Meadow Valley Wash. From his description of the canyon, I guessed where he had been; I described the stovepipe, and he said it was exactly like that. I remembered the stovepipe, but not the Franklin.

> *Clyde Brundy says Charlie and Sam Beal started their ranch in Cottonwood Canyon in 1913, and they became successful cattlemen. They rode mules. They shod the range bulls to protect their feet from the rocks. Jim Bradshaw says, "Sam Beal was a true friend".*

Nellie Cox provides details of a story that we knew in very sketchy form. When Charlie was foreman of the Bar Z, he hired Sam Beal to live at Cane Beds and take care of the ranch. We were told that Sam (and Bill Garrett and Art Coleman, of Gold Butte, in Clark County) had been involved in the 1892 cattle war in Johnson County, Wyoming, which might have had some significance in the incident described by Cox.

A saddle tramp showed up and stayed a while with Sam, but something wasn't right about it, and Sam concealed a gun in a wood box just outside his door. One day Sam went out to get some wood, and when he turned around, the man had a gun on him. He demanded money, but Sam threw the armload of wood at him and ran around the corner of the house. He made some noise, and while the would-be robber was running from window to window, looking for him, Sam got back to the woodbox, got his gun, and killed him. Sam rode 9 miles to turn himself in, and that was the end of the story; he didn't even come to trial.

We knew Sam Beal as a quiet, pleasant old fellow, and we took that story as further proof that a person can make a serious mistake misjudging someone.

This is not really something that pertains to Carp, but here is a reminder of two men whose names were on the tip of every cattleman's tongue in southern Nevada: Preston Nutter and George W. "Jockey" Hail (or Hale, depending on whose story you are reading).

Pres Nutter moved into the Arizona Strip in 1890. He built up the Grand Canyon Cattle Co., and he took over the Bar Z as part of it. Jockey Hail's outfit was the Walking X. Nutter went on to run cattle through Utah, all the way to the Uinta Mountains. He died in 1936, and in 1937 or 1938, Hail bought the Grand Canyon Cattle Co. from the Nutter estate. He ran cattle as far west as Groom; Dick Tennille helped on the final roundup in 1927. According to the *Lincoln County Record* on March 3, 1927, Jockey Hail and John C. Benson had "bought all the cattle of Henry Lee". They had previously bought the cattle of Henry and James Hammond, of Eagle Valley.

I think, but I couldn't swear to it in court, that in about 1940, Hafen & Frei sold a herd to Jockey Hail and trailed the cattle to Pahranagat Valley. When my father sold part of our herd in about 1937 to pay medical expenses, we loaded several cars at Carp, consigned to Badger Livestock Commission Co. at the Los Angeles stockyards. I worked the Hafen & Frei roundup, and I don't remember loading any cars for them.

Charlie Dimmick's ranch near Carp, the former Lyman ranch, had a well on the edge of the creek bed. A big Aermotor windmill pumped the water from the well. The wheel was 14 feet in diameter, and the windmill lifted 3 1/2 gallons at a stroke. The wheel turned so easily that my father said it would turn if you stood on the ground and waved your hat.

Elmer Middleton, a retired mine-hoist operator from Pioche, was living at Charlie's place when the 1938 flood hit; my father got him out of the cabin before the water reached it, and Mr. Middleton lived with us for a while, then he returned to Pioche, where he died on Oct. 4, 1939, age 67. The flood tipped the windmill over, and Dad wanted it for our irrigation well that had only a gasoline engine at that time. He asked Mr. Middleton to casually mention to Charlie that maybe Clint Averett could be talked into buying it. Mr. Middleton apparently didn't understand the concept of a bargaining advantage, because the next time Charlie came to Carp, he said to Dad, "I understand you want to buy my windmill".

Dad bought it, anyway. The tower, wheel, and tail were in good condition, and the motor was okay except that it was full of sand. Dad washed it out with kerosene and took it to the boiler house at Carp and steamed it out. We got sand every time we changed oil, but the motor still ran like a dream.

Dad's brother-in-law, J.H. "Nick" Nicolaides, came from Las Vegas to help us re-erect the windmill. We assembled the tower on the ground, with the base at the well and the top pointing away. We put up a gin pole by the well and ran a line from the top of the tower up through a snatch block at the top of the pole and down to the front bumper of Uncle Nick's car. Then he backed away (slowly) and pulled the tower upright. (Why didn't we take pictures?)

Ves Hulse had the ranch next to the Dimmick (Lyman) ranch. He had carried mail down the Meadow Valley Wash in the early 1900s, and he told us he camped by the creek, a few hundred yards from the future site of our house. He taught us to cut barrel cactus, roll it through a fire to burn the spines off, and chop it up and feed it to the cattle. (According to Edwin Way Teale, in Texas the spines are burned from the pads of prickly pear cactus so they can be fed to the cattle.)

Cacti have spines to defend against animals that nibble and browse, but they have another defense as well: they are loaded with calcium oxalate, which typically forms small crystals that burn the mouth of man or beast. People who sample wild plants without a proper sense of caution soon learn what happens. Prickly pear has about the least calcium oxalate of the cacti, and the young pads are edible. However, barrel cactus has substantially more. The common wisdom of the desert is that if you run out of water, cut the top out of a barrel cactus and drink the liquid; my father tried it once, and he thought he would die. The liquid was sticky and sweet, and it almost choked him. Maybe the cattle can eat a barrel cactus, but I don't recommend serving it in a salad.

Mr. Hulse was born at Pinto Creek, Utah, son of Benjamin R. and Mary Jane Hulse. The family moved to Panaca in 1868. He married Kate Gleason in 1878 and moved to Arizona, then in 1908 he moved to Carp. In the 1930s he was the Brand Inspector at Carp, and he stamped the beef that we butchered and took to Safeway in Las Vegas. He was a fine old man; I cannot recall ever hearing a word spoken against him. He died in his cabin on his 80th birthday, Nov. 10, 1939. Al Smith, an old man who had been living on the Montgomery place, was staying with Mr. Hulse, and he brought word to us that Mr. Hulse didn't wake up that morning.

Walter Conk bid in the signal maintainer's job at Las Vegas in March 1933, and he was replaced by Charles O. Maxwell. The Vernal A. Anderson family lived on the Conk ranch until about 1936. They were followed by the Clarence Elroy Jagger family, from Joplin, Missouri. Doran Fox, a Jagger stepson, was my age. As we were coming home from school one day, something was said about the fields of dried tumbleweeds on the Conk, Huston, and Mabey ranches, and he commented, "I'm going to set fire to those tumbleweeds". Within a few days, if not that same day, the fields did burn in a spectacular fire, and I decided perhaps he wasn't joking. The Jaggers moved to El Paso in March 1939.

The Montgomery ranch had a house that was built as a single room by A.L. Hilburn. Fred Montgomery converted it to a rock house in 1932. He also installed an Aermotor windmill. He moved to Los Angeles, then to Arden, in January 1933, and Ed and Mildred Sparks lived there for several months. Al Banks and L.L. "Pete" Rose and their families lived there in about 1939, followed by Al Smith. In the late 1930s, Fred Montgomery bought the Mabey and Huston ranches.

Archie William "Walt" Huston was born on June 8, 1878, at Breckenridge, Mo., and he died in Caliente on Aug. 13, 1946. He used to talk about his days with the 101 Ranch in Oklahoma. He came to Lincoln County in 1904 and for several years he caught wild horses for Charles Culverwell. He bought a ranch at Barclay in 1909, then in 1920 he moved to Carp. His wife, Edith Pearl Huston, was born in Winterset, Iowa, on Feb. 7, 1879, and she died in Stockton, California, on Aug. 6, 1947. She came to Nevada in 1911 with her son, Clifford Freemeyer. She married Jack Johnston and with their son, Samuel Jay Johnston, came to Caliente. Mr. Johnston died of influenza in 1918, and she married Walt Huston in 1919.

Sammy Johnston was commonly called Sammy Huston, but Sam Johnston was his legal name, and it was often misspelled "Johnson". I will use the version given in a news item when drawing from it as a source, and Johnston otherwise.

An item in the *Caliente News*, Nov. 1, 1920, said John Conaway, Archie Yoacham, William Culverwell, and Otto Olson were moving 700 head of cattle to Carp so Walt Huston could winter them.

In the early 1930s, people were trying to get the Rainbow Canyon Route accepted as the route between Caliente and Las Vegas—-down the canyon, across Tule Flat, to Mormon Mesa, and then to Las Vegas. Don Bradshaw says his father, Rube Bradshaw, thought it would happen. Using lumber salvaged from concreting Tunnel 4, Rube put up a false-front building on the hill, near the water reservoir, that was the Carp store and post office. It had an "oil station", a single hand-pumped gas pump with the glass reservoir at the top. Lynn Beatty, his brother in law, ran the store for him.

The Rainbow Canyon Route was not accepted as the road to Las Vegas, and Rube sold the store to Mrs. Huston. She ran it, with help from Sammy Johnston, Pres McKnight, and Lynn Beatty until Jim Davis took over.

The Hustons split up in early 1929, and she had moved away (to Stockton, I think) by 1938. Walt was living at Elgin by then, calling himself a prospector. The Eubanks family moved to the Huston ranch and lived there a year or so.

The original road from Caliente to Carp came down the Meadow Valley Wash all the way to Carp. (According to Clyde Brundy, in 1924 his brothers Todd and Dave drove a Buick from Caliente to Elgin, the first auto to make the trip.) From below Elgin to below Leith, the road was rough and rocky, and there were numerous creek crossings that were unpredictable and difficult.

The people at Carp and Elgin thought a better route must exist, and in 1928 my father, with Charles Walsh and Brad Stuart, took County Commissioner Tom Dixon over a route they thought would work. From where the original road crossed the wash at present Lyman Crossing, the proposed

Carp post office, 1956. Photo by Earl Pampeyan.

road went through our 40-acre desert entry, under the wooden railroad bridge, past our upper windmill, up a long dry wash, up onto and across a mesa, down a steep hill into Leith Canyon, up Leith Canyon to a summit at the east edge of Kane Springs Wash, then eastward down Riggs Wash to join the original road just below Elgin.

Kane Springs Wash was visible from that summit, and one summer night when we were going to Carp from the Elliott ranch, we stopped there to watch sheet lightning illuminate the long, wide valley—a fond memory from times past.

The route became the road "over the hill" or "over the summit". At the upper end of Leith Canyon, it went through a stand of junipers; the area was called The Cedars. A fire started in The Cedars just after the scouting trip, and people said Brad caused it when he knocked the ashes from his pipe. He swore to me he didn't do it, but he said he got blamed for it anyway.

Charles Walsh says a fine crop of loco weed covered the burned-out area the next spring. A band of sheep was trailed through there, and many of them died from eating the loco weed. He says loco weed doesn't hurt the animal until it drinks some water, then the alkaloid in the plant can be fatal. The sheep died after they reached the Meadow Valley Wash and drank at the creek near Carp.

He said the law then forbade sheep in that area, and the night the band of sheep arrived, some of the ranchers met with the owners and told them what the law said, and asked them to please move the sheep out. They agreed, but when the sheep were found dead the next morning, the ranchers were concerned that they would be accused of poisoning. However, no trouble came of it. (I think a Nevada state law prohibited sheep on cattle range at that time.)

The *Caliente Herald* had a brief news report on April 9, 1931, with the headline "600 Sheep Killed by Grass at Elgin, Nev." Sheriff Culverwell had been called to Elgin to investigate the death of 600 to 800 sheep that belonged to Warren Bullock and Tate Brothers. The dead sheep were scattered over a 5-mile area near the summit west of Elgin, and at least 400 were in a single group. According to the news report, "it is believed that the animals died from grazing on Filaree weed which had been frost bitten, the animals after grazing bloated up and died in a short time". The owners skinned the sheep for the wool, and the sheriff arranged to have the carcasses buried.

We cannot account for the 2-year difference between 1929 and 1931. Charles says the names in the paper were the same as the ones in 1929, so were there two separate incidents? It seems like one more mystery of the Wild West. However, Jim Bradshaw remembers when the sheep died near Elgin.

❖ ❖ ❖ ❖ ❖ ❖ ❖ ❖ ❖ ❖ ❖ ❖ ❖ ❖ ❖ ❖ ❖

The road was built in 1929 as a cooperative effort between people at Carp and Elgin. It was improved in 1933 by the Public Works Administration. It went up the dry wash from our windmill, following a dugway for some distance. My father was a foreman on the construction of the dugway.

The road wasn't a bad pull, except where it climbed out of the wash to the top of the mesa that had to be crossed before dropping down into Leith Canyon. In about 1940, Dad bought a 1939 Chevrolet 3/4-ton truck that we drove between Carp and the Elliott ranch. The radiator was usually boiling by the time we got to the top of the hill; we turned around there and pointed the truck back into the breeze so we could run the engine and cool it down.

Loco weed and "frost-bitten filaree" were not the only hazards for livestock. A story in the Caliente Herald on May 2, 1935, said the new spring buds of rabbit brush are very poisonous to sheep. Three pounds eaten at one time, or smaller amounts eaten regularly for several days, are fatal to mature sheep. The symptoms might not appear for 24 to 36 hours, but all affected sheep will die. After the plants have matured, they are no longer dangerous to sheep.

The road across the mesa was usually in good condition. Four-o-clocks bloomed between the wheel tracks in season, and badger holes were everywhere on the flat. The mesa was high enough that we could see for many miles; at night we could look to the south and see the airplane beacon light at Apex, just north of Las Vegas.

The original road down the canyon from Elgin was on the east side of the canyon from near Leith to where it crossed at the place now known as Lyman Crossing. West of the crossing was the junction where the road over the hill went its own way west and north. The road from Lyman Crossing to Carp ran between the railroad right-of-way and the various ranches. An older road, which was usually in poor condition, went down the east side of the valley and joined the main road at the lower end of our ranch. It was used mostly for access from Carp to the Montgomery ranch.

When my wife and I went down the Meadow Valley Wash in 1972, all the creek crossings between Caliente and Carp had been converted to culverts, the road over the hill was apparently abandoned, and instead of crossing the wash at Lyman Crossing, the road continued down the east side to Carp. Much of the improvement of the road down the Canyon was started in 1955, when Don Bradshaw was County Commissioner in charge of roads. By 1994, the road was oiled all the way to Elgin. It's a good graveled road from there to Carp, allowing for dry creek-crossings that are subject to damage by floods.

❖ ❖ ❖ ❖ ❖ ❖ ❖ ❖ ❖ ❖ ❖ ❖ ❖ ❖ ❖ ❖ ❖

Charles N. James wrote to me that in about 1926, Capt. Felix Steinle crash-landed an Army DH-4 De Haviland in the hills east of Leith, and no attempt was made to salvage the plane. Steinle later worked for Western Air Express, and he crash-landed a WAE Douglas M-2 near Elgin. The plane was salvaged and was shipped out on a flatcar.

Charles Walsh remembers seeing a barnstormer at the Mabey ranch, and the pilot was doing okay until he landed wrong and demolished his plane (without harm to the pilot or passenger).

In about 1930, two or three Navy planes landed at the Mabey ranch when they ran low on fuel. My father said the pilots were angry about the poor quality of the gasoline available from the ranchers, but their choices were to use it or wait until the Navy could ship in some aviation gasoline; they decided the scenery wasn't very exciting, so they used what they could get.

These various automobiles were part of life at Carp: Shorty Monford's stripped-down Ford; Walter Condiff's touring car with side curtains; Tom and Anna Anderson's Pontiac Eight sedan with the trunk on the back that looked like a trunk; my father's Model T truck with a Ruxtell rear end, and his Willys-Overland (which was before my time); and Ernie Wright's Ford V-8, the first "forked 8" we had seen. When my father was on a train one day, someone looking out the window at a set of wheel-tracks on a dry wash said that a person could be sure those tracks were made by a Model T, and my father said on the contrary, he had made them with a Willys-Overland.

For a while our Model T was fitted with a hoist just behind the cab. When the casing in our irrigation well needed to be cleaned out, my father backed the truck up to the pump house and cleaned the well with a bailer that was attached to a cable that ran from the hoist through a sheave at the top of a gin-pole and down into the well.

Several passenger trains went through Carp each direction every day, and one of them was the mail train. It often blazed through in a cloud of dust, and the mailbag was thrown out of the mail car just about the same time the steel arm snatched the outgoing mailbag from the mail hook beside the track. My mother received a pair of shoes by mail, and they didn't fit; the postmistress refused to accept the package for return, because she said the box would break the man's arm when he reached out to grab the mailbag.

In the days of rimlock wheels and high-pressure tires, the postmistress borrowed a wheel and tire from my father. She returned it by Railway Express, but when Dad got it, the tire was flat. He struggled through the process of removing the tire from the wheel, but he couldn't find a leak. The next time he saw her, he asked when it went flat; she said there was nothing wrong with it, but she wasn't going to pay express on 60 pounds of air!

THE AVERETT RANCH

Our ranch was a 160-acre homestead and an adjoining 80-acre desert entry. The 240 acres extended from the railroad eastward beyond the creek, and it ran from the Mabey and Montgomery (Hilburn) ranches almost to Carp.

We had a 40-acre desert entry about 3 miles up the valley, just beyond present Lyman Crossing. We had a corral and a well with a windmill on the west

Overall view of Averett ranch, looking northwest. Carp is out of sight to left. Ranch buildings and corrals in center, fields to right. Light streak in upper left is the road over the summit to Elgin.

side of the railroad, and we tried to irrigate some land east of the railroad to prove up on the desert entry. I recall it as a forlorn effort, and from the file of General Land Office records, evidently we didn't prove up (though we did have a water appropriation permit for the well).

The well on the desert entry was 60 feet deep, with 3-inch casing and an Aermotor windmill that Charles Walsh brought from Austin in 1931 and helped my father erect. It had a tall, 4-legged tower. It pumped water into a 2000-gallon galvanized iron tank that supplied a cowtrough, the one that I had once thought might be a howcroft. The windmill also filled a reservoir that was scooped out of the ground.

At the peak of our ranching, we had about 170 head of Hereford cattle. They wintered on our range and worked back down toward our ranch in the summer. Our fields included a 10-acre field next to the main well and an "east field", east of the creek, that was sometimes in white sweet clover, oats, or rye. We always had one field in alfalfa; we had oats, corn, cane, barley, milomaize, or wheat in other fields. (At one time I couldn't get it straight whether corn and wheat were both grain or whether corn and grain were both wheat.)

The 10-acre field was so sandy that the ditch banks washed away as fast as they could be repaired. My father diverted flood water onto the field, and after the silt from a flood had dried, he would plow it in. After a while, he made a good field out of it.

An old railroad grade, probably the one built

Averett windmill #2, near Lyman Crossing, 2 miles north of Carp ranch, 1937. Road over the hill came through that trestle; road was impassable if the dip under the trestle was filled with water from a cloudburst.

after the 1907 flood and abandoned after the 1910 flood, is still visible on our ranch and on various other ranches above Carp. Someone once told me that several miles of rails between the Lyman and Kiernan ranches had been buried by a flood and never recovered. I thought of looking for it, but being a man of few words and little action, I left it for someone else.

The railroad was fenced partly with cast concrete posts of triangular cross-section, partly with cedar posts, and partly with railroad ties. (We knew the cedar posts were really juniper, but it's "cedar" in the vernacular). Some railroad ties were used in the railroad fence, but once the fence was built, the railroad didn't have much need for all the ties that were taken out of the track when new ties were put in. But the ranchers sure could use them—-for fences, buildings, corrals, firewood, or whatever. A few of the ties were redwood, and we kept them for special use.

My father built our houses of railroad ties that he stood on end and framed top and bottom. The house we lived in was built in 1928, finished inside with gypsum wallboard. ("Sheetrock" and "dry wall" were not in our vocabulary). The outside was gray stucco, applied by J.M. Ford, of Las Vegas, in 1928. It had two bedrooms, a kitchen and living room combined, and a screened back porch. It faced the railroad.

My father drove a 1928 Chevrolet sedan. To haul ties for our houses and fences, he took out the back seat, opened both back doors, and put the ties in crosswise. I wonder what he did when he met another car.

Under the provisions of the Bankhead-Jones Farm Tenant Act (see the later description of the Meadow Valley Scattered Settlers Project), all the improvements were to be removed from the farms that were purchased by the Government. I saw the house on the McGuffie ranch torn down, but the houses and corrals on our ranch were left in place. The house is still there.

Corrals at Averett ranch, 1937. Fields in the distance. View from top of tank house, looking north, away from Carp. When we butchered cattle, we hung them from high crossbeam in center for skinning.

Averett ranch at Carp, viewed from the corral, looking toward Carp. Main house right, auxiliary houses to left, tank house farther left. Mormon Mountains on skyline. Early 1930s.

Near the upper end of our ranch, a low, boggy area along the road extended out into our property; we called it "the slough". My father used a team and a Fresno scraper to put a dike across the lower end of the slough, and then he diverted floodwater into the area above the dike. After the area had been filled several times and the water had evaporated during the interval between floods, enough silt had been deposited to make a good field. We called it the "lakebed field", and the alfalfa crop was great. In 1938 we let the alfalfa in that field go to seed, and we threshed out the seed.

Occasionally the county would send a road grader down to smooth out the washboard roads and restore (or wreck) the creek crossings. In about 1939 the operator tried to cut a drainage ditch beside the road, just above our lakebed field, and he broke through the alkali crust into the mud below. I remember the sight of that Austin-Western Senior 77 motor grader bogged clear to the axle.

Then in about 1943 the railroad sent Dutch Schlarman's B&B gang to install a wye so the helper engines could be turned at Carp instead of Leith, and they picked our lakebed field for the place. (It wasn't our ranch any more.) We heard a variety of exciting stories about breaking through the crust, building timber mats to hold the construction equipment, and losing a Caterpillar tractor into the muck. We were told it disappeared and was never recovered.

In 1941 the Western Remount Area was asking for registration of all horses and mules between ages 3 and 10 as part of defense preparation. My father had only two work horses and two saddle horses, but shortly before, he had seriously considered whether he might round up some wild horses for the Army remount. He had run wild horses when he was younger, and it was exciting. He said that when you got started, it was hard to quit. He had seen too many fellows going after wild horses instead of trying to make something of themselves, and perhaps that's one reason he dropped the idea.

Wyman, in "The Wild Horse of the West", says that former mustangers talk about the thrill of chasing mustangs for both fun and money. He comments that even the ones who tried to make money really ran mustangs for adventure and for the attraction of that kind of life.

My father believed the cattle should be brought to top condition in the summer so they went into the winter in good shape. Other people let their cattle start the winter in poor shape, then they had to be fed all winter. On April 10, 1930, the *Caliente Herald* reported that a speaker at a Farm Bureau Association meeting had said the large numbers of sheep from out of state had

Chasing wild ones was a favorite cowboy sport

overgrazed the range so much that cattlemen had to feed their cattle in the winter instead of having them on winter range. After my father established his range, he never would allow sheep to enter.

Our range extended north from about Vigo Canyon to Leith Canyon and west from the railroad to the great escarpment that drops off into Kane Springs Wash. The main problem was on the north side, where our cattle could stray onto Parley Henrie's range. The difficulty was resolved when the Grazing Service constructed a drift fence to separate the two ranges.

We had two springs, Averett Spring and Hidden Spring, near the west edge of our range. In late 1930 or early 1931, my father built a masonry dam across a ravine to collect water, making Averett Reservoir. (Topographic maps of the U.S. Geological Survey show "Avertt" Reservoir, but through the U.S. Board on Geographic Names and the State of Nevada, the name has been corrected to "Averett".) Charles Walsh and Jim McKnight built another reservoir in the summer of 1931.

In 1945, Sam Johnston and Oliver Fitchett filed a series of perlite claims close to our reservoirs. We were out of the cattle business by then, and I haven't been to the reservoirs since before 1940.

After we had left Carp, someone told me about having been to our reservoirs and finding that the round rocks in the area had been cracked open by someone who was looking for rocks with crystals inside. Some time after that, I learned about geodes, which often contain quartz crystals (sometimes the amethyst variety), and I concluded we had been walking across geodes all those years.

Some of the ranches between Elgin and Vigo provided a full-time living for the owners or occupants. The ranches required irrigated fields of alfalfa or grain, and they usually had a garden. Milk cows, pigs, and chickens were generally part of the effort to be as self-sufficient as possible.

We had a long diversion ditch that took water from the creek, but the creek did not flow enough water for irrigation of our fields. The ditch also captured floodwater while it lasted, and we always hurried out to irrigate with that water. We supplemented the water from the ditch with pumped water.

In the summer of 1930, my father and Charles Walsh dug an irrigation well about 12 feet, lining it with 2x6 sheet piling. They drove a casing down into the sand at the bottom, and I think my father deepened the well afterward. The water was pumped by a 6-inch centrifugal pump that was belted to a Fairbanks-Morse 6-horsepower one-cylinder gasoline engine. I enjoyed many long summer days by myself at the pumphouse, tending the lubricator and the cooling tank on the engine and being there to go after Dad if anything went wrong.

After 1938, we had the big Aermotor windmill to supplement the centrifugal pump. The water could be delivered into the ditch that ran to the fields, or it could be pumped into an open reservoir that fed the ditch. The windmill made the reservoir especially useful, because it could deliver to the reservoir all the time; when we were running the engine, someone had to be there almost constantly.

We had various other 6-horsepower one-cylinder engines around the place, including a hothead diesel that seldom ran and an Alamo vertical-cylinder gasoline engine that never ran that I remember. The Alamo might have been a good engine, but it needed parts, and the company had gone out of business. The hothead diesel had a dome-shaped starting chamber that was heated with a blowtorch, and then, if all went well, the engine started when you kicked the flywheel over. Things seldom went well.

We sawed our firewood with a 24-inch circular saw that was sometimes powered by one of the gasoline engines or the hothead diesel, but was usually belted to a rear wheel of an automobile. We liked juniper wood, but mostly we used what we could get, which was railroad ties. I had heard stories about the disaster that could occur if the saw hit a rock, and when I thought of all the pebbles embedded in those ties, I was uneasy. Ellen Johnson, our teacher one year at Carp, moved to Ursine and married Sam Hollinger, and a few years later he was killed when a circular saw broke up.

Hothead diesel, Averett ranch, 1933. Note the Model T loaded with railroad ties.

One-cylinder 6-hp gasoline engine, Averett ranch, 1933. Engine, on skids, being moved by Bonnie, Snip, and Brownie.

Now, in the 1990s, we pay dearly for a few railroad ties to use around the yard, but in those days, railroad ties were only a disposal problem once they were pulled out of the track. If nobody used the ties, they were burned. We were returning from Carp to the Elliott ranch one night in the 1940s, and when we passed Tunnel 5, we saw pile after pile of railroad ties burning along the railroad right of way. The flames and the coals were beautiful, but think of the waste of material that would be valuable today!

In 1930, my father dug a well by the abandoned railroad grade below our house. He had accumulated some sheets of galvanized iron, and his brother-in-law, J.H. Nicolaides, helped him make them into a tank about 10 feet diameter by 4 feet deep. They built a tank house about 12 feet high, and they got the tank up on top. They put in a pipe to the house, and later to the corrals, and we had running water! Cold water, anyway; the house had a closet by the stove for a hot-water tank, but we never did get the wood stove hooked up for hot water.

The water tank was open-topped, and it would fill up with moss and all kinds of water bugs. Every now and then in the summer, we drew the water level down, climbed into the tank, and fished out the moss.

The water was pumped first by hand, with a 4-inch double-throw hand-operated "man-killer" pump that was replaced by a pump jack and a small one-cylinder gasoline engine. We also had a windmill that worked the pump jack.

My father and Charles soldered together pieces of galvanized iron to make a shallow square pan that held about 10 gallons of water. They punched small holes along the sides, just above the bottom. Then they put the pan on top of an open-sided wooden frame that was covered with burlap over window screen. Water in the pan flowed through the holes and over the burlap, and evaporation of the water gave us a desert cooler. We kept pans of milk and other containers of food on shelves in the cooler. It wasn't an icebox by any means, but it was sure better than no cooler at all.

In August 1939 I saw a world-class cloudburst at our ranch. The rain fell for an hour or so, and when the storm was over, tin cans in the yard had 9 inches of water. A dry wash came in from the west, just beyond the railroad, and a dike had been built to protect the railroad; we could see water splashing above the top of the dike.

We had stacks of alfalfa hay in the corral that were soaked to the ground. My job was to place shocks of hay on the stack as my father pitched them up from the wagon. I kept the sides of the stack true and then topped out the stack. We covered the finished stack with a plant we called "cow-weed", which made a tight thatch that usually kept the stacks dry. Not this time, though.

The hay was soaked, and we thought it might catch fire by spontaneous combustion; but nothing happened. When we cut into the stacks later that year, the hay was dark brown, and it had a pleasant tobacco-like odor. Even more surprising, the cattle acted as if it was the best food they had ever had.

And it probably was; the Department of Agriculture said that we had accidentally obtained a "tobacco cure", a rare occurrence. Livestock generally voted it their favorite brand.

❖ ❖ ❖ ❖ ❖ ❖ ❖ ❖ ❖ ❖ ❖ ❖ ❖ ❖ ❖ ❖ ❖ ❖

We normally raised alfalfa to feed to the cattle, and most years we raised corn or cane or both that we turned into silage. We fed the stalks into a silage cutter, and the resulting fragments were fed down into a pit silo. I have a vivid recollection of the day the cast-iron flywheel on the silage cutter flew apart, scattering pieces everywhere.

We spread the silage out evenly and kept it wet. When the silo was full, we put a lot of multi-wall paper bags over the whole thing, then we piled on about a foot of dirt or straw. (The paper bags were lime sacks from

> Sometimes we received a slow, steady rain that soaked the ground with little run-off. Laura Gilpin, in "The Enduring Navajo", says the Navajo personify the winds, lightning, thunder, rain, fog, and mist; the rain is described as "He" rain and "She" rain. The "He" rain is the violent cloudburst that drives seeds into the ground; the "She" rain is the gentle rain that nourishes the land and encourages crops to grow.

the water softener at Carp.) When we opened the silo, the partly-fermented organic material had a rather pleasant smell, unless it had begun to sour. I was always amazed that the pit would be warm and steaming, no matter how much snow and ice were on the ground.

We put the silage in old wash-tubs to feed the cattle, and those cows came on the run when they heard the tubs begin to clatter!

When the silo was full, we leaned the rest of the stalks of corn against the haystacks in the corral. My sister and I used to crawl back into the space of perhaps 18 inches that was left between the bottoms of the stalks and the bottom of the stack. I still have a vivid memory of the fragrance, sound, and feel of those dry stalks and the dim light.

Besides the field crops and the garden, we had a reliable crop of Russian thistle (a tumbleweed), greasewood, sandburs, stinkweeds, cow-weed (the name we used because the cattle liked it so much, and also a tumbleweed), puncture vines or tack vines, Jimson weed, and cockleburs. I heard of someone in southern Utah who sold cockleburs to tourists as porcupine eggs. The guy who told me about it kept a straight face, so I guess he must have been serious.

The creek bed through our ranch was wet and green, with mostly salt grass and a reed called wire grass. We had one place that was wet enough to have water cress. Now and then my father would see some Johnson grass in the meadow, and he dug it up at once. In the years since we left Carp, much of that creek bed has been taken over by tamarisk.

❖ ❖ ❖ ❖ ❖ ❖ ❖ ❖ ❖ ❖ ❖ ❖ ❖ ❖ ❖ ❖ ❖

As a kid, I knew the name Mojave Desert, but I thought it was probably somewhere beyond Mountain Pass, on the road to Los Angeles. Some maps of the geologic regions of the United States show a little projection into southern Nevada, but how far in? The answer just recently came to me. In "The Mysterious Lands", Ann Zwinger explains that creosote bush and Joshua trees characterize the Mojave Desert; where the creosote bush stops and sagebrush begins (allowing for the probable existence of a transition zone), the Great Basin Desert begins, a cool steppe desert that is generally cooler and higher than the Mojave Desert.

Sagebrush thrives at the Elliott ranch, only a few miles north of Tunnel 4, so I lived in the Mojave Desert and moved to the Great Basin Desert without even realizing it.

Wire grass

Tongues of the Mojave Desert extend north, depending on moisture and average temperature. Desert willow, Joshua trees, and creosote bush grow in the Meadow Valley Wash just below Elgin. The creosote bush and Joshua tree association extends up the St. George Corridor into Utah, past Washington. Delamar Flat has abundant Joshua trees, and they grow at Goldfield. The ones that are common in the Mojave Desert are *Yucca brevifolia*, but the ones on Delamar Flat are *Y. brevifolia* var. *jaegeriana*, named for Edmund C. Jaeger, one of the foremost naturalists of the Mojave and Great Basin deserts. I have drawn extensively from his articles in "Desert Magazine".

The Joshua tree is a tree lily. It starts with a straight trunk, but soon it will develop branches. The cause of branching seems to be mainly damage to the terminal bud by the yucca-boring weevil or by death of the terminal bud after flowering.

When we were riding after the cattle in cold weather, we used to look for what we called "petrified yucca" (although we knew it wasn't really petrified). The hard, dark chunks made a fine, hot fire. According to Jaeger, the larvae of the weevil get ready for pupation by making tough cases of frass at the ends of branches. The plant deposits silica in the cell walls to defend against injuries by the borers or injuries from fire or wind.

Mining & Scientific Press, April 18, 1903, says the Southern Nevada Mine, at Searchlight, sometimes burned Joshua trees in their boilers; they burned 20 cords a day. I'm surprised any Joshua trees were left in southern Nevada!

Zwinger says she once saw a man on a distant hill, a pack on his back and an arm raised in greeting, so she waved back. Finally she realized the "man" was a Joshua tree. I never did mistake one for a man, but Joshua trees in the dusk can take the form of anything you want (or don't want) to see. When I was perhaps 8 or 9 years old, we pushed a herd of cattle out to Tule Flat, and we didn't get there until after dark. As the twilight deepened, those Joshua trees became all kinds of strange and sometimes ominous things. My imagination ran at full speed in those days.

The desert around Carp has abundant filaree and bottlestoppers, and our range had white sage (winter fat). Filaree is a crane's bill, a member of the geranium family. Our cattle liked it as much as they liked alfalfa. White sage, a halophyte that grows in good soil as well as saline soil, is good cattle forage; it has almost as much protein as alfalfa does. It was common on Tule Flat until the sheep herds were allowed to come in; the sheep killed it off. My father never did let any sheep on our range, and white sage was becoming plentiful when we left Carp.

Bottlestoppers (as they were known at Carp) are widespread in the deserts of the West. The common names are derived from a hollow enlargement in the main stem and in branching stems in the upper tiers. After the plant dries out in the summer, the gray or purplish plant stands all through the winter. But in the spring, when the plant is soft and tender, it has a delicious tart flavor. At least, us kids thought so; evidently the cattle have a different opinion.

Creosote bush is common around Carp. We knew it as "chaparral", and many years passed before I learned that chaparral is a general term for stiff or thorny shrubs or dwarf trees that are difficult to pass through. Creosote bush is a stiff shrub, but the plants regulate their growth so they are widely spaced, certainly not difficult to get through. Their roots may be 30 to 40 feet long. Evaporation of water from the plant is retarded by the resin coating on the leaves. Animals that might browse on the leaves are discouraged by the bitter sap and the odor. (There is no creosote in the creosote bush, but it has the name, anyway.)

Creosote bush often occurs in large, evenly spaced, pure stands that look brownish-green from a distance. The bushes have small, yellow blossoms in March or April that turn into little fuzzy white balls when they go to seed. Stems of the plants may have round, brown or green galls that are produced by the creosote gall-midge.

The stems harbor large numbers of the creosote bush lac-scale insects concealed under warty-looking patches of reddish or brownish resinous material. The Indians separated the lac resin by boiling the plants in water and skimming off the resin. It was used for mending pots and waterproofing baskets.

> *Zwinger says the creosote bush is unpalatable because of resins in the leaves. The resins emit such a pleasant aroma after a rain that she thinks that's what the desert should smell like. I agree, for the Mojave Desert; I think sagebrush after a rain is what the Great Basin Desert should smell like. Stebbins notes that the desert iguana eats fresh leaves, buds, and flowers of the creosote bush.*

Brown cocoons among the branches of creosote bushes are the pupal stage of the creosote psyche or bag worm. A most unusual grasshopper is Bruner's silver-spotted grasshopper, which is said never to land on the ground; if it is disturbed, it will fly to another creosote bush. It has rich green wings with spots of brown and mother-of-pearl. (I don't recall ever seeing one; this is based on Jaeger's description.)

Another strange and interesting thing to be seen in the desert (not necessarily associated with creosote bushes) is the home of the lycosid spider (wolf spider). It is a small chimney of sticks and silk, often seen in sand and clay patches, that marks the deep, tubular hole in which the spider lives. The spider comes out at night for its insect prey.

When we lived at Carp, I knew that "purple sage" is the Nevada state flower, and when I saw a small shrub with an extravagantly beautiful purple flowers, I concluded it was the purple sage. Later I learned that the shrub with the purple flowers is Fremont dalea (smokebush). However, a purple sage, a true Salvia, does grow in southern Nevada; it isn't what I saw.

We had two kinds of mesquite: honey mesquite, with large, bean-like pods, and screw-bean mesquite, with the seeds in tight, screw-like rolls. Mesquites need water, but their roots may travel 50 or 60 feet to get it; a mesquite in the bed of a dry wash is a reliable sign that water is nearby. The trunk of a screw-bean mesquite can be fairly long and straight, which makes it useful for posts or construction.

Cattle and horses eat mesquite leaves and beans, and the beans were ground into flour by the Indians. Mesquite beans are rich in sugars and proteins. The desert weevil breeds in the beans of screw-bean mesquite, and the weevils leave exit holes where they leave the twisted pods.

We had black willows, which are real willows, and we had desert willows and arrow willows, which are not willows. Desert willow, which is related to the catalpa, has a lovely white to pink or lavender flower. The plant is often found in and along washes that have deep, sandy soils that retain water below the surface.

The arrow willow has willow-like leaves, but it is in the sunflower family. The pungent odor, especially after a rain, certainly makes it seem kin to sunflowers. The straight stems grow as tall as 12 feet, and they often form thickets. Between the Carp school ground and the creek was a steep bank that was covered with arrow willows, and I had passageways that never saw sunlight in summer.

Heliotrope, which was common on our ranch, has little, purple blossoms on a curving stem; when I first saw a Paisley print, I was reminded of those little plants that were so common. I still think "Paisley" when I see a photo or drawing of heliotrope.

Another plant we knew was the sand lily, which I am not able to remember well enough to recognize in a book. However, I wonder if perhaps it could have been the evening primrose, which was common. I believe I remember seeing the curved structure of the dead plants, the birdcage primrose.

❖ ❖ ❖ ❖ ❖ ❖ ❖ ❖ ❖ ❖ ❖ ❖ ❖ ❖ ❖ ❖ ❖

We had such an abundance of lizards that my father called our place a "lizard ranch". We had horned toads (actually a lizard), side-blotched lizards, western whiptails, zebra lizards (also called gridiron-tailed lizards), and desert spiny lizards (fence lizards). The western whip-tail, in common with numerous other lizards, sheds the end of its tail when it feels threatened, and the lizard runs away while the end of its tail flops and squirms like something alive. A small one ran up my pants leg, and I don't know who was more excited, me or the lizard. He emerged with his tail truncated.

According to the Zuni Indians, a circus bug was about to be attacked by a coyote, when the bug put its head to the ground and said it heard the gods planning to punish those who defiled the trails. The coyote realized he was one of the guilty ones, so he hurried away to avoid being caught.

The spiny lizard is a burly fellow who pumps up and down on his front legs, displaying a blue patch on his throat. We called him a bull lizard. I remember a bull lizard pumping up and down while watching Dad milk a cow, and Dad pointed a teat and squirted the lizard with milk. Was that a nice thing to do?

Big, red harvester ants were everywhere. My father killed off ant hills by pouring a solution of sodium cyanide into the hill at night, after all the ants were in, and plugging the entry hole. And we had goldsmith beetles, so big and noisy I was intimidated by them.

We never saw a circus at Carp, but we had plenty of circus bugs, which we knew simply as stinkbugs or tumblebugs. They are beetles in the general group called darkling beetles. Stinkbugs are dark black, and they are active in the heat of the day. They are vegetarians, and they often scavenge fragments of seeds and flowers around ant hills. They stand on their heads, with the tip of the abdomen pointing upward, and when threatened, they emit a foul-smelling oil. If that doesn't seem to work, they may fall over and play dead; the next choice is to hurry away, when they are likely to tumble end-over-end. Thus they are tumblebugs or circus bugs.

❖ ❖ ❖ ❖ ❖ ❖ ❖ ❖ ❖ ❖ ❖ ❖ ❖ ❖ ❖ ❖ ❖

Dry bogs, apparently the home of kangaroo rats, are common in soft ground such as abandoned fields. Numerous holes or tunnels run just below the surface, and the top will collapse under the foot of man, horse, or cow. A person who steps into one unexpectedly has trouble keeping balance, because with every lurch as the surface gives way, the next step is no better, and the result is to reel along or perhaps fall down. Riding a horse at a run across a dry bog (or trying to) is a risky maneuver. I rode Prince into one, and he fell and banged his head. I wasn't hurt, but his head swelled up and we think he probably had a king-sized headache.

The kangaroo rat is a feisty little creature that has big hind legs and a long tail. It can jump much like a kangaroo and, by using its tail as a rudder, it can change direction in mid-leap. It travels on all fours when moving slowly, but it is bipedal when in a hurry. It stands on its large hind feet and uses the tail for balance when feeding, looking just like a tiny kangaroo.

Large, black birds were part of life at Carp; we knew them as crows, but now I know they were ravens. Edmund Jaeger says, "There are no crows in the desert". (I thought only Edgar Allen Poe knew a raven on sight.) We often saw them flying in evasive patterns, trying to get away from little birds that kept pestering them in the air. We called those little birds "picky birds", because they were always picking at the ravens. Now that I have learned a thing or two, I know that the "picky birds" were very likely Western kingbirds. We see them harassing the ravens in Grand Junction, too. Ravens eat the eggs of other birds, and numerous birds, even as small as hummingbirds, harass ravens.

By the time I remember the creek, bullfrogs were common in it and in the pond near the school grounds. The pond had lots of tules (cattails), and we enjoyed hearing the red-winged blackbirds calling among them. In the summer of 1927, a railroad conductor brought a 5-gallon container of bullfrog tadpoles from Chicago, and Charles Walsh and my father spread them from our place down to Matt Reese's place. They thrived.

Jack rabbits, cottontails, mourning doves, and Gambel's quail were plentiful. In season we had mallards, canvasbacks, and teal. We ate lots of rabbit and quail. Dad had a 12-gauge Winchester Model 97 shotgun, I had a 20-gauge single-shot Stevens, and my sister, Mary Lou, had a 410-gauge shotgun and a pump-action Remington .22 that jammed as often as not.

The game season wasn't taken very seriously there. Sometimes we had visitors who hunted a little; one attorney would come from Pioche to "open the season" on quail for a few hours.

Things were different in 1937 or 1938, when the County Commissioners decided not to open the season on quail. Maybe the quail had been scarce somewhere, but not at Carp. As a result, our valley became badly overpopulated with quail. The few we shot were so thin and emaciated that we gave up for that summer. Even our cats wouldn't eat them.

One afternoon Dad and I heard what we took to be the sound of a heavy truck some distance away, but no truck showed up. Finally we realized that the sound was made by enormous flocks of quail in flight.

We had planted oats in our 10-acre field that year. We cut and shocked the ripe grain, then we went to Las Vegas overnight. The next afternoon, the shocks of oats had been leveled, and most of the grain had been eaten. Too bad for us, but maybe it helped the quail.

My father was proud of his barb-wire fences. He used a block and tackle to pull them really tight, which meant the corner posts and gate posts had to be well braced. He said sometimes a wire was so tight that it would snap when the staple was driven home into the post.

At the lower end of our ranch, the railroad went through a cut that had been blasted in the point of a hill. When we would be working on the fence where it was washed out by high water in the creek, sometimes I would climb around on the broken rock from the cut. I remember seeing rusted cylindrical cans with a hole punched in one end, and my father told me the cans had held black powder.

Anyone who writes about a desert area such as southern Lincoln County is expected to throw in a few sensational stories about the summer heat. Let's pass on that, and hear a little about the cold.

About 1927-1930, when my father was active in the Odd Fellows Lodge in Caliente (where he rode the goat in May 1927), my parents often made trips to Caliente. My mother's mother and stepfather (Dr. & Mrs. O.F. Waldram) lived in Panaca after June 1929. Mom and Dad drove to Caliente or Panaca winter and summer, and they had some tough wintertime experiences.

They described two or three winters that were especially cold. Some of the creek crossings between Carp and Caliente would be frozen over, and the ice would crack and let a wheel drop into the water. Dad had to get out and break a path through the ice so he could get the car across. Heaters didn't amount to much in those days, and when you got wet and cold, you stayed wet and cold.

Once when Dad was returning to Carp with a telegraph operator as a passenger, the radiator froze after they passed the Kiernan ranch. Dad got out to hunt for someone with a team or another car to tow him in, and his passenger decided to "limp on in". The engine overheated and threw a connecting rod and was ruined.

The folks got into exceptionally cold weather on one trip to Panaca. The highway from Caliente to Pioche has a fairly straight stretch before it reaches the "Y" where the road to Panaca branches off to the right. The steering linkage was coated with so

> *We often worked without gloves, even in the summer heat (except when handling barbed wire). The tools would get awfully hot in the sun, and then we needed gloves. We accepted the advice to stand iron tools on end so they wouldn't get so hot, but I was not convinced it made any difference. Still, what harm could it do?*

much ice when they got to the "Y" that the car wouldn't make the turn. Dad had to back and cut several times to get around the turn. They slept that night in a bedroll on the kitchen floor and kept a fire going in the stove, and yet a pan of water on the back of the stove froze before morning.

Severe winter weather can affect birds and animals, as well as people. For example, the *Caliente Herald* reported on Jan. 3, 1928, that a snowstorm on Dec. 13 had left 10 inches of snow and "thousands" of dead birds. They were identified as Western grebes; evidently they had been caught in the blinding storm, and while in flight they had crashed into trees and houses.

Ellen Johnson and her father came from North Dakota, and she taught one year at Carp. They told of the winters there, with houses buried to the eaves in snow. In January 1937 we had a taste of weather that seemed like North Dakota.

The year 1936 ended balmy and warm; Christmas was a shirtsleeve day. Then came the winter, immediately after Jan. 1. People claimed to have read the temperature at -36° that month. I don't know about the temperature, but I do know the ponds in our meadow had the thickest ice I ever saw at Carp. A washtub of water on our screened back porch froze solid one night and pushed the bottom out of the tub.

My first experience with the freezing process is still vivid in my memory. I knew what ice was, but I had not seen water turn into ice. One day I was in the yard and I saw water from a dripping faucet becoming ice. I was fascinated by the formation of ice, but the fascination has worn off by now.

The water for our house came from an overhead tank that was filled by a windmill or a pump jack run by a small one-cylinder gasoline engine. When the packing gland at the top of the casing began to wear out, each upward stroke of the pump would force water between the packing and the pump rod, and water could spray all the way to the top of the windmill tower. January 1937 caught us with the packing gland leaking, and the spray of water began freezing on the tower. The three-legged tower became coated with ice, forming an icy pyramid. The wheel was finally immobilized, and for a while we got our water by chopping pieces of ice from the tower and melting the ice in pans on the kitchen stove.

I was a little kid then, and it was a Great Adventure; now I hope I may never again see thirty below!

THE MEADOW VALLEY SCATTERED SETTLERS PROJECT

As early as the 1920s, programs were proposed that were intended to deal with perceived misuse of land resources. H.H. Wooten, in "The Land Utilization Program, 1934 to 1964", summarizes the development and operation of the Land Utilization Program. The Bankhead-Jones Farm Tenant Act of 1937 authorized the purchase of lands, "including lands which are submarginal or not primarily suitable for cultivation in order thereby to correct maladjust-ments in land use". Isolated settler projects were part of the program. The management of the program was transferred to the Soil Conservation Service in 1938. The Meadow Valley Scattered Settlers Project was one very small part of the Land Utilization Program.

A headline in the *Caliente Herald* for March 30, 1939, said "LAND PUR-CHASE TO BE MADE IN LINCOLN COUNTY". A new program for "submar-ginal land purchase and land use adjustment" had been announced for parts of Lincoln and Clark Counties. Prices to be offered would be based on appraisal of the land. About 30 "scattered farms" in the Meadow Valley area had been proposed for purchase, and about half of them were considered abandoned. Purchase would be through the Soil Conservation Service (SCS).

H.H. Bennett, chief of the SCS, said flood damage and soil erosion in the area had been severe. As a result, "the costs of maintaining irrigation facilities are prohibitive, while much of the range land has been depleted through unwise grazing". Most of the crop land in the area was in fields that were too small to make cultivation profitable. He said about 1700 acres had been classi-fied as crop land; 425 acres were used for hay production, 100 acres were used for grain and other crops, and the remaining 1145 acres were idle or abandoned.

Bennett said the land would be retired from cultivation and developed for grazing. Unnecessary buildings and fences would be removed, and stock watering facilities would be installed where they were needed.

In about 1939, two SCS appraisers, named Salvage and Johnson, came to see my father at Carp. Their appraisal resulted in an offer that my father believed he should accept. The 1938 flood had not washed away any of our land, but the next one might; other ranches were seriously damaged. He did not think our ranch was submarginal, but everything considered, the prudent man would not pass up that kind of ready cash during the Depression.

The other ranches in the Meadow Valley Wash that were purchased under the Project included the Black, McGuffie, and Conk ranches. I don't have good information on any others, but extensive purchases between Lyman Crossing and Elgin are indicated by the Clover Mts., Nev.-Utah, 1:100,000 Surface Management Status map, 1978, of the U.S. Bureau of Land Management.

All the improvements were to be removed from the farms that were pur-chased by the government. I saw the house on the McGuffie ranch torn down, but the houses on our ranch were left in place. They are still there in 1994.

SCHOOL DAYS

These school districts have been significant in this part of the Meadow Valley Wash: Bullionville, Caliente, Carp, Clover Valley, Cottonwood, Henrie, Kiernan, Meadow Valley Wash, and Red Rock. Bullionville was a smelter town near Pioche, but the Bullionville school district extends from Caliente down to about Boyd. The Bullionville school was at Etna, but the Red Rock school was there first. (Another of the many fires destroyed the school at Etna on Sept. 22, 1935.) Kiernan school was at Elgin. Henrie school was at Kyle; it was discontinued in February 1942.

My parents moved to Carp in early 1925, so they saw some of the early days of Carp school. Besides what I remember, my information has come mostly from what they told me, what Charles Walsh remembers, and what I can get from the Caliente and Pioche newspapers.

My mother told me that she thought Mrs. Pearl Huston taught school at Carp, and the classes were in the Huston home or the Mabey home. However, the *Caliente News*, Dec. 2, 1920, said, "The inhabitants of Carp are impatiently awaiting the completion of the schoolhouse being erected by V.K. Mariger". About 1932 a two-room apartment was added at the back.

In 1975 I wrote to the Nevada Board of Education about Carp school. The Public Information Officer said Carp School District was 1 of 18 new districts that were started in the 1917-18 school year under an emergency warrant. The following list of teachers at Carp is based on their list; I have modified it on the basis of other information, such as news items in the *Caliente Herald*. Their reports skipped some years, and I have not tried to connect names with dates if I have no other information. Dr. D. Don Francom, Lincoln County School District, has added names since 1944 to the list.

Year	Teacher	Year	Teacher
1917-18	Rena Gannon	1933-34	Grant Hafen
1918-19		1934-35	Grant Hafen
1919-20		1935-36	Grant Hafen
1920-21	Mary West	1936-37	Miss Ellen Johnson
1921-22	Marguerite Rice	1937-38	Howard L. McMullen
1923-24	Laura Gentry	1938-43	Miss Fannie Daniel
1924-25	Grace M. Lewis	1943-44	Miss Sara McElwee
1925-26		1944-45	Miss Sara McElwee
1926-27		1945-46	Etta Titus
1927-28	Katharine Wells	1946-47	Agnes R. Roberts
1928-29	Mrs. Clara Holbrook Brown	1947-48	V. Howieson
1929-30	Wilma Schofield	1948-49	Janette E. Erway
	Bernice Geiger	1950-51	Mrs. Gladys Martin
1930-31	Miss Artie Macy Henrie		and A.J. Nelson
1931-32	Miss Artie Macy Henrie	1951-52	Mrs. Gladys Martin
1932-33	Harold O. Tabor		

Charles Walsh attended Carp school during part of the 1927-28 year and all of 1928-29 and 1929-30. He says the teacher in the fall of 1929 was Wilma Schofield, whom he remembers as a beautiful young blonde, just out of college, with a sweet disposition and personality. He says he and Don Reese and Mathew Reese fell in love with her immediately. After about 2 months, the Department of Education notified the school board that she lacked one-half credit of being qualified to teach, and she must be replaced.

Schoolhouse at Carp after teacher's apartment was added. Tom Anderson's Pontiac at right. This building burned in 1938.

Bernice Geiger, an older woman, was the unfortunate person who was brought in to continue the year. Competing with the perception of Wilma Schofield, she didn't have a chance; the rest of the year was "a shambles and a running fight" between her and the older pupils. Afterward, Charles realized that she wasn't really as bad as they thought.

Macy Henrie was one of the Henrie girls from the Henrie ranch, a daughter of Mr. & Mrs. Parley Henrie. She taught at Kyle (Henrie school district), and in early 1933 she married Thomas Reece. Clyde Brundy says that one of the pleasant things about the Henrie ranch was all the attractive Henrie girls.

Schoolhouse at Carp, 1946. This building was built in 1938. Look at all those windows on the south side! Photo by Andy Bohn.

Harold Tabor was studying law and was teaching school to help finance his education. During his year at Carp, he arranged with Lincoln County High School to teach the first year of high school there. Lincoln County High School, in Panaca, was too far away for most kids from a place like Carp.

My father had only favorable comments on Mr. Tabor, but he did have one interesting story. When he was staying at our house, Mr. Tabor built a rather large dog-house, and he put on a shingled roof. The only problem was that he began at the ridge pole and shingled down, a sure way to get the rain to run into the house.

Grant Hafen was one of the Hafens from southern Utah. He taught me to tell time, using a pocket watch that I realized later was a Hamilton railroad watch. Gloria, the little daughter of Grant and Eva Hafen, had long, golden blonde hair.

Howard L. McMullen was the teacher for the year 1937-38. My impression of him is that he was not a very inspiring teacher. He had some strange stories that he appeared to think we would believe. Here is an example:

He had been in the Ozarks, where he saw a bear that was chained to a log. The bear picked up the log, carried it to a bank, and threw it over. The chain jerked the bear's collar, and the bear went over the bank. He was not the type to be easily dissuaded, so he carried the log back up to the top and threw it over again, with the same result. And he tried it again a time or two. Well, that's what the man told us.

Carp is about 35 miles by railroad from Moapa; Jim Davis said Mr. McMullen used to send letters air-mail to Moapa.

He normally started the school day by having us gather at one end of the room while one of us read aloud. One morning in April, Eugene Anderson arrived late and said the roof was on fire. We knew a tall story when we heard one, and nobody paid any attention—-not until smoke began drifting into the room. By golly, the building *was* on fire!

McMullen ran into his apartment to salvage what he could, leaving us outside in the yard. Louis Leavitt and I were the oldest and tallest pupils, and we went back inside to bring out books and the big map-case from the wall. Men from Carp soon arrived to learn the cause of the smoke, and they squelched our salvage operation.

He had a Ford parked near his door. It had a locking steering wheel, and the wheels were turned and locked; he couldn't find the ignition key so the steering could be unlocked, so several men had to push the car a few feet, pick the front end up and set it over, and push again.

The building burned to the ground. We finished out the rest of the year in Mrs. Anderson's front porch.

A new schoolhouse was built that summer by Harold V. Freedman. It had windows all along the south wall, and it was a pleasant place. And that's quite an endorsement from someone who didn't like school.

Memory is a fine thing, but sometimes I am uneasy about relying on it with no corroboration. In the 1980s I thought I would like to confirm some of the details about the new building, including the name of the contractor. I was no longer in Nevada, so I wrote to the Nevada Board of Education to ask if they could provide any information. They didn't even know the schoolhouse had burned!

The schoolhouse was used for dances, parties, and Sunday School, and it was the polling place during elections. The ballot box, ballots, and other supplies for Carp Precinct came from Pioche by mail in a sealed mailbag, and one side of the bag was covered with postage stamps. After the polls closed, the Election Board would work into the night by the light of Aladdin kerosene lamps, counting the votes and preparing the return so the mailbag could be sealed and returned. Us kids slept on the floor while that was going on.

When my father was in grade school in Logan, Nevada (that was before it was Logandale), he had a teacher who told about two aviators (as pilots were called then) who crashed in Egypt, close to the Sphinx. They were attacked by a gang of gorillas, and things were not going at all well. (Civilization then was not as advanced as it is today, and "guerrilla" was not an everyday word.) The men were losing the fight, when suddenly a weird whistle frightened the gorillas away. The explanation soon became obvious: The whistle was produced by the wind whistling through the teeth of the Sphinx.

The standard answer to a question from a pupil was "That's for me to know and you to find out".

TRAGEDIES

Places as remote as Carp have their tragedies that are aggravated by the remoteness. Here are a few that I know about in the Meadow Valley Wash.

The railroad was just across the road from the Mabey house, and in early February 1920, Clarence Mabey's little girl crossed the road and went up onto the railroad grade as a train was passing by, and the step of a car struck her on the head. The injury was a terrible one, but not immediately fatal. (From the 1920 Census report, I conclude her name was Sarah.) The *Pioche Record*, Feb. 20, 1920, said, "The 4-year-old child of Clarence Mabey, who lives near Carp, was killed by a passing freight train about 10 days ago". The article said a step of the caboose struck her in the head.

Dr. Lynwalter, the railroad doctor in Las Vegas, came in on the next train and took her to Salt Lake City to the hospital, but she died on the way. Dr. Lynwalter's wife told my mother that the case affected him the worst of any case he ever handled.

I remember walking through the brush on the Mabey ranch and seeing a small oval of white stones; later I learned that the oval of stones marked her grave . . . a forlorn grave in a lonely spot. I wonder if that is why the Mabeys left Carp.

When the tunnels were being concreted in 1929-30, a serious cave-in occurred at Tunnel 9. William Benson was killed; Fred B. Fisher, a 7-year-old girl, and nine other people were injured.

James E. Frazine, a passenger conductor, died of apoplexy at Guelph (Farrier) on Dec. 19, 1924, according to the *Pioche Record*, Dec. 27, 1923. He was the conductor on eastbound Train #4, which was in the siding waiting to meet westbound Train #3. He went up the track to see if #3 was coming, and when he saw it, he started back and collapsed on the track. The rear brakeman ran to ask what was wrong, and Frazine replied, "I'm all in". He was helped back to the train, and the crew went through the train, looking for a doctor. They found a Dr. Bulette, who had been called from Las Vegas to attend a sick child at Carp. Dr. Bulette did what he could, but Frazine died in a few minutes.

"Called to attend a sick child at Carp"; Flight For Life helicopters didn't exist then, nor could anyone call 911, nor were there antibiotics. For someone sick at a place such as Carp, the only option was to try to hang on for 6 hours or 8 hours or 12 hours, or however long it took to telegraph a message to Las Vegas or Caliente to a doctor who would wait for the next train and make the trip to Carp or wherever.

The *Caliente Herald* for April 30, 1936, had two stories of tragedies in the Meadow Valley Wash, both of them mysteries.

The coroner's jury had been called to examine the body of a man found in a mine tunnel about half a mile west of Caliente. He was identified as Leo Girard, a needle salesman who had visited homes in Caliente about a month earlier. He had registered at the employment office at Pioche on March 10. He had evidently been living in the tunnel. The cause of death appeared to be pneumonia. He had been dead 3 or 4 weeks. He was buried in the Caliente cemetery.

The other death was at Carp. As Tom Anderson was making the daily inspection of his section of the railroad, he found a man lying by the tracks about 3 miles west of Carp. He put the man on his motor car and took him to Carp to be taken to Caliente by train, but he died before anything else could be done. Sheriff James B. Tennille and Coroner Evan H. Edwards came to Carp and summoned C.L. Averett, Charles O. Maxwell, and George Ely as a coroner's jury. The man was identified as Oliver Newton Staats, a veteran of the Spanish-American War. The jury concluded he had died of injuries sustained when he fell from a train at milepost 416.50.

A work train overturned about 17 miles west of Caliente (between Boyd and Elgin) on March 14, 1938, as gravel was being dumped. Four men were injured and another, Blair Williams, was killed.

W.N. Sexton, a brakeman, was killed near Boyd on Aug. 29, 1938, when he was flagging traffic during railroad rip-rap work and failed to get clear of a helper engine. Sheriff Tennille and Corner Edwards summoned a coroner's jury of Carl Scannell, R.D. Taylor, and Dr. J.F. Hill. They concluded there was no evidence of foul play. He had plenty of time to get off the track, and nobody could understand why he didn't.

On July 15, 1939, a colored man was found dead underneath a railroad bridge at Galt. He appeared to have been 70 to 75 years old and to have died of a heart attack perhaps 10 days to 3 weeks before. His identity could not be established.

Ralph Hughes, head brakeman, fell from a freight train near Elgin on Feb. 26, 1941. He was taken by automobile from Elgin to Caliente, but he died of internal injuries on the way.

The end came for Jim Davis, the storekeeper and postmaster at Carp since 1935, on April 10, 1943. He was found alongside the tracks where outfit cars were spotted at the west end of Carp siding; both legs and one arm had been cut off when he fell or was pushed under a moving train. He lived a few hours.

He had talked about his years running a donkey engine in the Ruth copper pit. Sometimes his brother Ira came to visit. We learned that Jim was really John Ernest Dawley, and we heard he had been blackballed from his job in the copper pit.

Walt and Pearl Huston's son Robert, almost 5 years old, died of interstitial nephritis at their ranch on Dec. 3, 1926. The body was taken to my parents' house (the pumper's house). My father went to Las Vegas to get a coffin; my mother sat up all night, with some other women, "rubbing his face and hands with camphorated oil to keep his skin from darkening". They had lost a 9-month-old son, Walter Hugh Huston, to bronchial pneumonia at Carp on Feb. 8, 1921.

Something that is common to stories of medical emergencies in the "good old days" is the amount of time that elapsed while a patient was being taken to a medical facility by wagon, auto, train, or whatever. When we lived at the Elliott ranch, I broke my ankle at school, and the bone was set and a cast was applied by Dr. J.B. Demman in Caliente; but I bumped the cast and dislocated the ankle and the fracture. My foot began to swell, and I was in misery all night. The creek came up during the night and we couldn't get back to Caliente, but we did get to Stine, where Dad flagged a train and we went to Las Vegas. The doctor said it would have been gangrene in a few more hours; the swelling was already splitting the cast.

An incident on the Conk ranch was close to tragedy, but tragedy was averted by good luck and quick thinking. Here is how it was reported in the *Caliente Herald* on Aug. 31, 1933:

> *There was a near tragedy on the V.A. Anderson ranch last week. The children, while playing, dug a cave, and it caved in completely covering little Ross and partly covering Vernal, Jr. Vernal got out and he and Arnold dug Ross out. The boys are to be commended for their quick wit and the way they acted in an emergency. Had they not worked fast Ross would have smothered. The little fellow was ill from swallowing dirt but is better now.*

Another story in the *Herald*, dated Jan. 28, 1932, had the headline "Thought Kidnapped; Was Sleep Walker". Sheriff Charlie Culverwell had been called to Stine to search for Arthur Chavez, 10 years old, who was thought to have been kidnapped. By the time the sheriff and Railroad Officer E.F.

Sherwood got there, the boy was back safely. The parents thought he had been kidnapped, when they found him to be missing, and they thought perhaps the kidnappers had actually been after their 18-year-old daughter in the next room. But the boy came back, with his feet cut and scratched. He was in his underwear, and he had been walking in his sleep. He crossed the bottom of the Meadow Valley Wash, where the icy water was 2 feet deep and 35 feet across, walked through the snow up the bank on the other side, crossed a patch of slide rock, and then walked back. (I never did see the creek that deep and wide except during a flash flood.) He didn't wake up until he was crossing the creek and heard his parents shouting. The sheriff followed the tracks, and nobody else's tracks were there. The only possible solution was suggested to be that he "had been quite sick with influenza and it was probable that, slightly delirious and in a sound slumber, he had made the long walk in the cold night and across the icy waters of the creek". Don't give me that fishy look; I'm only relaying what the newspaper said.

CARP ITEMS

Most of our news came by radio (mainly KFI, Los Angeles; KNX, the Voice of Hollywood; or KSL, Salt Lake City) or from the *Caliente Herald*. Some excerpts from "Carp Items" are copied here, with comments and elaboration.

June 22, 1933: ". . . Mrs. Maxwell and the boys came Sunday evening to make their home in Carp. . . . Mr. Maxwell has a new DeSoto car. . . . Mr. Ewing has bid in the operator's trick and will move to Carp with his family."

Charles Maxwell had replaced Walter Conk as signal maintainer; the Maxwell boys were Tom and John. Albert Ewing had been an operator at Elgin. The Ewing children were Betty and Billy.

Aug. 31, 1933: ". . . Mr. and Mrs. Tom Anderson and Sonny are spending several days vacation in California. . . . V.A. Anderson is the relief foreman while Tom Anderson is away." Vernal Anderson later worked with other section gangs. He was killed in January 1937 near Brant, California, when a light engine collided with the section gang's motor car, killing eight men. John Jansen was a relief foreman for Tom Anderson in the late 1930s.

Aug. 29, 1935: Sam Thompson, from Caliente, was "signposting" roads in the Carp area.

Oct. 3, 1935: "Jerome and Wright McKnight returned from Cedar City last week with a new Chevrolet coupe. . . . Mr. Graff is visiting at the Hafen and Frei ranch. . . . Jack Fullam and his helper, Mr. Kennedy, are stationed at Carp with the dragline repairing the damage done by last week's cloudburst."

Jerome, Pres, Jim, Harrison, Lawrence, and June were Wright and Rozena

McKnight's sons, and Vivian, Evelyn, and Sarah were their daughters.

Lynn Graff, of southern Utah, drove a stock truck, and sometimes he hauled cattle in or out of Carp. Hafen & Frei Brothers were usually the ones who hired him, as I recall.

Jack Fullam was a dragline operator who worked a lot between Caliente and Carp.

Oct. 31, 1935: "E.K. Wright, Mrs. Leisander and Dorolene motored to Panaca Friday evening to bring Dorothy home for the week. . . . Mrs. Mary Averett, Walter and Mary Lou returned home Saturday after spending the last week visiting in Las Vegas. . . . Rev. A.G. Shriver spent Saturday and Sunday at Carp reorganizing the Sunday School there. . . . Leon Averett and his son Ramon of Las Vegas arrived in Carp Saturday evening. Ramon is visiting at the ranch while his daddy and C.L. Averett are on a hunting trip."

Leon Averett was my father's younger brother. Sometimes a friend or relative would come to Carp to go hunting with my father in the Clover Mountains, though I don't remember much venison resulting from those trips.

When I read about mineral resources of the Mormon Mountains, I look for a clear reference to the Paint Mine (also called the Jasper Mine), but I don't find it. But I was at the mine, although I was very young. It was examined by Dr. J.D. Von Galscale, the Union Pacific geologist, in the late 1920s. By my recollection and the descriptions by other people, it was toward the eastern end of the range. The mine was owned by Matt Reese and Cliff Whitmore.

The ore was trucked to the Meadow Valley Wash below Carp and was loaded on railroad cars at the west end of Carp siding. Monroe "Roe" Thomas, of Las Vegas, shipped a car of ore in May 1933. Leon Averett drove a truck for a while, hauling the ore. The mine was shipping jasper or hematite to American Asphalt Corp., in Salt Lake City, for use in roofing.

Salt was hauled from the Moapa Valley in the old days by a road that crossed Mormon Mesa and went east of the Mormon Mountains, then west to the Meadow Valley Wash. From there, the salt was hauled to Delamar or Pioche for use in chloridizing mills.

Tom and Anna Anderson's son was Eugene, but he was commonly known as "Sonny". After he was graduated from high school, he enlisted in the Air Force. He was killed in a plane crash near Las Vegas on Sept. 7, 1955.

Hafen & Frei had a road from Vigo to Tule Flat, perhaps following the old Salt Road. The ore from the Paint Mine came out by that road, and that was how we got to the mine.

Adam G. Shriver was a Presbyterian minister who came through Carp now and then. He had lantern slides and a projector and a portable generator to run the projector where electricity was not available. The main things I remember from his visits were the slide shows (but not the slides themselves) and the reorganization of the Sunday School that usually followed a visit. After a visit in 1932 the attendance was 12, and after a visit in 1933 it was 26.

Mr. Shriver was a native of Canal Fulton, Ohio, according to Anne Shriver, in "The Jack Rabbit Missionary". He had worked in Montana, Alaska, Washington, and Oregon before he was transferred to Carson City, Nevada, in 1927, when he was 46 years old. He was a Sunday School missionary for all of Nevada and part of Utah and California until his retirement in 1955.

The schoolhouse was the only public building, so dances, elections, and Sunday School were all held there.

E.K. "Ernie" Wright was the first-trick operator at Carp, probably the one who replaced Tom Casey. The Wrights lived in the house the Caseys had occupied. Dorolene and Dorothy were daughters of the Wrights. Lincoln County High School is in Panaca, and no doubt Dorothy was in high school then.

Ernie had musical ability; together with his son Billy, my father, and perhaps someone else, they played for the occasional dance. My father played violin, and Ernie played guitar and later the trumpet.

Ernie Wright got me started collecting stamps in about 1940, and it has been one of my interests ever since. Thank you, Ernie.

Jan. 9, 1936: "C.L. Averett left last week for Los Angeles, where he expects to receive medical attention. . . . Owen Frei returned to Carp after spending the holidays in Utah. . . . Lillian Prince of Pioche is spending the winter there with her sister, Mrs. Workman. . . . Mr. and Mrs. Tom Anderson and Mrs. Workman were visitors in Caliente on Sunday."

My father was in ill health in 1935, and because his teeth weren't very good, he thought dental trouble might be his problem. He went to a dentist in Las Vegas, and the dentist was going to pull all his teeth. For a reason that I don't recall now, my father didn't do it; he went instead to Los Angeles, to Dr. Lewis Gunther at Good Samaritan Hospital. The diagnosis was toxic goiter, very far advanced, and the doctor said extraction of his teeth would have killed him. He had the goiter removed in 1936, and for years afterward he took Lugol's solution. However, the goiter returned, and he had a second operation for goiter in Las Vegas in 1940.

Hafen & Frei Brothers, of Santa Clara, Veyo, and Gunlock, Utah, had various people on their ranch at Vigo. Val Hafen, Vivian J. "Viv" Frei, J. Claude Frei, Owen Frei, Duane Leavitt, and A.M. Workman are the ones associated with the ranch I can recall. The Hafen & Frei outfit was locally called "the Dutchmen". The Hafens and the Freis came from Switzerland as Mormon converts (see Bradshaw, "Under Dixie Sun"). They spoke German, and "Deutsch" (the German word for themselves) was garbled to "Dutch", as in Pennsylvania Dutch.

Oct. 29, 1936: "Our school opened Sept. fourth under the very efficient management of Miss Johnson. . . . She and her father live in the apartment at the school house. Mr. Johnson has recently come from North Dakota. . . . Charles Walsh has been visiting with his uncle at the Averett ranch the last week. He has just finished two years in the Hawaiian Islands. He served in the Aviation dept. of the Navy. He is now on furlough and is visiting his mother, Mrs. Nicolaides, and grandmother, Mrs. Mary Averett at Las Vegas. . . Mrs. Huston is spending the winter in California. . . . Mr. James Davis has charge of the post office and has put in a store and oil station."

Ellen Johnson was my favorite teacher in grade school. Her father worked for us sometimes, and he was a good worker. He said, "I'm like a steam shovel; I shovel a while and I puff a while".

Charles Walsh is my cousin, the son of my father's sister, Mrs. J.H. Nicolaides. He stayed with us at Carp when he was a teen-ager, and he often returned to visit. I quote him a lot in this narrative; he has been one of my main sources of information.

Jim Davis liked his liquor, and when he would go to Las Vegas or Caliente, nobody was surprised if he didn't get back until he had been on a bender and had spent a few days in jail. He arranged for my father to run the store and post office in his absence, and during

C.L. Averett at Carp store and post office, 1945.

one of those absences, Dad looked out the front window and saw a man coming up the path from the station with a determined gait and fire in his eye. He was a Postal Inspector, from Sacramento. The postmaster was to send in a daily report, but Jim hadn't happened to mention that to Dad. When the reports stopped, the Post Office Department had to take action. The difficulty was cleared up, and nobody went to prison over it.

The Hustons lived on their ranch long enough to prove up on the homestead. They split up, and Walt moved into the Mabey house. In 1930 or 1931, it caught fire and burned to the ground, almost trapping him inside. The story was that he had piled a bunch of newspapers too close to the stove. Other fires included Bert Lyman's house (after Bert had left) and a house on Walter Condiff's ranch.

My father drilled a well for the Hustons, and they installed a Dempster windmill. My father said Mrs. Huston complained to him that it didn't seem to be running very much. He told her the problem was that too many windmills had been put up; they were using up the wind.

Nov. 5, 1936: "Western Union men are here on inspection for some repair work to be done. . . . Mr. and Mrs. Harris, recently from Missouri, are employed at the Averett ranch. . . . Mr. James Banner was a business visitor in Carp several days last week. . ."

Jimmy Banner was a districtman in Caliente, and he lived in a house on Company Row. He was an officer of the Mt. Vernon Encampment No. 8 I.O.O.F. in 1931, when my father was a member. My father was also a member of the Meadow Valley Lodge No. 48 I.O.O.F. in 1931.

Paul Harris was a man with an interesting story. He and his wife, Corinne, came to our ranch in the fall of 1935, and Dad hired Paul. After a while, Paul told his story. The substance of it was that his father had been killed in an accident on the Rock Island Railroad near Joplin, but Paul's mother received bad legal advice and did not enter a claim for compensation. She blamed the entire legal system, and her children grew up believing the Law was corrupt and ineffective. They got a reputation as troublemakers, and everything was blamed on them.

An old man was beaten and tortured to force him to tell where he kept his money (and he probably didn't even have any), and Paul was one of the accused. He was put in jail, and a state trooper beat him with a shot-filled rubber hose until he confessed to something he hadn't done.

He got away from Missouri somehow, and he and Corinne made their way to Nevada. They happened to drive through Carp, and they intended to steal some gasoline from the pump at the Carp store. Then they realized that perhaps Carp was so isolated that they could lie low for a while.

My father contacted a lawyer in Missouri, and the information corroborated Paul's story. Word of Paul's whereabouts got back to Missouri, and a warrant for his arrest was sent to Nevada. Buck Tennille was sheriff, and he came to Carp more than once to get Paul. Somehow, Paul was never there when Buck showed up, except once. Paul wound up in jail in Caliente. He was released the next morning by mistake, with the drunks who had been locked up overnight.

New officials were elected in Missouri, and Paul returned on the promise of a fair trial. He was acquitted or the case was dropped, and he came back to Nevada under his real name, Paul Strothcamp.

Dec. 3, 1936: "Mr. Stucky of Santa Clara had the misfortune to have his truck turn over at the Carp crossing Sunday afternoon. It was loaded with steers from the Hafen and Frei ranch for the California market."

I remember a truck load of cattle having turned on its side at the crossing just below Carp, and this is probably the one. The one I recall was a sleeper cab truck, and some water got into the sleeper compartment; either a relief driver was in it or else the driver was alarmed at what might have happened if someone had been. Things like that were big news at places such as Carp.

Feb. 18, 1937: "Carp is recovering from the storm of last month, and all the stalled cars have been brought in. [The big storm is described in the "Lincoln County Stories" chapter.] The road over the Summit is open, but is still very soft. Operator F.W. Davidson is relieving Mr. Condiff and operator A.D. Paglia is relief man on the third trick. . . . The people of Carp were glad to know that Mr. Paul Harris was vindicated of the accusation against him and we wish him good luck. . . . Mrs. Wright and Lorraine Morford are each the proud possessors of Police pups. . ."

Lorraine Morford; to me, 9½ years old, she seemed much older and more mature – she was probably at least 12. She wore a Cashmere sweater sometimes, and it made her my idea then of the ultimate in femininity. That childhood world – where did it go?

March 4, 1937: "At last the road to Las Vegas is passable so the ones that have cars can have the pleasure of driving there but the road to Caliente is almost impassable and we of Carp are afraid to make the venture in trying to get there."

Sept. 16, 1937: "Mr. McMullen, Carp school teacher, is getting his classes organized for the term . . . . Mr. McMullen and Bill Wright went to Caliente Saturday night, dodging rocks, washouts and what ever we have in our road to Caliente. They have more nerve than most of us." Things seem to have been much the same in 1892; the *Pioche Record*, June 9, 1892, reported, "The road down Meadow Valley Wash, never at any time good, is about as ever – that is, dreaded by those who have once traveled it." So what else is new?

Oct. 7, 1937: "Lucille Metz of Las Vegas is spending a week at the Averett ranch at Carp."

When my father was in the Good Samaritan Hospital, he became acquainted with Lucille Metz Shearer, a nurse. She came from Los Angeles (not Las Vegas) twice to visit us. In 1938 she brought her daughter Frankie, who was about my age. Lucille rode cattle with us, helped haul and thresh alfalfa for the seed, and went on a hunting trip with my parents to Bunker Peak. Friends of long ago; where are they now?

Threshing alfalfa, Averett ranch, 1938. A Dodge pickup powered the thresher. Lucille Shearer on top of load, Mary L. Averett and Frankie Shearer on horses.

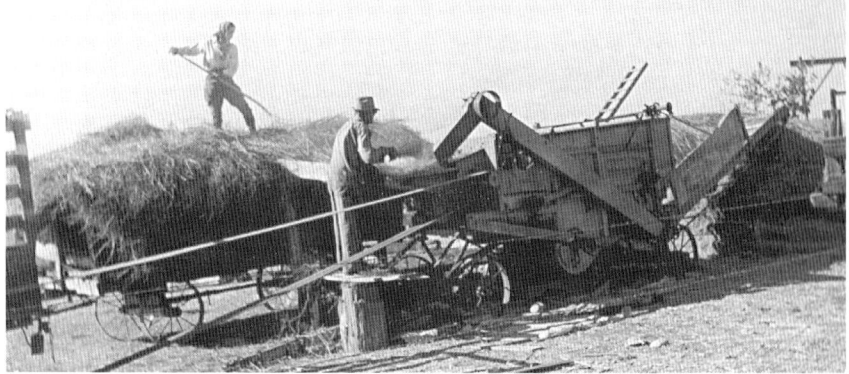

Threshing alfalfa, Averett ranch, 1938. C.L. Averett feeding thresher, Lucille Shearer pitching alfalfa from the load.

The statement has been made that you can't go back, and I think the statement is right. My wife, Marjorie, and I drove down the Meadow Valley Wash from Caliente to Carp in 1972, the first time since 1945 that I had been down the Canyon except on the train. The landmarks were still there, but sometimes I had trouble recognizing them. When we came out of the canyon below Leith, and caught sight of the Mormon Mountains ahead, I knew Carp was near. I wasn't prepared to find that the road went down the east side instead of crossing the wash at the old Dimmick ranch. We passed our old house, but seeing it from the east side, I wasn't oriented yet. After we passed it, I saw how rapidly the valley narrowed down and I realized where we were.

I wanted to drive to the Carp depot, but the open area that was beside the depot was fenced off. We drove up on the hill, where the store used to be, and we found only the ruins from a fire that did not appear to have been recent. I looked down on the buildings where Walt Huston used to live and keep his horses and braid rawhide ropes and quirts, and across to the school yard, and as I walked among the debris, the ghosts of the past walked with me.

North from site of Carp store and post office, 1972. Averett ranch extended north from big curve in the creek at right. Clover Mountains in distance.

Marjorie and I returned in 1994 to talk to people who remembered the old times. We found changes since 1972, just as dramatic as the ones we saw then. According to the *Lincoln County Record* on Dec. 13, 1973, the Carp school was to close on Dec. 21 because of low enroll-ment and the cost of repairing the building. We learned that the post office was later moved into the school building; after the post office closed, the building became a source of miscellaneous building materials until it was final-ly torn down. All the hous-es have now been removed from Carp siding. Three temporary buildings were put in to house the section gang, and they are to be removed and the section

Carp bridge and school, 1972, looking northwest from site of Carp store and post office. The center pier of this bridge sank in the 1938 flood. Streamliner wreck in 1943 was just beyond bridge.

will be discontinued. The section gang will work out of Caliente.

So what is there now is today's reality. The world I knew is gone, and there's no going back, at least not for me. But that's fine; it still lives in my memory as it was, and I enjoy seeing the Meadow Valley Wash as it is now and remembering it as it used to be.

Section houses at Carp, 1994, about where Tom Casey's house stood; view is to the south.

Signpost at Carp, Oct. 1994.

CHAPTER 5

THE SALT LAKE ROUTE

BUILDING THE RAILROAD

The railroad through the Meadow Valley Wash was completed in 1904 as the San Pedro, Los Angeles and Salt Lake (SPLA&SL), but the railroad story begins much earlier than that. The Union Pacific had built a railroad from Salt Lake City to Milford, and in 1889 a subsidiary, the Oregon Short Line (OSL) started building south from there. Construction was interrupted until 1899, when the OSL extended the tracks to Uvada, on the Utah-Nevada line, and graded on down Clover Creek to the Culverwell ranch, which later became Caliente. Then the OSL let the grade go back to Lincoln County, Nevada, for taxes.

Now meet Senator William A. Clark, of Montana, a copper millionaire whose ambition turned to railroading. In particular, he wanted to build a railroad from Salt Lake City to Los Angeles. He had a real railroad, the Los Angeles Terminal Railway, and he had a railroad on paper, the Utah & California. All he needed was to fill the gap.

Senator Clark and his associates tied everything together in 1901 by organizing the SPLA&SL, commonly known as the Salt Lake Route. (The corporate name was shortened to the Los Angeles & Salt Lake in 1916.) As part of their railroad empire, they bought the tax-delinquent grade of the OSL from Lincoln County. The maneuver provoked the OSL, which challenged the transaction.

This very brief account barely hints at the conflict. To learn the details, these two books are indispensable: David Myrick, "Railroads of Nevada and Eastern California", Vol II, and John Signor, "The Los Angeles and Salt Lake Railroad Company; Union Pacific's Historic Salt Lake Route".

Legal actions were started, and stories are told of physical conflict. For example, crews of the SPLA&SL were said to have laid track during the day, and crews of the OSL would tear it up that night.

The first stage of construction was down Clover Creek to its junction with the Meadow Valley Wash at the Culverwell ranch. The succession of names was Culverwell, Clover Junction, Calientes, and finally in about 1903, Caliente.

The railroad was completed from Uvada to Caliente in 1901, to a point 2 miles west of Boyd in 1903, and through the Meadow Valley Wash in 1904. The last spike of the entire road was driven in 1905 some distance beyond Las Vegas.

A story, or yarn, as the case may be, concerns the first train to arrive at Caliente. I was told by an old-timer that the first train of any kind was a work train on the SPLA&SL, bringing in supplies. When the train reached the place where the section houses were later built, the engineer stopped at a fence that had been put across the tracks. The crew began unloading supplies, and several OSL men with guns stepped out into sight. The men of the SPLA&SL went running up the hill to get away. There is a lot more than that in the story of the struggle to be first to Culverwell, as it was then called.

William Andrews Clark was born in Connellsville, Pa., on Jan. 8, 1839 and died in New York City on March 2, 1925. He worked as a mucker in Central City, Colorado, in 1862, then he moved to Montana in 1863 and began accumulating a fortune in the merchandising and freighting businesses. His investments in the copper mines were very profitable, and his huge fortune enabled him to build the San Pedro, Los Angeles & Salt Lake Railroad and also the Las Vegas & Tonopah. He put together a large collection of paintings and other art objects, and the collection was bequeathed to the Corcoran Art Gallery. He served in the U.S. Senate for the 1901-07 term, so he is widely known as Senator Clark.

The SPLA&SL grade between Calientes and Kiernan's ranch was nearly complete on Nov. 1, 1901. The OSL had four grading camps below Kiernan's; two of them were as far as Cane Springs, about 80 miles from Caliente.

When Uvada became the railhead, mining men traveling to and from Searchlight, Eldorado Canyon, the Yellow Pine district, Delamar, and Pioche began riding the train between Salt Lake and Uvada and taking the stage connection at Uvada. By April 1902, the "Muddy stage", to the Muddy Valley, was operating three times weekly. J.A. Denton had the Uvada & Delamar Stage Line, and Ed Clark was operating his forwarding company from Uvada. Later he moved to Caliente, and finally he went to Las Vegas, where he became a prominent business man.

Both companies were grading down the Meadow Valley Wash below Caliente for at least 40 miles. They finally agreed that instead of having their grades cross each other in the narrow canyon, the OSL would keep to the west side and the SPLA&SL would keep to the east side, and the two grades would not come closer than 20 feet from each other. Just below the present Tunnel 5 the old OSL grade can be seen on the west side of the canyon; it is now the county road. The agreement did not concede to either company the right to operate a railroad; it merely kept the construction crews out of each other's way.

The conflict between the two railroad companies was settled in early 1903 by an agreement that gave the SPLA&SL rights to the railroad from Salt Lake City to Los Angeles, but the Union Pacific became half owner of the SPLA&SL. The arrangement was commonly said to have been Senator Clark buying out the Union Pacific, but it meant the U.P. could veto his plans. Eventually the U.P. bought him out.

On Oct. 25, 1901, the *Lincoln County Record* reported that a lot of mining men were riding the stage from Caliente to Las Vegas. Business was so good that in February 1902, Sanford Angell, of Overton, announced he would open a store and hotel at Pockets, about 5 miles below Carp. A side canyon with reliable water-pockets comes in there from the east, and travelers had relied for years on the water at Pockets. Robert O. Gibson told me he remembered making an overnight stage stop at Pockets on a trip from Las Vegas to Pioche.

The SPLA&SL had a construction camp there for about a year. Holt's construction camp was also at Pockets. The camp lasted perhaps a year.

Angell had a mail contract when the mail came down from Caliente to St. Thomas. Before that, Bill Perry had a stage line from Panaca to Pioche and to Milford, Utah. His line carried mail, and he had an extension of the mail route down the Meadow Valley Wash. Ves Hulse and Charley Nelson carried the mail for him; it was loosely (and incorrectly) called "Pony Express".

The power plant for Delamar had been built at the mouth of Rock Springs Canyon, at a location first called Bamberger and then Stine, and wood was burned until coal became available at Caliente. The *Lincoln County Record* reported on July 31, 1903, that the road between Caliente and Bamberger had been damaged by so much coal being hauled; the boilers required 30 tons of coal daily. On Aug. 14, twenty-two 3-ton cars of freight for Bamberger Company at Delamar had been received at Caliente. By April 1904, Bamberger was expected to be the shipping point for Delamar freight.

Work on the railroad had slowed down until the settlement was reached in 1903, but it quickly speeded up. A temporary water tank had been put up at Caliente, the yards had been surveyed, and ties, rails, and bridge timbers were being received. A

> *Pockets was also where the mail bags were exchanged by mail riders from Panaca and the Muddy. The riders would meet there, stay overnight, and return. They made three trips a week.*

regular passenger train between Salt Lake and Caliente was soon to be put on. Utah Construction Company had received the contract for the railroad for 85 miles from Caliente (to Moapa).

By September, 800 men were at work between Caliente and Pockets, and the number was expected soon to be 1500. Cory Brothers had 200 men on a 12-mile subcontract at Pockets. Construction camps were located at Pockets, the

Kiernan ranch, the Bradshaw ranch, The Narrows, the Caldwell ranch, the Carson ranch, the Pippin ranch, the Conaway ranch, and the Ryan ranch. Utah Construction Company had received 75 tons of material in the past week.

Caliente had 19 saloons, 5 eating houses, 4 barber shops, 2 merchandise stores, 2 blacksmith shops, 2 hotels, a livery stable, a butcher shop, a bathing resort, and a school.

Grading had continued until the dispute between the companies was settled, but track had not been laid beyond Caliente. Now tracklaying was in progress; the track had reached Conaway's ranch on Nov. 5, it was expected at Pump Station (the Bamberger power plant) by the end of the month, and it should be at Kiernan's by Christmas. The "track-laying machine" had laid 11,000 feet of track on Dec. 1 and 2, and track had reached Caldwell's ranch on Dec. 5. A big cut had to be dug there, and when it was completed in about 3 weeks, track could be laid for the next 40 miles.

Empire Construction Co. had "boarding cars" at the Power Plant in late November. They had a grading contract that would last all winter, and the cars would be kept there.

The railroad bridges had been completed nearly to Moapa in February 1904, and the rails were 12 miles beyond the Kiernan ranch (which would have put them close to Carp). The steel gang was laying 2 miles a day.

On March 4, the *Lincoln County Record* said Utah Construction Company had the contract for grading 85 miles beyond Moapa. The construction train was running to Pockets. The first 75 cars of material had arrived for the telegraph line between Caliente and Las Vegas. By April 15, trains were running to Moapa.

In May, construction trains were carrying passengers and freight between Caliente and Moapa. The train left Caliente every night, arrived in Moapa by midnight, and was back in Caliente by 4:00 am. On March 30, 1905, *Mining Reporter* said, "For the present passengers and freight between Caliente and Daggett are handled by the railroad construction department. This fairly adequate service will give way to regular through service from Salt Lake to Los Angeles in about sixty days." On April 28, 1905, the *Lincoln County Record* said the passenger train had made the 136-mile run from Caliente to Las Vegas in 2 hours and 20 minutes.

The tracks between Salt Lake and Caliente were being re-laid to 85-pound rail in 1904. The existing rail would be used in sidings, spurs, and other applications that were not part of the main line. Track beyond Caliente was using 85-pound rail. Only 135 miles remained to be completed; through trains to Los Angeles were expected by Jan. 1, 1905. Western Union had completed its telegraph line from Caliente to 7 miles beyond Kyle in July, and it was expected in Moapa by Aug. 15.

The railroad was built with sidings at about 5-mile intervals. From Las Vegas, the general rule was a bare siding at 5 miles, a siding with a section gang at 10 miles, a bare siding at 15 miles, and a siding with a section gang, telegraph operator, signal maintainer, and pumping plant at 20 miles. Then the sequence starts over. Section gangs could be placed at successive sidings. Elgin sometimes had an East Section and a West Section.

According to the *Lincoln County Record* of Aug. 26, 1904, the railroad was soon to appropriate $200,000 for permanent structures at Caliente, the division point. The construction would include 12 dwellings (Company Row), a round-house, a "fine station building", a water tank, an oil house, and an artificial ice plant. (Company Row had 24 houses when it was complete.) On April 14, 1905, the newspaper said the dwellings were "for use by the freight crews between Caliente and Los Angeles". On June 9, the paper reported that the roundhouse was to be enlarged from 18 to 34 stalls. The 200-ton coal chute had been com-pleted at Caliente, large enough to coal 10 engines at once. (The *Pioche Record* on Feb. 17, 1924, said eight new stalls, to handle large engines, had been added to the roundhouse, making a total of 23. A boiler-washing plant had also been installed.)

Caliente shops and roundhouse, 1944.

Coal-burning locomotives were originally used on the SPLA&SL. The locomotives were converted to oil in 1912 and back to coal in May 1917. LeRoy Thacker, an engineer, told me in the 1950s that all the locomotives burned coal until 1924, when the road converted back to oil. The *Las Vegas Age*, March 13, 1928, said oil standpipes had been installed, and oil-burning locomotives were being brought in.

Is there a difference between a steam engine and a steam locomotive? The two terms are widely used interchangeably, so there is no difference in common usage. However, a technical difference does exist. A steam engine, strictly speaking, is the cylinders, pistons, rods, drivers, frame, valve gear, and other components that make up the propulsive unit; a locomotive is one or more engines with the firebox, boiler, cab, tender, and whatever else was needed to make up the complete mechanism. An articulated locomotive may have two engines, but in ordinary language, it is still called either an engine or a locomotive, whichever word comes to mind.

Through the narrowest parts of the Rainbow Canyon, the railroad was built so close to the cliffs that rocks were certain to fall on the tracks. Here, as in similar circumstances on other railroads, the hazard was met reasonably well by the installation of "rock fences". Heavy wire netting is attached to tall posts between the railroad and the cliffs to catch rocks that are dislodged from behind the fence. Angle arms at the top extend toward the tracks so the fence can be carried farther from the cliffs. Signal wires run along the fence to detect any rocks that are large enough to break through the fence; if a signal wire is broken, the signals are thrown red to stop traffic coming from either direction. According to *Railway Age* in 1928, the rock fence had been completed between Farrier and Etna. It's still there.

RUNNING THE RAILROAD

Train crews ran from Los Angeles to Yermo, California; Yermo to Las Vegas; Las Vegas to Caliente; Caliente to Milford; and Milford to Salt Lake City. Caliente was the end of the Western Division in the 1930s. Crew members who lived in Las Vegas would lay over in Caliente, often overnight. Some of them had shanties for sleeping quarters near the depot. We used to visit Sam Wengert, my father's partner, at his shanty. His front door had a loose panel and a padlock on the inside. The padlock was a dummy; it didn't have a locking mechanism. Sam said a padlock only keeps out children and small animals. The presence of a padlock will bluff most adults out of trying anything, and if a man won't be bluffed, a padlock won't stop him.

When there were more enginemen or trainmen than were needed for assigned runs, the men with the least seniority were put on the "extra board"; they took their turns being called for whatever assignments were available. The engineers and firemen of helper engines were often "bucking the extra board".

The following information about helper engines draws more heavily on Signor than on any other source. He gives much more detail than this, of course.

The railroad climbs 4321 feet in the 110 miles from Moapa to Crestline; between Carp and Crestline the grades reach or exceed 1.5%. According to the U.P. track diagrams, the grade is 2.06% east of Little Springs, in Clover Creek Canyon.

Caliente is halfway between Carp and Crestline, which gave it vital logistic significance. Helpers were dispatched west from Caliente to Carp (turning on the wye at Leith, later at Carp) to wait for trains that needed them. One or two helpers would be cut in at Caliente. The Carp helper would work past the 2% grade above Minto and be dropped at Islen. Any other helpers would continue to Crestline to be cut out. A wye and a beanery were located there. The helpers ran light from Crestline or Islen back to Caliente. (A single engine traveling on the main line was "running light".)

Helpers might work as far east as Modena, because some help was needed westbound on the 8-mile stretch of 1.0% grade between Uvada and Crestline. Westbound trains had to stop at Crestline so the retainers could be set up, then inspection stops were necessary at Islen, Elgin or Carp, and Rox. The retainers were knocked down at Rox.

This was in the days of steam. Diesels, with their exceptional power and dynamic braking capabilities, made it a whole new story, and I'm not qualified to talk about diesels.

Some eastbound passenger trains didn't pick up helpers at Carp, but almost all the other trains did. Trains of 25 cars or less usually put the helper in front of the road engine. Longer trains (freight trains, because passenger trains weren't that long) could have the helper at the rear end, just in front of the caboose and any outfit cars that were in the train. (As I understand it, a locomotive was not then allowed to push from behind a car in which people were riding.) Sometimes a long train came in from Las Vegas as a doubleheader or with a helper cut into the train, and it would leave Carp with at least one more helper on the point.

Passenger trains that would have been too long to run as a single train were divided into "sections", such as First #7 and Second #7. All but the last section carried green flags on the engine to indicate that another section was following on the same schedule and having the same superiority. In other words, the main line wasn't clear until the last section was past. Dougherty describes a bad wreck at Whitehouse, Utah, on the Denver & Rio Grande Western, when a freight train pulled out into the path of the seventh section of an opposing passenger train fleet.

Westbound passenger trains had odd numbers (such as Number 7), and eastbound passengers had even numbers (such as Number 8). The practice on the Union Pacific was to put the train number on the indicator boards on each side of the smoke stack. Thus Train #7 would have a 7 on the indicator board, or First #7 would have 1-7. An unscheduled train (an "Extra") took the engine number with the X- prefix. If engine 3547 was pulling an extra, the train number was X-3547. If engine 3547 was the helper for an extra, the train number became X-3547 until the engine was cut off. The engine of a train running extra carried white flags. This is a pretty simplified explanation, and many details are omitted.

The directions "east" and "west" in the Union Pacific lexicon refer to the complete Union Pacific system between Omaha (the eastern terminus) and Los Angeles (the western terminus). The east end of Carp siding, for example, is the end that is in the direction of Omaha. In the Meadow Valley Wash, east in railroad terminology is approximately geographic north.

Besides the usual rolling stock, we often saw two special pieces of equipment. One was an inspection vehicle we knew as the "official car", formally identified as the B-41. It had a passenger body and a 6-cylinder Buick engine, and it was used by officials who were on inspections.

The other was a Sperry car, a rail-inspection vehicle that travels slowly along the tracks and takes readings that will show cracks or defects in the rails and mark such places. Those yellow cars are still a common sight, creeping slowly along the tracks of a railroad.

On January 6, 1917, the *Las Vegas Age* announced that the Salt Lake Route was to spend more than $5,500,000 on improvements, including these: 200 miles of 90-pound rails, $1.5 million; additional ballast, $50,000; installing automatic block signals, $390,000; bridges, $120,000; 790 self-dumping gondolas, 6 cabooses, and 6 giant locomotives, $1.8 million.

In 1917 the railroad began installing 3-position Edison-type electric automatic block signals supplied by Federal Signal Co. The system was to be installed on 287 miles of railroad, at $2000 a mile. Trains still depended on telegraph operators to relay orders from the dispatcher, but between stations the crews had at least some idea whether another train was in the vicinity. Brundy says the first automatic block signals were installed between Leith and Modena because of the deep canyons, sharp curves, and tunnels.

When a train occupied a section of track (a "block"), the automatic block signal at each end of the block was thrown red to tell approaching traffic to stop before entering the block. The next block each direction had a yellow signal, telling approaching traffic to proceed at restricted speed and be prepared to stop before entering a red block.

During World War II the railroad installed Centralized Traffic Control, which enables a dispatcher at a control board to throw switches to sidings and to control signal lights at considerable distances. For example, the dispatcher in Las Vegas controlled trains as far away as Caliente. The section from Carp to Elgin was cut in during January 1945, finishing the job.

My recollection and understanding of the train control system at Carp is about like this:

The telegraph operator sent and received railroad telegrams, took train orders, and sent and received Western Union telegrams. By 1930, the train orders were received by telephone. When an order was received, each number was read back by the operator and then repeated, and the names of sidings were spelled back to the dispatcher. For example, if Number 21 was to meet Extra 3547 at Vigo, the dispatcher would tell the operator, and then the operator would repeat, "Number twenty-one two-one to meet Extra thirty-five forty-seven three five four seven at Vigo V-i-g-o".

One operator pronounced "Elgin" as "Elgine", and he would repeat it as "Elgine E-l-g-ine". Or so I was told.

The semaphore mast, about 20 feet high, stood right against the front of the depot. The top of the mast had two arms (the "order board") that were controlled by levers inside the depot. One arm was for eastbound traffic, and the other was for westbound. When an arm was down at about 15° from the vertical, it showed a green light and it meant the train was not required to stop for orders. When an arm was horizontal, it showed a red light, and it meant the train had to stop to pick up orders or to take the siding. (Taking a siding was called "heading in" or "going in the hole". If you took strong exception to what someone said or did, and you vigorously expressed your disapproval of the action or statement, you "told him where to head in at".)

If a train had orders but no stop was required, the operator handed them up "on the fly". The orders, called "flimsies", were written on yellow onion-skin paper. The paper was rolled and folded into a small doubled cylinder and attached to the order stick. One set of orders had to be handed up to the engineer and another to the conductor.

Until about the mid-1930s, the operators at Carp used "hoops". They were made of bamboo with a straight section about 4 feet long and a loop about 18 inches in diameter at the end. The orders were put in a spring clip where the bamboo loop came back and crossed the straight stick. The hoop was held at arm's length, with the loop at the top, and the engineer or fireman leaned out from the cab window and put his arm through the loop—-that is, everyone hoped he did. If he missed the hoop, the engineer had to stop the train, back up, and get the orders. If he got the hoop, which he usually did, he dropped it back on the right of way, and the operator had to walk down the track and retrieve it. The conductor picked up his set of orders from the vestibule of a passenger car or the caboose of a freight.

The hoop was replaced by a Y-shaped stick with a string that ran along the legs of the Y and across the open space. The orders were tied in a loop in the string, and when a man's arm went through the string, he got the string and the operator still had the stick. However, sometimes the string broke, and the result was the same as when a hoop was missed: Stop, back up, and get the orders.

Carp was a flag stop, which meant that most passenger trains could be flagged to stop and pick up passengers. (Trains such as the Streamliners did not respond to a flag at a flag stop.)

Inside the depot was a rack that often contained some manila envelopes that had holes punched in them and a string tie at one end. In recent years, I have worked where those interoffice correspondence envelopes are used, and when I use a "holey Joe", I often remember seeing them at Carp and not knowing or thinking to ask what they were.

TUNNELS

The relocation of the railroad after the 1910 flood required construction of eight tunnels between Carp and Caliente. Six tunnels had been bored in Clover Creek Canyon by the OSL in 1889-90, and two more were bored by the SPLA&SL in 1911. All the tunnels were timbered originally, and in about 1930 all but Tunnel 3 were lined with concrete; it was converted to an open cut in 1944. In the 1920s the Union Pacific had considered putting in double track west from Salt Lake City, and when the tunnels were concreted, most of them between Kyle and Brown were widened for double track. The following information was supplied mainly by Harry Bennett and the U.P. track diagrams:

TUNNELS WEST OF CALIENTE

Tunnel No.	Location	Year Built	Year Concreted	Width, Tracks	Length, Feet	Milepost West end
4	West of Kyle	1911	1931	Double	1096	433.56
5	Between Elgin and Boyd	1911	1925	Single	500	441.90
6	West of Stine	1911	1930	Double	456	449.01
7	East of Stine	1911	1929	Double	431	450.89
8	Just east of Tunnel 7	1911	1929	Double	264	451.33
9	West of Etna	1911	1929	Double	612	453.25
10	East of Etna	1911	1928	Double	745	455.91

TUNNELS EAST OF CALIENTE

Tunnel No.	Location	Year Built	Year Concreted	Width, Tracks	Length, Feet	Milepost West End
11	West of Eccles	1911	1927	Double	1324	462.66
12	Just east of Tunnel 11	1911	1927	Double	502	463.22
13	West of Little Springs	1889	1924	Single	571	471.32
14	West of Big Springs	1889	1924	Single	693	472.75
15	East of Big Springs	1890	1926	Double	232	473.95
16	Just east of Tunnel 15	1890	1926	Double	387	474.23
17	East of Tunnel 1	1890	1925	Double	299	474.61
18	West of Brown	1890	1927	Single	301	487.87

Tunnel 3, near Leith, was converted to an open cut in 1944. It had been left a timbered tunnel when the other tunnels were concreted.

As an example of the need to fix up the tunnels, consider Tunnel 13. It was a timbered tunnel, built in 1889, and according to the *Pioche Record* on Jan. 4, 1924, the center of the tunnel had caved during the previous Saturday, closing the railroad. Train #19 might have been wrecked, but a track walker saw the problem and flagged the train. The clean-up required 250 men, working 2 days. Altogether, 12 trains were held up, and about 4000 passengers were involved. On Jan. 7, William Billings was injured when he was helping remove loose ground at the tunnel and the rocks and dirt caved on him.

Many men would be at work on a tunnel, and their living quarters in the vicinity of the tunnel came to be called Tunnel Camp. The men working on the tunnels called themselves Tunnel Stiffs. In 1928 and 1930, Tunnel Precinct was an established precinct for the Primary and General Elections.

All of those tunnels seemed to be strategically vulnerable points during World War II; the answer was to put guards at each tunnel. We saw long train-loads of big, wooden boxes that were said to be aircraft parts going to Douglas or Lockheed, and many a string of tanks, trucks, and artillery passed through Caliente. We never knew how much ammunition went through. Troop trains (called "main" trains because they held the main line) were commonplace. What an opportunity for sabotage by blowing up some tunnels!

Civilians or soldiers were stationed at every tunnel, night and day, with instructions to require identification of anyone on foot or on a motor car and to prevent mischief and enemy action in general. A guard was stationed at each end of Tunnel 4, the longest tunnel west of Caliente.

My father was a guard at Tunnel 6 for perhaps a year, and he was briefly at Tunnel 5. The guards were deputized, and one of them at Tunnel 6 insisted that a guard's authority must be proclaimed by keeping the deputy badge out in sight at all times. Dad's opinion was that anybody who was a real threat would not be intimidated by a tin badge; he said, "This .30-06 will assert my authority".

The guards weren't to stop trains or any engines that were running light, but the man on duty was expected to be out in sight, with his rifle, for every passenger train that went through. This meant staying at the tunnel, regardless of weather, which called for some sort of living quarters.

The shelter was originally a wall tent at each tunnel. I remember the tent at Tunnel 6 being boarded up about halfway to help protect against the build-up of snow. Some tents, if not all, were replaced by one-room prefabricated houses. After the war, my father bought the one at Tunnel 10, moved it to our house in Caliente, and turned it into a garage.

Civilians were hired as tunnel guards west of Caliente, but the Army was not satisfied. A job as a guard required a military man, and the Army forced the decision to assign troops to guard the tunnels east of there.

Still the Army wasn't happy, so they pulled a surprise inspection. Some Army officers and railroad officials got a light-weight, quiet-running motor car at Las Vegas, and they made a nighttime run through the Rainbow Canyon from Leith to Caliente. They got past one tunnel unchallenged, but they were stopped at all the rest.

The Army changed the rules there. They got the type of big, heavy, noisy motor car that is used by section gangs, and they went on east. They were seldom challenged by the reliable Army guards; most were inside their tents, asleep or playing poker. The Army men were quickly replaced by civilians.

No tales of sabotage ever reached us, though somebody thought a mysterious person was seen near Tunnel 5. Some cattle were reported to have blundered down the hill by Tunnel 10 one night and provoked a fusillade. But not one of the tunnels was blown in.

TRAINS

Passenger service was important to the Union Pacific in those days, and the U.P. was always looking for improvements in its service. One innovation was the introduction in February 1934 of the "Speed Train". It was a three-unit articulated train from Pullman Car & Manufacturing Co., a lightweight streamlined train that featured construction with aluminum alloys. It was also known as the "aluminum train". It had a 600-horsepower distillate Winton engine, and it was said to have reached 110 miles per hour. Its successors would mean the end of steam.

The information on the trains described in this section comes from Kratville, Kratville & Rank, Signor, and the *Caliente Herald*.

The Speed Train was officially designated M-10000. It toured the United States, including a trip to Boulder Dam. In January 1935 it was put on the run from Kansas City to Salina as the "City of Salina".

According to the *Caliente Herald*, March 15, 1934, the Speed Train arrived in Caliente westbound at 5:30 am on March 9 and stayed about 15 minutes. I remember seeing it come through Carp. Aluminum medallions were distributed to the people who came to see it, and I still have mine. The *Herald* article said 1 million of them had been made.

After the introduction of the Speed Train, the next advance in passenger service was the "Challenger", which was intended to provide first-class accommodations to coach and tourist sleeper passengers. It had stewardesses who were trained nurses; cars reserved for women and children; free porter service; and low-priced meals. It was running as Second No. 7 and 8 (the "Los Angeles Limited") in 1935, and by 1937 it was No. 717 and 818, the "Challenger". My clearest memory of the "Challenger" is the 3700- and 3800-class Challenger-type articulated engines that often pulled the train. The steamboat whistles on those locomotives always thrilled me. (They still do.)

"Aluminum Train" medallion.

While Lucille Shearer was visiting us, probably in 1938, Dr. "Red" Lombard, a friend of hers, came in from Los Angeles on the "Challenger" to visit. I still remember the excitement of watching that big engine bring the train into Carp and seeing him get off. Passenger trains were always my reminder that there were faraway places to see someday; a passenger train in the night, the lighted windows glowing, told me that a big world was waiting for me.

With the Speed Train established, more Streamliners followed. The "City of Los Angeles", M-10002, was put into revenue service on May 15, 1936. It was an 11-car train, with all but the first 2 cars articulated. Its schedule was just under 40 hours between Chicago and Los Angeles. The *Caliente Herald* reported on June 11, 1936, that the Streamliner had averaged 57.25 mph between Salt Lake City and Las Vegas. Its only stop was at Caliente to change crews.

One other train deserves a note. When the movie "Union Pacific" was made, a special old-time train was outfitted for scenes early in the history of

Eastbound passenger train as seen from front door of the Averett ranch house at Carp. Photo by Lucille Shearer, probably 1938.

the railroad. The *Caliente Herald* announced on May 18, 1939, that the train would arrive in Caliente westbound on May 21, stay overnight, and continue the next day. We saw it come through Carp, and we got medallions that were distributed from the train.

WRECKS

Derailments, rock slides, collisions, boiler explosions, the Meadow Valley Wash saw them all.

Moapa was the scene of a head-on collision between Train #81 and Extra 3874 on July 24, 1909. A rockslide derailed a train at Galt in July 1912, and conductor Walter Clay and brakeman Geyer were killed. Another rockslide caught Train #2 at Guelph on Oct. 4, 1912, and derailed Engine 3415. Engineer "Jap" Matthews had a sprained ankle, fireman Nicholson had a broken arm, and baggageman A.E. Barger's back was seriously injured when a stack of trunks in the baggage car fell on him.

Another derailment at Galt on Sept. 2, 1915, put the "Pacific Limited" on the ground; engineer Mitchell and conductor George A. Goodwin were uninjured. At Galt again, on Oct. 20, 1917, nine cars of freight were wrecked; engineer Hogan and conductor O'Leary were not hurt.

The *Las Vegas Age* reported on April 28, 1917, that at 2:50 am on (apparently) April 22, X3656 West had hit a rockslide in a small cut near milepost 450, about 2 miles east of Stine siding. The engine and one car were derailed and went down the bank. A story on May 5 gave further details. As the engine came through the cut, the headlight caught the rockslide, but too late for the engine to stop. Engineer Ed Long jumped, but he landed on rocks and was badly injured. The train was just the one car, and the derailment left the main line clear. Train #7 was following, and Long was put on the train. He died on the train between Barstow and San Bernardino. The fireman rode the engine almost to the bottom and then jumped; he wasn't hurt.

Engine 3656 derailed by a rock slide east of Stine, April 22, 1917. Photo from Harry Bennett.

Another fatal wreck occurred on Jan. 15, 1923 at Valley siding, about 15 miles east of Las Vegas. (This isn't in the Meadow Valley Wash, but it's the same railroad.) Extra 6050 east, a mile-long freight, was to go in the hole at Valley to meet Extra 2725, a mile-long westbound freight. Engineer Bradford, on Extra 6050, thought he had time to spare, so he decided to pull on past the siding and ease in backward, downhill, to avoid an extra start of the heavy train on the long grade out of Las Vegas Valley.

However, his train broke in two before the caboose had cleared the east end of the siding. The air brakes were set automatically when the air line parted, thus blocking the main line. He sent a flagman ahead to stop Extra 2725, but engineer Tartar couldn't get his train stopped in time on the downhill grade. The engine crews jumped to safety before the two engines met head-on, with Engine 2725 moving just fast enough to dent the smokeboxes and rattle a few cars.

An open gondola of sheet steel was coupled right behind Engine 6050, and the engine was shoved backward with enough force to collapse the end of the car onto the steel—-and kill three men who were riding in the open space between the steel and the front of the car. A fourth man, Arthur Wearne, of Pleasant Grove, Utah, was fatally injured. He was rushed to Las Vegas to the care of Dr. Hal Hewetson, but he could not be saved.

Another wreck in 1923 might have been much more serious. The *Pioche Record* had a detailed account in the issue of Nov. 30, 1923.

Westbound Train #19, the "Continental Limited", derailed at about 30 miles per hour at the east end of the newly constructed passing track at Leith on the previous Sunday night. Evidently a bolt was missing from the switch, causing the derailment. The 7800-class engine and the mail and baggage cars stayed on the track; the next car, a chair car, swung into the passing track and was derailed, followed by several standard Pullmans. All the cars were stopped by soft ground, narrowly avoiding falling into a dry wash. Some of the trucks were buried so deep the car steps touched the ground. The last Pullman and the observation car stayed on the track.

The Caliente and Las Vegas wreckers were dispatched to the scene, and the main line was cleared in about 3 hours. An eastbound freight train had taken the siding at Rapelje, or it would probably have been in the siding at Leith.

In early November 1925, a work train was cleaning out cuts beside the tracks, where mud and gravel had washed down, and half a mile east of Vigo, the ditcher cut a trench too close to the ends of the ties. The work train went in the siding at Vigo to wait for a westbound freight train, Second 261, but the freight didn't quite get there. The track gave way under engine 5508, which rolled over on its side. The tender was thrown across the tracks, and the following flat car telescoped into the cab of the engine. Engineer W.H. Paulus, brakeman H. Downey, and brakeman C.T. Tyson jumped to safety, but fireman Fred S. Horner was killed instantly by a broken beam that pinned him in his seat.

Two flat cars and three tank cars were derailed. The Caliente and Las Vegas wreckers cleared the tracks in about 7 hours. Train #3 was held at Caliente and #4 was held at Las Vegas; when they were released, they passed at Vigo.

My father was pumping days at Carp and nights at Moapa. He would fill the reservoir at Carp during the day, eat supper, and catch this particular freight to Moapa. Then he ran the pump all night, catching what sleep he could and taking a train back to Carp the next morning. He usually took the fireman's seat on the westbound freight and fired the engine from Carp to Moapa. But Mom was late with supper that evening, and Dad missed his train. He was still eating supper when Horner was killed. That was 2 years before I was born.

A little mishap occurred near Farrier, probably also in 1925, that resulted in damage but no serious injuries. The section gang had removed a rail, but a double-headed freight approached before the new rail had been put in place. The flagman had not gone far enough out, and the short flag didn't give time for the train to get stopped. The engines were derailed, and they turned on their side. Engineers Van Santongue on the helper and A.J. Hanna on the road engine were almost unhurt. Many freight cars were derailed and damaged, and cars of hogs broke open and the hogs jumped out and began looking for something to eat.

In November 1926, Train #27 hit a rock slide at the west end of Tunnel 8, and the engine and two cars jumped the track but didn't go down the bank into the creek. None of the crew or the 400 passengers were hurt.

Serious trouble came on Jan. 18, 1926, when Engine 6079 blew up, just west of Carp. Engineer H.O. "Holly" Johnson was badly burned by escaping steam, but the other members of the crew were not hurt. Evidently this is what happened, as my father reconstructed it: The tracks had a sag, about half a mile west of the west switch at Carp. The water in the boiler was low enough that when the engine started down into the sag, the crown sheet was exposed above water and became very hot (maybe red-hot). As the engine started up the other side of the sag, the water surged back and cooled the crown sheet so rapidly that it split open and the steam blew back and into the cab. That's what was known as "dropping the crown sheet".

A near-calamity occurred in late December 1928, when Engineer Tom Fanatia barely avoided wrecking a passenger train. Just west of Kyle, he saw a large boulder (7 tons of it) that had fallen onto the tracks, and he applied the brakes. His engine barely bumped the boulder. The railroad was then installing rock fences, and the work had not yet gotten to Kyle.

Automatic block signals and switch interlocks were intended to keep two trains from trying to be in the same place at the same time, but sometimes those safety measures weren't enough.

For example, consider Moapa siding. The home signal at the end of the siding could operate as an automatic signal, or the operator could control it and thus control trains approaching the siding. But this is what happened on Aug. 20, 1942, as described in ICC Report on Investigation No. 2618:

Eastbound freight train Second 154 headed into the siding, as directed by the signal. The train stopped in the siding. The engineer on eastbound Train #8 had the throttle in drifting position and was proceeding at the prescribed 30 miles per hour to pass #154 on a clear signal. Apparently the interlock failed when the operator cleared the signal, and nobody knew the switch was still lined for the siding.

The engine on #8 lurched as it took the siding, and the surprised engineer applied the emergency air brake; the freight train was just inside the siding, and #8 didn't have time to stop. The engine was derailed and landed on its left side. The engineer, flagman, conductor, 10 dining-car employees, and 112 passengers were reported injured.

The final wreck described here was at Carp, on July 13, 1943, and involved the eastbound Streamliner "City of Los Angeles", Train #104, the hottest hot-shot train on the U.P.; anybody who delayed the train could be in serious trouble. Some background information here will set the stage.

Wrecker picking up cars of Train #8 at Moapa, Aug. 20, 1942. Photo by Tom Anderson.

Wreck of Train #8 at Moapa, Aug. 20, 1942. Photo by Tom Anderson.

Caliente wrecker picking up Train #8 at Moapa, Aug. 20, 1942. Photo by Tom Anderson.

Centralized Traffic Control was being installed in 1943, but it had not yet reached Carp. The railroad in that area still operated on train orders and automatic block signals. The system normally provided enough warning to keep two trains from colliding.

Each signal mast had an arm at the top, with three colored glass lenses that moved past a light. With the arm straight up, a green lens was in front of the light, saying the track ahead was clear. (Even in daylight, it was called a "green block".) When the arm moved so it pointed outward from the mast at 45°, a yellow lens moved in front of the light; a yellow block was a warning that certain precautions were to be taken because some sort of traffic represented a possible hazard. When the arm was horizontal, pointing straight out from the mast, a red lens moved in front of the light; a red block meant that something was so close ahead that an immediate stop was required. A train would normally have been traveling in a yellow block before coming to a red block, and the speed was supposed to have been reduced enough to allow a complete stop before any part of the pilot of the engine passed the red signal.

A train had to stop for a red block, but under some

circumstances, it could proceed against the block. For example, a train that was only a short distance from a siding might be able to get into the siding and thus clear the main line. The movement against a red block was allowed only if a flagman was sent ahead with a red light and a red flag to stop any oncoming traffic, and if the train moved no faster than the flagman could walk. That maneuver was called "flagging the block" or "leading it in".

Now comes the day of the Streamliner wreck. Extra 3825 west, a freight that was pulled by Challenger-type articulated steam engine 3825 (widely but incorrectly called a Mallet), broke an air hose about 2 miles east of Carp and was delayed while a new hose was installed. The train got rolling again after midnight. The eastbound Streamliner was due at Carp at 1:24 am.

Dan Curran was engineer on X3825, making his first trip as engineer in the district. A.J. Brimacombe, an engineer who knew the district, was riding with him as the pilot. Curran was reportedly advised to run on into Carp to meet the Streamliner. Because Curran was facing a yellow block, he could proceed at reduced speed; the Streamliner would be stopped at Carp by the red block that would be thrown by Curran's train. The flaw in the logic lay in the fact that the Streamliner had been exempted from the rule concerning entry into a red block, and it could proceed at reduced speed against a red block after making the required full stop. The events of the next few minutes led to deletion of that exemption.

Art Wengert, engineer of the Streamliner, was a long-time engineer on steam engines on that road, now trained to operate diesel engines, and his sense of caution made him uneasy as he approached Carp in a yellow block. He expected to see the order board (the semaphore) at Carp set against him, directing him to stop there for orders. However, the order board was clear, and he eased on past the depot.

> *Anatole Mallet, a Frenchman, got the idea in 1874 for a locomotive made up of two engines connected in tandem by a pin under the boiler, with the engines working in compound expansion. That is, the steam exhausted from the rear engine went to larger cylinders on the lead engine to be used again. This locomotive was powerful, and it was flexible for use on sharp turns. We adopted his idea, but in time the principle of compounding was abandoned in favor of simple expansion. We commonly call all articulated steam engines "Malleys", though the term is incorrect if they are simple expansion. His name was pronounced "mall-ay", but we turn it into "malley".*

Dale Hunt was in helper service out of Caliente, and he was waiting at Carp with orders to help an eastbound freight that was following the Streamliner. Most of the rest of this account is based on first-hand information from him and from Art Wengert.

Hunt had his engine at the west end of Carp siding, to be ready to couple onto the rear of the freight train when it stopped at Carp. The Streamliner went by, right on time, and he expected to be on his way to Caliente soon. But he was surprised to see the Streamliner stop, and Max Patterson, brakeman on the Streamliner, hurrying back down the track; he had to flag the freight train that was following. Hunt asked him what was wrong, and he replied, "I don't know, but I think we hit something".

After Patterson had stopped the eastbound freight, he came back up the track, and Hunt said, "Jump on, and I'll run you back". When they approached the depot, they saw the Streamliner standing there, with people milling around the telegraph office. Bert Ayers, Traveling Road Foreman, who had been on the Streamliner, was talking by phone with someone in the head office in Omaha.

This is what had happened:

The east end of Carp siding is close to the steel bridge over the creek, with block signals at the west end of the bridge; when Wengert got there, the signal for the Streamliner was red, because X3825 was so close.

Wengert brought the Streamliner to a full stop, as required. He started forward and had crossed the bridge when he saw the bright light of an oncoming locomotive swing around the bend about a quarter of a mile away. He thought it might be a helper trying to sneak into Carp ahead of him, so he stopped his train again so he could back up and let the helper into the siding. As soon as the Streamliner passed the signal, the signals for X3825 also turned red, but the engine had already passed the last signal before Carp.

And then things happened in a hurry. His diesel was rocked by a terrific crash, and he was thrown to the floor. He tried to get up, but he was thrown down again. He tried again, and was thrown again.

Dazed and rattled, he concluded he had been derailed, and his only thought was to blow his air horn to warn the "helper", but the air horn didn't work. He managed to climb out through a door, and he was amazed to see the big steam engine standing on the tracks above him. The diesel was in the borrow pit below the grade.

His next thought was to blow the whistle of the steam engine to warn the freight train that was following him, but its whistle wouldn't blow, either. The leading unit of the Streamliner's diesels had ridden right up over the pilot and air pumps of the steam engine and then on top of the boiler, shearing off the bell and whistle. Then it rolled off, bouncing off the engine and the roadbed and finally coming to rest, headed back toward Carp.

As reported in the *Las Vegas Evening Review-Journal*, July 13, three cars of the Streamliner were derailed, and two of the three were jammed together and had to be set out at Carp. Seven cars of the freight train were derailed, six of them being piled up in the railroad cut. Only one car was damaged beyond repair. The freight that followed the Streamliner came on into Carp siding for water and oil, then it backed down to Vigo to clear the main line.

A war was on, and the railroad was burdened with heavy traffic in war materials and troop movements. Every hour's delay in clearing the tracks added to the backlog of trains waiting to get through or being

> *The force of the impact broke many rails under the cars of the freight train. A tank car of lard turned over, and lard ran out on the ground. The workmen who picked up the wreck said they rendered the lard out of their clothes every night.*

diverted to other railroads that were equally busy. The wrecker trains from Caliente and Las Vegas were rushed in to start picking up the pieces. (For a good look at life with a wreck train, although not on the Union Pacific, see Dougherty's "Call the Big Hook".)

The wreckage of the diesel had cleared the tracks, and the Streamliner was pulled back into Carp siding so the Las Vegas wrecker could reach the wrecked freight train. The wrecker was derailed twice during the morning of the 13th because of heavy sideways pulling without enough blocking. (Dougherty describes the limit of lateral pull that could be tolerated without wrecking a wrecker.)

The crews worked all day and through the night, throwing wrecked and damaged equipment to either side, and about 4:30 am, July 14, the track was cleared. The rails were gauged and spiked, and trains began to move just after 5:00. Steam engine 7019, a 4-8-2, took the Streamliner out of Carp. The other passenger trains began to move, and then the freight trains. Hunt says he was away from Caliente about 52 hours, "just to make a 40-mile help on a freight train".

About 15 passenger trains and 12 freight trains were tied up. Gene Anderson was on the diner crew of Train #38, the eastbound "Los Angeles Limited - Pony Express". The train was held at Las Vegas, parked in the freight yard. The air conditioner picked that July day to quit. People on the train sweated there all through the day; they were the first train into the yard and the last one out. Late that night they left Las Vegas and were held several hours near Carp. Early in the morning they began moving again; they were 27 hours late at Caliente.

What about the people who were involved? According to the newspaper articles on July 13 and 14, no passengers were injured; some were shaken up, and some slept right through the crash. The injuries were to crew members, as follows: Fireman Charles Keene, of Engine 3825, jumped just before the collision and broke his ankle. Engineer Art Wengert had cuts about the leg and minor abrasions. Bert Ayers, Traveling Engineer and road foreman on the Streamliner, had a sprained back. He said he was walking toward his seat in the engine, and when he next saw his seat, it was bent and broken. Conductor Gergen, of the Streamliner, had a severely bruised hip. Fireman Price and brakeman Max Patterson, of the Streamliner, had slight cuts and bruises.

Two of the passengers were Dr. A. Schroeder, of Los Angeles, and Miss Florence Twomey, a Registered Nurse at White Memorial Hospital. They treated the injured people and went through the train to check on the passengers. Union Pacific physician Dr. Hale B. Slavin was sent out on a special train with railroad officials and work crews. He brought the injured back to Las Vegas on the special train.

The article on July 13 concludes, "The tiny depot at Carp was jammed with passengers for several hours, as they stood inside the little vestibule delivering messages to be wired to relatives to notify them that they had escaped injury in the crash of the trains".

We heard stories and claims about the things that happened and why they happened and who was to blame. As I recall, the most persistent questions were, "How fast was the freight train going, if it was to head in at Carp?" and "Why did Brimacombe let Curran proceed that way against traffic, and especially against the Streamliner?" Art Wengert continued his career as the engineer of the Streamliner, and Dan Curran continued running steam engines; A.J. Brimacombe was pulled out of service.

Work train, Big Springs, 1917. Photo from T.C. Himstreet.

Extra 3508 at Big Springs, Clover Creek Canyon, 1917. Note X3508 and white flags of an extra. Photo from T.C. Himstreet.

Steam shovel at Islen pit, Clover Creek Canyon, 1917. Photo from T.C. Himstreet.

Streamliner wreck at Carp bridge, July 13, 1943. Eastbound "City of Los Angeles" collided with westbound extra 3825 that was running in a red block. Demolished leading engine of the Streamliner is looking back the way it came. Photos by Dale V. Hunt, engineer of a helper engine at Carp when it happened.

Rails through the canyon.

CHAPTER 6

WHAT HAPPENS WHEN THE CREEK RISES?

"NATURE TO BE COMMANDED MUST BE OBEYED"

The original grade for the SPLA&SL was so close to the creek the rails were hardly out of the water in places. Washouts were common; for example, on March 24, 1906, a 4-day storm caused numerous washouts between Minto and Hoya. According to the *Caliente Express*, March 29, 1906, a Southern Pacific piledriver had been sent from Salt Lake City to assist one that had already arrived, another was working between Elgin and Carp, and another was working just above Rox. Three gangs of men were repairing damage to the telegraph line. A double-headed freight train of 20 cars of oranges was held up at Eccles, and only part of the train was iced cars. An engine was trapped between Eccles and Minto. Passenger service had been extended as far as Acoma on the 28th, but trains into Caliente were not expected for 10 days yet. Acoma is about 25 miles from Caliente, and wagons were used to move passengers and freight between the two.

A lot of riprap was put in, and dikes were built, in the belief that the existing grade could be protected. A year later, 83 miles of track between Barclay and Guelph were badly damaged by a month-long series of rain storms. Winter snow was still on the ground when rain began on Feb. 22, 1907, and the rain kept falling for 12 hours. The flood took out the railroad.

E.G. Tilton, the Chief Engineer of the SPLA&SL, was sent from Los Angeles to see how bad it was, and it was so bad he had to ride horseback from Hoya. He reached Eccles, and on March 5 a flood that was 3 feet deeper than the one on Feb. 22 added to the damage. The water was a foot deep in the houses on Company Row in Caliente, and it covered the entire floor of the canyon above Elgin. The storms had wrecked a work train, and four men were killed. And it was not a local storm; severe damage had also occurred near Daggett, California.

Details of the flood were given in the *Caliente Lode-Express*, March 2 and 9, 1907. Eastbound train #2 was stranded at Etna on Friday, Feb. 22. The passengers took over the schoolhouse "and made merry". The train was moved to

Caliente on Feb. 25, after the Caliente bridge was repaired. Several freight trains followed, and the yards were crowded. Westbound train #7 was held about 5 miles east of Caliente and the passengers were brought to Caliente and housed aboard train #2.

By March 2, the railroad had 800 men repairing bridges, clearing slides, building grade, and laying track. The flood was said to have been the heaviest one known in the area, having been 2 feet higher than the one in 1906. "Along the stream are piles of drift wood, ties and bridge timbers etc. Many acres of orchards and gardens are now covered with silt and sand to a depth of two feet and numerous fence posts are almost covered over with the same." Rails and ties were left hanging across washouts, like an aerial tramway, and in other places the track was buried under 14 feet of sand, gravel, and silt. Several cars had been stranded near Minto by the first flood, and they were almost buried by the next one. By March 9, trains from the west were at Leith, and trains from the east were at Minto.

Another flood came through the canyons on March 19, but the first two had not left much railroad for it to attack. Traffic was resumed over a temporary line on April 12, and then came the time for what is called, in the vernacular of the 1990s, assessment of the damage done and the lessons learned.

A force of 1000 men was put to work to build a new grade 4 feet above the high-water mark. The grade was realigned, the stream channel was shifted, and eight new steel bridges were put in. But "Big Jim" Shanahan, the railroad engineer, rejected some good advice, and his new line was doomed. (The decision is also attributed to William Hood, the chief engineer of the Southern Pacific, who had been called in as an adviser.) An old Indian showed where the water had been even higher than in 1907, pointing to flood debris on the canyon wall, but old-timers didn't remember it, so the plan was retained. Too bad. The statement about obeying nature was made by Francis Bacon, and he was right.

THE 1910 FLOOD

Toward the end of 1909, heavy snow fell in Lincoln County. Then a warm rain began, a day or two before New Year's Day. By nightfall, Jan. 1, 1910, the railroad had lost 100 miles of track, almost an entire freight train, and $1 million worth of rip-rap that was put in place after the 1907 flood. Besides that, a passenger train was stranded at Elgin.

People in Las Vegas had no inkling of difficulties to come when eastbound train #8, the "Los Angeles Limited", left at 9:30 pm, Dec. 31, 1909. Nobody would have believed the train would take 5½ months to reach Salt Lake City.

Then the telegraph line went dead, and trains from the east failed to appear, and a 12-foot wall of water swamped the $185,000 gold dredge on the

Colorado River, 3 miles below Eldorado Canyon. People began to suspect something might have happened.

Finally the stories began to come in: Four feet of water in the roundhouse at Caliente, the east and south walls having fallen in where they were undermined; two bodies found below Caliente, one a section hand and the other an employee at the roundhouse; passenger train #4 marooned at Eccles, though the passengers were safe; Train #81 with more than 30 cars of merchandise and 2 cars of horses lost at Boyd; the river 1½ miles wide at Logan; 4 feet of ice on the tracks between Caliente and Pioche; the "Los Angeles Limited" stranded at Elgin and a baby born during the flood; John Averett's house at Logan, never before touched by flood, now standing in 18 inches of water; a relief train marooned above Moapa as it tried to make its way up the canyon; a flat car found at Logan, 10 miles from the railroad. The passengers from the train at Eccles were able to return to Acoma, which could be reached by trains from Salt Lake; the train itself, consisting of a baggage car, two Pullman sleepers, two chair cars, and a dining car, was not released to return to Salt Lake until May 16.

The major damage began at Barclay, in Clover Creek Canyon, and extended all the way to Guelph. Flood water coming down the Meadow Valley Wash and the flood in Clover Creek Canyon merged at Caliente. The creek bed was very shallow, and debris quickly built up at the railroad bridge and sent the flood around the bridge and into town. Bridges were out, several houses at Caliente were lost, the depot was undermined, and at least two men were swept away and drowned. And the better part of 110 miles of track was gone.

When water was diverted by debris lodged against the Pioche bridge, an attempt was made to blow up the bridge and release the dam; an employee was badly injured when dynamite exploded prematurely.

Robert Graham, editor of the *Caliente Prospector*, risked his life to cross the flood so he could walk to Panaca to send out the news. One of the Wadsworths took the message across the mountains to Modena, and from there it went by telegraph to Salt Lake City.

Caliente yard during 1910 flood. Photo from T.C. Himstreet.

Walter Thomas, the section foreman at Pioche, walked the track from Pioche to Caliente and reported that it was in good condition except for being covered with ice and water and having a few washouts.

Old Elgin, built down in the creek-bed, was practically washed away. The stranded "Los Angeles Limited", a double-header, was safe, and the two engi-

Debris behind Company Row, Caliente, after the 1910 flood. Porch is gone from #12; the Himstreet family lived in #11. Photo from T.C. Himstreet.

neers were helping salvage what they could from the houses. They were also called upon to act as midwives; Mrs. Schroeder, the section foreman's wife, was in the last stages of labor. The Schroeder house was already partly undermined when the two men carried her through the rain to high ground.

When we lived at the Elliott ranch, we were told that the railroad bridge near Etna was threatened by the high water, so a train was run across the bridge to hold it down. According to the story, the bridge and the train were lost. If it really happened, it escaped the notice of the newspapers. The railroad ran down the creek bed, not at its present alignment, and there were plenty of low bridges that were vulnerable to high water.

Train #81, a westbound freight, actually was caught by the flood. About a mile west of Boyd siding, the track was gone from in front of the train, and by then, the track behind was also washed out. The crew got to safety and watched Engine 3657 and the entire train, except for five cars and the caboose, disappear into the flood.

Fireman Lou Martin, writing in *Railroad Magazine* in 1942, tells the story, and I refer to him as the authority; he was there. (You should read his complete story; my summary barely hints at what he went through.) He says he was called for an extra west out of Caliente, a 42-car train. The train had to wait in the yard for the arrival of two eastbound trains, #4 and #8. When #8 arrived, the conductor told the dispatcher in Las Vegas that he should not send out any more westbound trains, but the extra was given orders anyway.

They had some adventures before they reached the washout west of Boyd, where the track was suspended in the air. George Ramey, the engineer, and George Ferris, the conductor, left the train to make their way on foot to Elgin, about 5 miles down the canyon. Martin went back to the caboose, arriving soaked to the skin and nearly frozen. Martin and the brakeman, with several men who were riding drover service with the cars of livestock, walked to Caliente after daylight. After they waited 2 weeks in Caliente, Martin and the brakeman walked to Barclay, where they could catch a train to Salt Lake City. They went by train to Salt Lake, then to Ogden, San Francisco, Los Angeles, and finally back to Las Vegas. They had been 125 miles from Las Vegas, but they went almost 2100 miles to get there.

Martin says the 3657 was dug out of the mud after about a year and rebuilt, and he says, ". . . she was one of the best engines they ever had."

Afterward, people down the canyon wore clothes made of goods from the train, and they built houses, barns, and fences of lumber that still had railroad lettering. The barn on the Elliott ranch had several beams in box-car red with the letters SPLA&SL in white.

The trucks from the cars of Train #81 were left where the flood buried them until after scrap iron prices went up as World War II approached. Jim Bradshaw and his father, Rube, dug the trucks, cut them up with a torch, and sold them for scrap. Rube bought a cab-over-engine dump truck with the proceeds.

The agent at Rox, a man named Butterfield, tried to fish a body from the flood, but the water caught him and he was nearly drowned. Sixty hogs were drowned at Capalapa, in the Moapa Valley, and S.H. Wells lost 60 acres of grain and 50 acres of asparagus in the ranch of the Moapa Improvement Company near Logan. The great surge of water swept into the Muddy River, then into the Virgin River, then into the Colorado, and swamped the gold dredge below Eldorado Canyon.

Crews from Las Vegas immediately began rebuilding the telegraph line to Caliente. L.W. "Pete" Mescher told me they faced bitter cold as they worked up through the canyon. The job was finished in 14 days, and Caliente was back in touch with the world. A stage line had been established to bring in supplies from Modena to Pioche, easing the predicament at Caliente.

Las Vegas had no train service from the east, and service from the west seemed to be cut off. The Pacific Electric was washed out between Redlands and Riverside (not part of the Meadow Valley Wash, of course; it was a big storm), and a landslide cut the railroad at Devore. The Tonopah & Tidewater was badly damaged near Tecopa. A washout cut the SPLA&SL west of Crucero.

One route was still open: From Los Angeles, a train could take the Southern Pacific to Colton, then follow the Santa Fe to the T&T at Ludlow, then north to Crucero, and finally to Las Vegas on the SPLA&SL. (As I first heard it, the route was the T&T from Ludlow to Rhyolite, then the Las Vegas & Tonopah to Las Vegas.)

Work trains started up the Meadow Valley Wash from the west, and the Utah Construction Company began rebuilding the line down Clover Creek Canyon from the east. The construction force reached 3000 men; a Bridge & Building gang was borrowed from the Santa Fe; and two pile drivers were brought in from the Southern Pacific.

Sixty teams and scrapers were at work by March 12, and 300 men were on the job. The tracks reached Hoya on April 2, and on April 16, according to the *Pioche Record*, trains from Salt Lake to Caliente were expected early in May. George Fetterman was hauling five carloads of bridge piling from Acoma to Caliente, where it could be loaded on cars and started down the canyon for repair work and construction of the temporary track. Construction trains could run to a point near the Pippin ranch, and the track was passable from Moapa almost to Carp.

Senator Clark said to speed up the job and double the work force. Finally the track was passable again; regular train service between Salt Lake and Caliente was resumed on May 21, and the "Los Angeles Limited" reached Salt Lake City on June 12, only 5½ months late. The same day the first through train, the "Overland", left Los Angeles eastbound.

The big question everyone asked, after the urgency of the flood had abated, concerned the fate of the SPLA&SL. All the old plans and speculations were dusted off and argued at length in the local newspapers. Some people said the Meadow Valley Wash route would be abandoned; a new route would run from Lund, Utah, through St. George, and then on to Las Vegas. Other people were equally sure the new route would run west from Crestline across the Meadow Valley near Panaca, then across Bristol Pass, and finally down into Pahranagat Valley and then to Las Vegas. Then again, it might run southward from Crestline through the Clover Mountains and across Tule Flat and Mormon Mesa to Moapa.

But what did they know? The people with the money had the last word; they owned the outfit, and they said the railroad would indeed be rebuilt through the Meadow Valley Wash.

Things were going to be different, though, this time. The company would spend $400,000 to put in a temporary line, then another $6 million to build a new roadbed that would be at least 15 feet above the creek.

The construction of the new railroad – the "High Line" – is beyond the scope of this story, but a few statistics will at least suggest the size of the job. The western half was to be built by Shattuck-Edinger Company, of Los Angeles, and the eastern half was to be built by Utah Construction Company. At least 1500 to 2000 men would be needed. Eight tunnels, ranging from 200 feet to the 1100-foot Tunnel 4, would be put in between Carp and Caliente, and 2 more between Caliente and Crestline; 24 steel bridges would be installed; and 74 miles of railroad grade had to be rebuilt. The job was to be complete on April 1, 1911, with a penalty of $100 a day for late completion and a bonus of $100 a day for an early finish.

According to the *Las Vegas Age*, Sept. 10, 1910, Utah Construction Company had a camp at Etna. They expected to have 1500 to 2000 men at work. The paper said on Sept. 17 that other camps were at Elgin, Carp, and Moapa. On Oct. 1, five contractors were camped at Elgin, with 1000 men working from there. Twenty camps had been established between Caliente and Moapa.

While reconstruction was under way, another flood caused trouble. The *Pioche Record* reported on Feb. 4, 1911, that "The heavy rains which prevailed in this section of Nevada last Monday and Tuesday have seriously crippled the Salt Lake Route in the Clover and Meadow Valley washes . . . . Both above and below Caliente, wide stretches of the track are gone . . . ." The flood crested about 6:00 pm on Jan. 31. A passenger train and a freight train were tied up east of Caliente, but the damage was far less than in 1910. Resumption of traffic within 2 weeks was expected.

According to the *Pioche Record* on Feb. 21 and 26, 1914, a flood had damaged the railroad in numerous places. Train #2 had been marooned near Barclay, but it soon made its way back to Caliente. Temporary repairs in Clover Creek Canyon had enabled traffic to be resumed between Caliente and Salt Lake.

The High Line was a good job well done, and it has fairly well resisted floods since then. "Fairly well" is the qualifier; the High Line is not secure against all damage. The events in March 1938 would show how bad the flood could get and how well the High Line could withstand floods.

THE 1938 FLOOD

The history of floods in the Meadow Valley Wash must include the two years 1910 and 1938. Although the 1910 flood did more damage, the 1938 flood had more water. The creek ran in a small channel in the flat bottom of the Meadow Valley Wash until 1910, but the flood cut a deep channel and washed away fields, houses, and the railroad. Summer cloudbursts and their flash floods were (and are) common. On Jan. 7, 1922, the *Las Vegas Age* reported serious washouts at Carp, the Kiernan ranch, and a mile west of Boyd that tied up the railroad for 5 days. The railroad was tied up for 60 hours in late September 1925 by a flood that was especially damaging in the canyon between Elgin and Leith. A flood came down Taylor Mine Canyon on Aug. 16, 1937, and filled the space under the bridge with mud and debris, moved the abutments of the bridge, and washed out about 25 feet of track on each side of the bridge. Simon Chavez, the section foreman at Stine, discovered the washout just in time to stop an eastbound freight train.

But the biggest flood was still to come; in February 1938 a lot of snow had accumulated on the Clover Mountains and around Panaca and Pioche, then a warm rain began on March 1, and the flood was on its way.

A story in the *Las Vegas Evening Review-Journal*, March 4, gave this summary of reported damage in the Meadow Valley Wash: "300 feet of track between Carp and Vigo buried beneath 10 feet of debris. One span of the bridge east of Carp washed out. 350 feet of track between Leith and Kyle (near Carp) under fifteen feet of debris. Numerous side washes between Kyle and Caliente pouring slides onto the track to depths ranging from a few inches to a few feet."

Sam Wengert was pulling a trainload of gravel and oil for a road construction job somewhere in Utah, and the dispatcher at Las Vegas put Sam in the hole at Moapa on the night of March 2 because of reports of high water in the canyon. Sam didn't think the weather looked bad enough for that, and he talked to the dispatcher by phone and got permission to feel his way through to Caliente. When he came through Carp early on the morning of the 3rd, he still thought the prospects for reaching Caliente were good.

The section foreman at Carp was considered to be an exaggerator, and on the evening of March 2, when he came out to our place and told us that the water was 2 feet deep in Tunnel 8, we took it with a grain of salt.

When we awoke on the morning of the 3rd, we could see water beyond the old railroad grade that ran between our house and the creek, and we knew we were seeing a rare sight. The top of the old grade was well above the creek bed, and the water was within about 5 feet of the top of the grade. Our house was higher than the top of the grade, so we could see the water beyond the grade. When we went out into the back yard, the water had crept up to within perhaps 100 feet of the house.

We walked down the railroad toward Carp to see what had happened there. The automobile road was under water a few hundred yards from our house, so the railroad was the only way through. The railroad goes through a rock cut at the lower end of our ranch, and as we came out of the west end of the cut, we thought the steel bridge at the east end of Carp siding, a two-span deck girder bridge, was washed out. As we got closer, we could see that the bridge was still there, but the center was down and the bridge was tipped to one side. The high water was splashing nearly to the top of the bridge.

Two block signals were at the west end of the bridge, one for westbound and the other for eastbound traffic. The arm on one signal was horizontal, which made it a red block, warning traffic to stop. My father thought the signal meant a train was approaching Carp from the east, and the engineer had to be warned that the bridge was not passable. (We didn't even think the bridge was safe to walk across.)

A train was coming, and it was Sam Wengert's train. He had his own story to tell.

After he passed Carp early that morning, he was on fairly level ground, some distance from the creek bed, until he got beyond Cloud siding. He knew that a bad flood could cut into that ground, but as he approached Tunnel 3, he had not seen any sign of trouble, and he still thought he was okay. The grade to Tunnel 3 is on fill that consists of rubble from boring the tunnel, and the grade had extensive rip-rap. He was certainly safe for a little while.

Sam had been straining to see any sign of trouble, and now that the train was on solid ground, he went over to the fireman's side to straighten his back and relax a little. Just then the conductor, Archibald, yelled from the engineer's side, "Big-hole 'er, Sam!" Without asking questions, Sam sprang over to the air-brake stand and big-holed her.

Then he looked out to see what was happening, and he got the fright of his life. The water was cutting away that "solid" grade almost under the locomotive, and there wasn't any track in front of them! It was all water!

To big-hole a train is to apply the emergency air brakes; the big hole is the notch on the control stand for the brake handle at the emergency position. The air is discharged from the release side of the air-brake cylinders, and the pressure in the application cylinders will force the brake shoes against the wheels. The release air pressure has to build back up to release the brake shoes, and for a train of that length, about 5 minutes were needed to release the brakes. All they could do was sit there and wait for the longest 5 minutes of their lives.

When the brakes had been released, Sam eased the reverse gear into reverse position and cracked the throttle as gently as possible to try to avoid any vibration that might dump them into the flood. He felt better when they could see solid ground again, but now he was concerned that the flood might have cut into the grade behind them. He was backing the train, so the conductor, in the caboose, was the person who had to see where they were going.

Everything went fine, and they had an uneventful journey until suddenly the block went red in their face. Because the red block meant traffic was close, Sam had to be suspicious; this just wasn't right. He would be throwing a red block for anything eastbound, but anything that could suddenly throw a red block for him had to be pretty close and running against his block.

What had happened was that the bond wires between rail ends had snapped when the concrete pier under the center of the bridge had sunk. The bond wires enable the signal current to flow through the rails and around the joints, and when the current is interrupted, the automatic signals go to the red position.

As Sam approached the rock cut at the lower end of our ranch, the conductor saw someone running up the track, waving at him to stop. That someone was my father, warning him that the bridge was impassable.

The track had many washouts between Moapa and Crestline, and obviously no trains were going to run for a while. Railroad officials talked to my father about stopping the train opposite our pumping plant and running pipe to get water, but we didn't have No. 6 fuel oil. The only reasonable choice was to pull into Cloud siding, kill the fire, and wait until they had a railroad again.

The train sat at Cloud while the extra gangs worked their way through the Meadow Valley Wash. As soon as the track was repaired as far as Carp, a work train was brought in with a B&B gang to jack up the center of the bridge, realign the spans, drive pilings, put in cribbing, and finally reopen the line.

When the center of the bridge was supported by pilings and cribbing, the center concrete pier was blasted out. It had rested on alluvium, and the turbulence of the flood was great enough to soften the creek bed deeper than the base of the pier. That was when the pier sank and tipped to one side. A new pier was put in, and it went deep enough to stay solid.

Bridge at Carp, 7:00 am, March 3, 1938. Center pier of bridge sank in the creek bed. Flood water has receded a little. View north from near west end of bridge. Photo by Tom Anderson.

I was attending Carp school then, and I remember the timber cribbing, the jackhammers, the pile driver, and the pumps that kept water out of the excavation for the new pier.

The flood was the result of an extensive storm system that reached all the way to Los Angeles. Major damage was done to the railroad in Afton Canyon and at Crucero, California. All eastbound traffic was held from March 2 until March 22, when Train #104, the Streamliner "City of Los Angeles", went through on a slow order, and then a rush of rail traffic followed.

Trains that were between Afton and Las Vegas were held in Las Vegas. Work went ahead rapidly on restoring the Carp bridge to service and to repair washouts at Minto, between Islen and Barclay, near Elgin, and between Carp and Vigo. The eastbound trains held at Las Vegas began to move 11 days after the flood, starting with five stock trains. (The damage in Afton Canyon was so bad that nothing could get through yet from Los Angeles to Las Vegas.)

RAIL SERVICE THRU VEGAS TO L.A. WILL BE STARTED AGAIN SUNDAY. That was a headline in the *Las Vegas Evening Review-Journal* on March 19. Service was to start the next day, when the westbound Streamliner "City of Los Angeles" would pass through. The eastbound Streamliner would leave Los Angeles the evening of March 21. Regular schedules would resume on March 22.

The immediate damage at the Carp bridge was repaired enough to get the railroad back in operation, but the permanent repairs took a while. The Carp Items of the *Caliente Herald* said that a snowstorm on Feb. 3, 1939, had delayed

Bridge at Carp, March 3, 1938. Caboose is the freight train stranded above Carp by the flood. Carp school ground at left; water tank, ruins of the recently burned school house, storage shed, outdoor toilets. Photo by Tom Anderson.

the work of the B&B gang on the bridge; on March 9, the news was that the bridge gang had completed work on the bridge and would move to Kyle quarry.

The managers could feel reassured by the durability of the High Line that was built in 1912. They could also feel desperation at the prospect of reopening a railroad that was nearly blockaded. Sidings were full of freight trains (such as at Cloud), and all the normal traffic as well as all those delayed trains had to move on the single-track railroad. Signor comments that veteran train dispatchers got gray hair over it, but they couldn't know that 3 years later the wartime traffic would routinely be that heavy.

Dramatic as the effect on the railroad had been, the flood of 1938 made a much bigger story in Lincoln County. *The Caliente Herald* had numerous stories during the rest of March that told what else happened in the Meadow Valley Wash.

High water from the Crestline and Barclay areas hit Caliente at 1:00 am on March 3, damaging the railroad and nearly taking out the highway bridge on each side of Caliente. Then it continued on down the canyon, taking out the county road, destroying farm land, and further damaging the railroad. Another surge from the Spring Valley and Ursine areas arrived the afternoon of March 3. For us at Carp, the flood was exacerbated by a surge that came down Cottonwood Canyon.

The Soil Conservation Service estimated the flood at Caliente to have been at least 27,800 cubic feet per second. Water overflowed the banks of the deep channel that had been cut by the 1910 flood and got into homes and buildings in town. In Caliente, the basement of the schoolhouse was flooded, fences were washed away, and the nearby Alice Culverwell Dixon athletic field was covered with debris and its fence was partly destroyed. (In 1941 my father bought the George Cram house, which was at the southeast corner of the field, and I wonder what it was like to look out from that house and see water creeping closer.)

On March 3, a story in the *Las Vegas Evening Review-Journal* said, "The Tom Betteridge, Robinson, Bishop Gurr, and Leslie Roberts families barely escaped with their lives when the flood came roaring down the wash and into their homes. They were awakened by the water lapping at the foundation of their homes and were forced to flee for their lives leaving all their possessions behind to be ruined by the raging water."

The fire department spent the next several days pumping out basements. Losses at 25 individual homes ranged from $50 to $1000. The sewage disposal plant was flooded, and the plant was out of service several days while new wiring was being installed.

By March 24, the damage was estimated to be $147,000, plus estimated damage of $2.5 million to the railroad. Some of the specifics (not including damage to the railroad) were as follows: Six bridges in Spring Valley and the Delmues area were washed away. The road between Caliente and Eccles was a total loss, and the road between Caliente and Elgin was damaged and two bridges were lost. Damage to land, ditches, irrigation diversion dam, and flood control work at the Conaway ranch came to $5000; the damage to the Tennille ranch was $3000, and damage to the Dula ranch was $2000.

The Nevada Congressional delegation asked that the CCC camps at Delmues and Panaca be authorized to provide emergency aid; the request was granted. Lincoln and Clark Counties asked for $750,000 in federal aid.

One of the consequences of the flood appears to have been the establishment of the Meadow Valley Scattered Settlers Project, which is described elsewhere. It didn't stop future floods, but it did get some people moved out of the area that was at risk of damage by flood.

IT WAS A BIG STORM!

In 1938 I was just a kid, and I don't recall knowing the extent of the damage. Just to give an idea how small a part we in the Meadow Valley Wash played, here is a summary of headlines from the *Las Vegas Evening Review-Journal*, March 2 through 8:

March 2: 4 DIE IN L.A. FLOODS; Control Dam Above Lancaster Reported Cracking; Hundreds Are Fleeing Homes In Southern

Section; City Of Venice Said To Be Completely Under Water; Hundreds Are Marooned; Altadena, Pasadena Flooded; All Land Between Los Angeles And Long Beach Is Under Water; Los Angeles River Threatens To Overflow Banks; No Relief Seen.

March 3: LOOTERS ARE ACTIVE IN L.A.; Death Toll Is Fixed At 45; Slackening Rains Reported And Crisis Is Thot Passed; 35,000 Square Miles Still Are Under Water In Area; City Of Las Vegas Isolated Today; All Power Lines From Boulder Dam to L.A. Said Down.

March 4: FOOD IS LOW IN L.A.; Death Toll Expected To Hit 200, And Property Damage Is Estimated $25,000,000 Today; Transportation In Area Halted; No Trains Into Vegas For Five Days, U.P. Says; Pair Battle Raging Torrents Of Amargosa River, And Save Lives; Virgin River Overflows Banks Washes Out Zion Park Road; Baker Is Facing Destruction As 6 Feet Of Water Roll Over Town; First Mail Out Of Vegas Moves Today.

March 5: FRESNO FLOOD DAMAGE HUB NOW; SAN BERNARDI-NO AREA WRECKED; Victorville And Barstow Sector Reported Razed By Big Floods; Train Service On Union Pacific Not To Be Resumed For Week; Los Angeles Digging Out; Looting Continues In L.A.; Water In Outlying Districts Is Condemned; Trains Begin Running Again.

March 7: Vegas Without Trains For 15 Days, Said.

March 8: BARSTOW UNDER MARTIAL LAW; Only Victims Who Seek Belongings Are Allowed In City; Victorville Is Badly Hit.

Section foreman Hilton Peters' house at Leith. 3-7-38. Photo by Tom Anderson.

Rockslide at Kyle. 1938 flood. Photo by Tom Anderson.

CHAPTER 7

LINCOLN COUNTY STORIES

WATER FOR DELAMAR

When Capt. Joseph R. De Lamar came into the Ferguson mining district in Lincoln County, before 1894, and began buying the properties that later became the Delamar group, he could not buy any water. The district is on the west side of the Delamar Mountains. The few springs nearby did not furnish enough water. De Lamar expanded the mill and installed the second cyanide plant in Nevada, and a cyanide plant has a powerful thirst.

He sent a crew to develop Riggs Spring in 1894. They were able to get about 3 miner's inches of water, which wasn't nearly enough. Several wells were drilled in the valley below the camp, in hope of finding an aquifer carrying water from the mountains, but even when drilled to a depth of 900 feet, the wells came in dry. (A miner's inch is variously defined by individual states of the West; the range seems to be from 38.4 to 50 miner's inches equal one cubic foot of water per second.)

One source of water was not yet tapped, and in the summer of 1895 he decided it was the only reasonable possibility: the Meadow Valley Wash, with nothing between it and Delamar except a range of mountains.

His strategy was to install a pumping plant at a place known as Kershaw, in the Meadow Valley Wash, and run a pipeline up Rock Springs Canyon, across the summit, and down Cedar Wash to Delamar, a distance of 14 miles.

Three booster stations would be needed to make the 2100-foot lift. The first was Rock Springs station, fairly low in Rock Springs Canyon. The second was Findlay station, several miles farther. The last was Cedar Wash station, not far below the summit.

By October the stations were finished and the 3½-inch pipeline was near completion. According to *Mining & Scientific Press*, Nov. 2, 1895, the pipeline delivered 100,000 gallons of water daily to Delamar.

In 1895 the April Fool Mine installed a 9-mile pipeline to Willow Spring to solve their water problem. Capt. De Lamar found that one water line from the Meadow Valley Wash to his mine couldn't supply enough water, so in

February 1896 he put in a second 3½-inch pipeline from the pumping station to Delamar.

He consolidated several properties into a single organization that controlled its own mine, mill, and water supply. Other capitalists liked that kind of operation, and the result was the formation of Bamberger-Delamar Gold Mining Company. The company began buying into the district in 1902, and they soon took over both the Delamar group and the April Fool.

The Delamar mill at that time included 13 Griffin mills; leaching tanks with a capacity of 9000 tons monthly; and a power plant with five boilers, a 500-horsepower compound engine with 22-inch high-pressure and 34-inch low-pressure cylinders, a crusher engine with 14-inch cylinder and 36-inch stroke, and a dynamo engine with 12-inch cylinder and 36-inch stroke. The dynamo engine ran a 60-kilowatt, 500-volt dynamo that powered the mine hoist and the stationary motors; the mill required 2800 horsepower.

The nearest railroad was at Milford, no coal was available closer than the Utah coal mines, and the desert had no great reserves of trees to be turned into firewood. The managers of the Bamberger-Delamar group concluded that a power plant should be built in the Meadow Valley Wash to save the cost of pumping water and hauling fuel to run the boilers at Delamar. The railroad would eventually reach the Meadow Valley Wash, but until its arrival made coal available, the boilers were wood-fired. Callaghan (1937) says the hills were stripped of trees for miles around. According to the *Lincoln County Record*, July 31, 1903, the eight boilers required 30 tons of coal daily.

By April 1902 the 500-horsepower engine had been dismantled. Soon afterward, a shipment of General Electric equipment was on its way to convert the Delamar mills to electric power.

About that time, the name of the pumping station was reportedly changed from Kershaw to Stine, in honor of Marcus Stine. The newspaper called it Bamberger, and I can't tell which name was official. Stine was a vice-president of Bamberger-Delamar, and he was with International Pump Co., which supplied pumps to the company. The name was retained as Stine siding.

A power line was run from the power station to Delamar, alongside the pipelines. I saw some of the wire and the big glass insulators, and what was left of the abandoned pipelines, in Rock Springs Canyon in 1944.

The *Lincoln County Record* reported on Aug. 14, 1903, that Frank Walker "had charge of the machinery department". The power plant had two 500-horsepower engines to run the dynamos that generated the power at 2000 volts, stepped up to 17,000 volts for transmission.

In 1904 the plant at Stine included Heine 1250-horsepower water-tube forced-draft boilers with mechanical stokers and two Reynolds-Corliss cross-compound condensing engines belted to 2300-volt dynamos. All exhaust steam was condensed in an open, fanless cooling tower and was returned to the boilers. Rube Acklin was the pumper.

The mines at Delamar produced millions of dollars in gold, but the ore couldn't last forever; in fact, it lasted only until 1909. The big mines and mills were shut down, but leasers operated on a small scale after 1909, and the big tailings pile from the Delamar mill was reworked. But the shutdown in 1909 was the end for the station at Stine.

The electrical power equipment was sold to Simon Bamberger, who used it on his Salt Lake & Ogden Railroad Co., an electric interurban railroad. According to *Mining & Scientific Press,* June 25, 1910, Fred Falkner was receiver for the Bamberger-Delamar Gold Mining Co. He was to sell the remaining mine and mill machinery about the middle of July. The power plant was being dismantled.

Frank Pace said Charlie Culverwell bought the building from Ed Dula in about 1923 and had it torn down and moved the bricks to Caliente. The foundations and part of the walls at the Stine pumping plant are still there in spite of the attacks of floodwaters.

Rock Springs station was about gone when I saw it in 1944. Findlay station had no machinery left, but the brick and concrete foundations were in fair shape. Cedar Wash station survived the scrap-iron dealers who scoured the land during World War II.

A former resident of Delamar gave this description of the final shutdown at Delamar: The fires in the boilers at the power plant at Stine were allowed to go out, and the whistle was tied down to bleed off the steam. As the pressure dropped, the generators slowed and the lights in Delamar grew dim. Finally the lights went out, the whistle was silent, and the days of Delamar were past.

THE CHEROKEE MINE

The history of the Cherokee suggests it is one of those mines that contain just enough good ore to cause people to put money into the hole without getting much of it back. Mineral occurrences were discovered by Phil Klingensmith, probably in the 1860s, and probably with the help of the Indians. (Numerous mines in the West were "discovered" when an Indian would see a white man admiring some particular type of rock and would offer to show where more of it could be found.)

A number of people from southern Utah wanted a remote location so they could keep out of sight after the Mountain Meadows Massacre in 1857, and this particular area was very remote. Brad Stuart said they built cabins or dugouts near where the Cherokee Mine was opened, and they lived there for a while. He said he had seen ruins of the cabins.

The Cherokee is several miles east of Leith siding in the Meadow Valley Wash. The Meadow Valley Wash between Leith and Carp was once called Long Valley, and in about 1900 the area that included the Cherokee appears to have been called the Long Valley district. The mine was located by Scott Allen in October 1900, according to Phil Dolan. Allen was a Cherokee; I have not seen any direct confirmation that the mine was called the Cherokee until some years later. The *Pioche Weekly Record*, Feb. 19, 1891, said John Kiernan had "large interests" in the Long Valley mines.

An item in the *Lincoln County Record* for March 7, 1902, said prospectors in the "old abandoned Long Valley Mining District" had organized a new district, the Viola, and elected Scott Allen recorder. The Viola claim was owned by John Kiernan and Scott Allen; it became the Cherokee Mine. (One of Kiernan's daughters was Viola, later Mrs. John Conaway.)

On March 20, 1902, *Mining Reporter* said the Viola claim had a 125-foot shaft with a 12-inch streak of ore that ran 115 ounces of silver per ton and 18% copper. Duffield said in 1904, "Along the route of the old wagon-road from St. George and the Virgin settlements to Pioche, whither the Mormons were wont to haul fruit and provisions to the miners, one small camp—-the Viola district, as it was called—-was started near Kiernan. A small stamp-mill was erected down in the main wash, to concentrate the high-grade sulphides. The veins occur along the contacts of different limestones, and the filling is quartz, through which are disseminated small stringers of silver sulphides (pyrargyrite), copper pyrite and occasionally some gray copper. They were proved unprofitable in the early days, affording only occasional shipments; but the best claims of the district have been held by re-location down to the present day, little or no development being done. . . ."

Dr. C.P. Harveille, general manager of the Cherokee-Nevada, expected to ship three cars of ore from Leith, according to the *Caliente Lode-Express*, July 20, 1907. John T. Hayes, a mining engineer from Las Vegas, bought the property in 1908 and set up the Cherokee Mining Co. The shaft was 200 feet deep in 1910, and two shipments were reported. Development work totaling $45,000 had been done by the end of the year, when the property was leased by a group from Utah called the Cherokee-Nevada Copper Co. The property was patented in May 1915, and a few carloads of ore were shipped during 1917, when the price of copper was high because of World War I.

In the years that followed, a variety of engineers, promoters, and owners poured money down the shaft. In the late 1930s, Roe Thomas was driving his big Packard to and from the Cherokee, stopping sometimes to visit my father. During those days of the Depression, every mine was worth another look, and he had great plans for that one. Some of those mines reopened then or later, at least for a little while, but the Cherokee seems not to have been one.

Garbled stories sometimes appeared in the newspapers, to which I would say, "Important, if true". For example, on Nov. 25, 1904, the *Lincoln County Record* ran an article "Roadbed of Gold". James Maun and Mike Smith, "a couple of prospectors from Arizona", had been traveling up the Meadow Valley Wash. They had an assay outfit with them, and they decided to take samples as they went, then run some assays. They collected about 80 samples that averaged $5.50 a ton in gold and another 40 samples that ran from a trace to $5.00 a ton. The area they sampled is not identifiable from the text, but it might have been between Pockets and Elgin. It does refer to "the old Fife millsite", a name I have not found anywhere else. Could it have been the stamp mill mentioned by Duffield?

THE BRADSHAW DISTRICT

From late 1928 to early 1931, the *Caliente Herald* had a number of items about the new Bradshaw district. On October 25, 1928, the headline was "New Mining District Struck Near Carp". John Bradshaw and Charles Culverwell had made a discovery at a site that was about 9 miles from the Cherokee and apparently about 19 miles northeast of Carp. They named the district for James Bradshaw, pioneer miner and the father of Rube and John Bradshaw.

The rocks were said to be "lime with igneous dikes". According to that report, three outcrops were found, with specimens that ran 30% lead and 29 ounces of silver per ton. The Lucky Boy prospect was identified, and it got most of the attention in later reports. An item on Dec. 6 said the owners, William and Charles Culverwell and John Bradshaw, expected it to be bonded; they could make a shipment at any time. They now reported ore that contained 60% lead, with silver "in proportion" and some visible hornsilver.

Joe Kutcher, who had been superintendent of American Clay Co., near Boyd siding, also had claims in the district. He was "a veteran mining man who has been in on every strike of importance in Nevada during the past 20 years".

On Jan. 24, 1929, the Lucky Boy was reported to have a shaft 40 feet deep. U.S. Smelting & Refining Co. sent an engineer to look at the area in March. The owners were to develop the Bradshaw mines, according to the item in the Oct. 10 paper. It said only a small amount of development work had been done, except for the Lucky Boy.

The next significant mention of the district was on March 6, 1930, when shipment of barite from the Lucky Boy was said to be a possibility; Minobras reports barite veinlets in volcanic rocks, but I doubt their commercial importance. Then the district vanished from the news, except that on Feb. 19, 1931, Joe Kutcher was working his claims. In 1933, Kutcher was back at American Clay Co., the kaolin deposit near Boyd.

The news reports gave confusing information about the location of the district. Evidently the principal route was from Carp to Tule Flat, then north to Garden Spring, then 4 miles farther to the Bradshaw area. Tschantz and Pampeyan give clues that might or might not lead anywhere. In their tabulation of principal mines in the Viola district, they list the Culverwell property, 19 miles northeast of Carp, a manganese occurrence that had been known for many years. There was no known production, they did not visit it, and the exact location was not known. It had a 10-foot shaft that was "entirely in manganese". They also list a Lucky prospect in the Viola district, containing lead, zinc, copper, and perhaps silver. However, it is only a mile or so from the Cherokee. They cite other prospects that might also fit the description of the Bradshaw.

Where the north end of Tule Flat becomes the foothills of the Clover Mountains, we knew Garden Spring, Sam's Camp, and West's Camp, in an area with many prospect pits and evidence of low-grade mineral occurrences that we took to be lead, zinc, and manganese.

Tschantz and Pampeyan also list the Wells Cargo fluorite deposit, discovered about 1957. The fluorite occurs as large replacement bodies in dark Carboniferous limestone (also see Minobras). Papke says it is 18 miles by road northeast of Carp, which puts it in the Bradshaw area. A group of 22 claims is called the Carp Mine. Various lessees operated it during 1968 to 1972. The fluorite was hauled by Wells Cargo, Inc., which he says has led to its being incorrectly called the Wells Cargo Mine.

Tingley (1992) also describes a Vigo district, an area of manganese deposits. It is east of the Cherokee area, close to the Utah state line, which seems to be too far east to take in the Bradshaw area.

PENNSYLVANIA

During his years in southeastern Nevada, Phil Klingensmith discovered the later Cherokee Mine, he started a ranch at Dutch Flat, on Clover Creek just above present Caliente, and he discovered the Pennsylvania Mine. Although the Pennsylvania probably hasn't made anybody rich, it is a respectable mine that still gets some attention now and then. The dumps and foundations are evidence that some serious mining was attempted in the old days, when some rich copper-lead ore was reported.

The Pennsylvania is up on the mountain near the head of Pennsylvania Canyon, a few miles northeast of Elgin. Klingensmith's twin sons, Phil and John, owned a sawmill on Elly Mountain, to the east, and in 1883 they owned the Pennsylvania Mine. It had a 45° inclined shaft that was 186 feet deep.

Old-timers in Caliente told me the brothers lost the mine after that, and a man named Barton staked it. He had a 5-stamp mill operating in 1886 and a nice little camp with a well-furnished bunkhouse, a boarding house, and an office. He couldn't keep the mine operating as he intended, and after about 1890 (perhaps the result of the Panic of 1893), all he could do was send a man in once a year to do the assessment work.

Heavy snows one year kept him from getting the assessment work done, and Jim Ryan and the Smith boys jumped the claim. Ryan's share was the furniture from the houses, and the Smiths got their mine back.

On Dec. 27, 1890, the *Pioche Weekly Record* reported that J. Poujade and Charles W. Roeden were suing Pat and James Ryan "to try the title to the old Klingensmith mine" in the Pennsylvania district. Poujade and Roeden lost their case in District Court in April 1891, but they said they would appeal.

Mining & Scientific Press reported on June 7, 1902, that Smith and Ryan had sold the Pennsylvania to J. Adams, of Bingham, Utah. A 10-stamp mill was to be installed. Samples from the mine ran $21 in gold, 60 ounces of silver, and 15% copper. The mine was reported in 1904 to have been optioned, probably because of the construction of the railroad through the Meadow Valley Wash. A representative of American Smelting & Refining Co. was reported in 1927 to be examining the property. In the late 1930s the property was owned mainly by Rube Bradshaw and Charles W. "Yam" Johnson, a railroad engineer in Caliente. Bradshaw owned the old Klingensmith claim, and Johnson owned adjacent property that had some gold, not found in the copper-lead ore of the Klingensmith. Tschantz and Pampeyan identify the Culverwell (Johnson) and the Pennsylvania as the mines of the Pennsylvania district.

On Oct. 25, 1934, the *Caliente Herald* reported that R.J. Bradshaw and Dana Conaway were taking out ore that ran 0.5 to 3.0 ounces of gold and 20 to 80 ounces of silver to the ton. On Sept. 19, 1940, John Bradshaw, Dana Conaway, and V.K. Mariger had made a test shipment of 6 tons of gold ore. The 8-mile road from Elgin was passable, but the road by way of Elly Spring was said to be better. Two cars of ore had been shipped by April 1941 from the South End group of claims. The paper said on Sept. 5, 1946, that a new road to Pennsylvania had been built from Eccles, and C.W. Johnston and H.H. Philips were to start shipping. (Jim Bradshaw says the only ore shipped between 1930 and 1941 was by way of Elgin.)

Early in World War II, Rube Bradshaw salvaged the trucks of the freight train that was lost at Boyd in the 1910 flood, sold them for scrap iron, and bought a cab-over-engine dump truck that he used to haul ore down from the Pennsylvania. Tingley (1984) cites a report that a Defense Minerals Exploration Administration contract had been issued for the Pennsylvania in about 1943, which is consistent with Bradshaw's work at the mine.

Tingley also reports that Bear Creek Mining Co. did some exploration in the district in the late 1960s, and other companies, including Homestake Mining Co., explored for gold. Maybe there's life in the old district yet.

TAYLOR MINE (EASTER MINE)

Taylor Mine Canyon drains eastward from the Delamar Mountains into the Meadow Valley Wash, just above Tunnel 8. About 2½ miles airline from the mouth of the canyon is the Taylor Mine, also called the Easter Mine. The mine was located in about 1906 by Joseph Taylor, Ben Henkle, and Clyde Bailey. The Easter Gold Mining Co. owned it in 1916, and Taylor was running it for the company. He had obtained equipment from the X-Ray Mine in the Highland district, near Pioche. The *Pioche Record* reported on July 16, 1910, that E.L. Godbe said, "The Easter is one of the most promising gold prospects I have ever seen. The great vein of clean quartz, in places 100 feet wide, is in porphyry. On one side of the mountain the porphyry is of a somewhat altered character, and it has eroded away, leaving the vein exposed to the depth of about 200 feet. It is at that point that the first cross-cut has been driven through the vein with remarkable results. To further prove the ore body, two more cross-cuts are being driven, and a winze sunk upon the eight-foot streak of richer ore." He said that if it fulfilled its promise, a large cyanide plant would probably be installed. The property had recently been taken under option by John R. Cook, William Lloyd, and E.A. Hodges.

It was known then as the Easter Mine, and the two names seem to have been used interchangeably. The *Caliente Herald* had news of the mine in 1930 to 1933, calling it the Easter Mine, but current maps call it the Taylor Mine. Take your choice.

Joseph Taylor, manager for the Easter Gold Mining Company, said arrangements had made for construction of a 100-ton mill at the property, according to *Salt Lake Mining Review*, Jan. 30, 1916.

A news story on Oct. 2, 1930, said T.E. Dula, the owner, was driving an exploratory tunnel after the mine had lain idle for 15 years. Later stories said the mineralized rocks of the mine were thought to be an extension of the Delamar gold-bearing formations. The gold was in veinlets of cherty quartz that cut a rhyolite ridge (Callaghan, 1937), and the vein was 3 feet wide in the stopes that were mined in 1934.

In the old days, the road from the Meadow Valley Wash to Delamar went through Taylor Mine Canyon, but the mine was not accessible through the canyon in 1930; because of the rough terrain, the road had to go in from near the Dula ranch, making about 6 miles of road that was being improved to accommodate the new activity. When completed, that 6 miles was a dugway.

In May 1931, a winze was reported to be in ore of shipping grade. By August 1933, the mine was under lease to Phil Dolan, Jim Hulse, and Jack Cole. According to Callaghan, they shipped a car of ore that ran 0.95 ounce of gold and 3.94 ounces of silver to the ton. Phil Dolan wrote to me in 1958 that the only ore shipped was three cars in 1934. (However, the *Caliente Herald* reported that Paul Shultz had shipped a fourth car in late December 1934). By the time we moved to the Elliott ranch in 1941, the mine was one more of those mines that had been worked in years past but were now idle.

MIKE'S CAVE

During the early 1930s, an old fellow and his dogs lived in the tunnel that is part of the mine workings across the creek from Caliente. The tunnel was once part of a promising gold mine, but when I lived in Caliente, we knew it as "Mike's Cave".

Andy Richard and Art Gentry found the outcrop of gold in 1902 that started the activity. Evidently they named it the Sunset Mine; the *Lincoln County Record* said on May 6, 1904, that it was "within pistol shot of the depot building". They worked it a little, then in about 1904 they sold it to the Caliente Gold Mining Company. The manager was George Fetterman, who had been at Delamar for several years. He was working the Sunset claim in April 1904, and in June he decided to put in a mill the next spring. The tunnel was 190 feet into the hill in August, and it was in good ore. (Aren't they always in good ore?)

Other properties were in the vicinity, but the stories don't describe them well enough to know how close they were to the Sunset. A news item in Sept. 1904 said that a 5-stamp mill was operating at the Hope and Jackson claims, somewhere near Caliente. Colorado parties were reported in May 1906 to be ready to put in a mill at the Blue Rock Mine, southwest of Caliente, and pipe water 3 miles to the mine. The *De Lamar Lode*, March 31, 1903, reported that a strong ledge, exposed for 700 feet and running from $8 to $28 a ton, was being opened between Antelope and Newman Canyons, about a mile from Caliente and about 6 miles south of the Chief district. This prospect was attributed to A.R. Parsons, A.J. Richard, and A.H. Gentry.

Caliente Gold Mining Company continued development, and in October 1904 they had free gold in a 40-foot drift on the Blue Bird claim. On Nov. 5, 1904, *Mining & Scientific Press* reported that the company had a 210-foot drift on a 4-foot ledge of gold that ran as high as $30 a ton. They had a crosscut running 135 feet from the 125-foot point.

The *Caliente Express* reported on Nov. 11, 1905, that L.F. Peer had discovered rich float 2 miles north of Caliente, evidently in Antelope Canyon. The Josephine Consolidated Gold Mining Co. was organized to work the property. The Little Johnnie was the best prospect; it had an orebody 5 to 50 feet wide, with assays of $20-$30 a ton. A 40-stamp mill was to be built.

David J. Cook had promising prospects adjoining the Fetterman property on the north. Fetterman had sold his holdings to C.B. Sibert (or Seibert or Siebert, depending on which newspaper story you read), and in early 1906 Sibert was sinking a shaft and planning a 50-stamp mill.

Many claims with free-milling gold ore "along the mountainside and east of the Siebert group of claims" were reported by the *Caliente Express* on Nov. 30, 1905. The Sunlight group, on the same trend as the others, was owned by Culverwell and Doyle. The Rev. Mr. Gamble and L.F. Peer owned the King Solomon, "a true fissure vein in quartzite". The Saddle Rock group, in Antelope Canyon, was owned by L.F. Peer.

A big explosion at the Sibert property occurred on Feb. 9, 1906. The story in the *Express* on Feb. 15 said that the Sibert tunnel had a lot of dynamite and equipment, and a tunnel next to it was used as a powder magazine by George Fetterman, a merchant in Caliente; on the 9th, someone detonated 3000 pounds of dynamite that was in the two tunnels. The someone was thought to have been Charles H. Roberts, a former employee who had a grudge against Sibert. Sibert's supplies and equipment were lost. The paper reported on the efforts to track Roberts down, but he had not been located by March 8, and people concluded he had been caught in the explosion and was buried in the rubble.

The *Caliente Lode-Express* said on Jan. 12, 1907, that Sibert had shipped two cars of good ore. *Mining World* reported on July 27, 1907, that the property of the Sibert Mining Company was within a mile of Caliente. A tunnel was being driven, and it had 8 feet of free-milling ore that ran $16 a ton in gold. Another story on Aug. 3, 1907, said C.B. Sibert was president and David Farnsworth was secretary-treasurer of the Caliente Gold Mining Company. The company owned four claims on which they had a 250-foot tunnel and a 60-foot tunnel. They had free-milling gold that ran $45 a ton. According to the *Caliente Lode-Express*, June 30, 1907, Sibert had "incorporated all the valuable claims between the now famous Sibert mine and Antelope Canyon".

The Rives brothers apparently bought Sibert out, and in 1908 they had a 30-foot shaft. According to *Mining Science*, Dec. 3, 1908, their vein was 600 feet from the railroad station. They cut the Fetterman workings in January 1909. One main tunnel existed in the 1940s, as well as a shaft that was said to cut the tunnel. Bill Newell told me free gold was still found sometimes on the dump.

Some distance back in the tunnel is either the shaft or a deep winze. The owners tried to keep it boarded over, but hoboes always stole the boards for firewood. A group of people was in the tunnel many years ago, when Mrs. Frank Pace's little dog ran ahead and fell into the shaft.

The shaft was timbered, with braces across the center, and she said it sounded as if the dog hit the braces. The dog was sure to be dead, but she said she would get it out, if it cost her $500.

Men brought ropes from town, and a call-boy was tied to a rope and lowered into the shaft. He found that a partial bulkhead had been put in at the 250-foot level, and a mattress dropped down the shaft had lodged on it. The dog had somehow landed on the mattress. When the boy dropped rocks down, they splashed in water below. He brought the dog up and put him on the ground, Mrs. Pace whistled, and the dog ran to her.

THE KAOLIN MINE

The canyon walls in Rainbow Canyon in the vicinity of the Elliott ranch are Tertiary rhyolite. East of the railroad, between the lower end of the Big Field and Boyd siding, one ridge contains a thick lens of clay (locally called kaolin) that was formed by hydrothermal alteration of the rhyolite. The ridge stands about 1100 feet higher than the canyon floor, and the lens is near the top of it.

The clay from the mine was sent to a loading station by a 550-foot inclined tramway on the east slope of the ridge. Then it was hauled to the railroad and loaded at a one-car spur (called Kaolin or Landis spur) near Boyd. These details are from Callaghan (1936, "Clay"). A loaded car descending the tramway pulled the empty car up; a side track in the middle allowed the cars to pass.

Harry Bennett told me the loaded car of clay would be pulled from the spur and an empty one would be spotted in its place. Harry said two railroad conductors, Nick Williams and Tom Parker, were the first owners of the mine. They sold it for $30,000 to a man who lived in the Overland Hotel, in Las Vegas. He operated the American Clay Company and shipped the clay to Burbank for use in dishware. Harry said the story was that the kaolin contained too much clay, and the finished ware soon developed check marks.

The *Las Vegas Age*, July 17, 1920, said that Nicholas E. Williams and Thomas J. Parker had sold their kaolin claims to I.R. Landis for $30,000. They had located the claims about a year earlier. Landis was said to have the contract to supply kaolin to Empire China Co., of Los Angeles.

The *Caliente News*, Dec. 23, 1920, had a story that implied that Charles Ginther and his brother owned the property. A long story, 2 weeks later, said I. Rohrer Landis was General Manager and Joe Kutcher was foreman for the American Clay Company. They expected to ship 1500 tons daily from the "kaolin banks". They were then building the camp and a railroad spur. The Empire China Co., of which Landis was General Manager, was building a factory at Burbank. The story said the research had showed "that from this china clay is now being manufactured a grade of china-ware and translucent semi-porcelain, which in compactness, strength, and whiteness, equals any of its kind heretofore produced in any part of the world". The market for the products was expected to be the restaurant and hotel trade.

Another story, on Feb. 3, 1921, said the deposits were "practically inexhaustible, totaling billions of tons", and they were "the only ores of any extent in the Americas so far discovered".

The *Pioche Record* said on July 7, 1922, that a grinding plant was to be installed so the kaolin could be cleaned and ground there. In 1922, another proposed use for the kaolin was in ceramic insulators. The *Record* said on Oct. 19, 1923, that payment of the first dividend was expected. An article on Feb. 29, 1924, referred to the grinding and washing plant in Los Angeles; the clay was to be used in firebrick and insulation. The summer of 1924 was so hot that the mine was shut down for part of August and September.

The *Caliente Herald* had numerous items about the American Clay Company from 1929 through 1933. Joe Kutcher was the superintendent until late 1930, when he went to the new Bradshaw district. Marion Sharp replaced him, then in 1933 evidently Joe Kutcher was back. The property was owned by F.E. Keeler, of Los Angeles, during these years.

On May 16, 1929, Kutcher said American Clay had "substantially" increased shipments; on June 6 he said they were shipping 4 cars a month. American Clay was making "large shipments" of china clay in August 1930; in November they were shipping to Pomona Tile Company. Nothing further was said until April 2, 1931, when Marion Sharp said the mine would resume shipping. There was no more news until July 27, 1933, when American Clay was to reopen and to start shipments soon. On Aug. 17, Joe Kutcher and Otto Olson were getting ready to reopen the mine. The American Clay Co. property was on the delinquent tax list in 1934 and 1938 and perhaps in years between.

A lens of low-grade alunite occurs less than a mile north of the "kaolin" deposit. O.M. Burt and Joe Kutcher were to open the alunite deposit, according to the *Pioche Record* on July 2, 1925. Callaghan (1936, "Alunite") says three carloads were supposedly shipped to Los Angeles to be used as fertilizer, but the date isn't given.

Joe Kutcher had other interests in clays. On March 14, 1925, the *Pioche Record* reported that Kutcher, with O.M. Burt and John Bradshaw, had found a deposit of Florida clay 4½ miles southeast of Rox and 1¼ miles from the railroad. The clay was suitable for use in roofing tiles, flower pots, and crockery.

THE CROSS AT KYLE

When we lived at Carp, I made only a few trips through the canyon between Carp and Elgin, but I remember a few scenes along that road. I remember the mouth of Cottonwood Canyon and the visible stonework of the Foreman ditch and the cross near Kyle. The first two are straightforward, but the last one eludes a clear explanation. My version includes information that Jim Bradshaw's father gave him.

The cross was a tall, wooden cross just west of the railroad, close to Kyle siding and Tunnel 4. My father told me it marked a mass grave for more than 40 Hungarians who were killed in a train wreck while the railroad was under construction. As Jim heard the story, the engine was getting low on water, so the engineer cut loose from the work train and ran to Elgin for water. When he returned, he misjudged the location of his train and ran into it, wrecking the railroad cars and killing or injuring many men. He hit the ground running and was never heard from again.

Years later, I was writing Sunday feature articles for the *Las Vegas Review Journal*, and I thought the cross would be an interesting subject. When I talked to old-timers, I was told that there were many casualties, and the survivors appeared to be looting the clothes of the dead. However, Brad Stuart said the men typically wore money belts, and the survivors were recovering the belts to send back to the families in Hungary.

It wasn't going to be much of a story, just one short paragraph. Or was it just one paragraph? I was also reading back-issues of the *Las Vegas Age*, and a note on Feb. 17, 1923, quoted a story from March 2, 1907, with the following information: " . . . a Salt Lake work train at the washout 20 miles from Caliente collided with a tie car with the result that 4 men were killed and 50 injured. The dead were all foreigners and they were buried in the Las Vegas cemetery by their friends."

If they were not buried at Kyle, the cross couldn't have marked the graves of 40 men. When I asked David Myrick if he knew anything about it, he found a story in the *Reno Evening Gazette*, dated March 1, 1907, that said a construction train had been in a bad wreck at Leith, and 42 Greeks were hurt.

Leith is 4 miles from Kyle, so an error in location is reasonable. The construction crews had many Hungarian laborers, and the cooks were Greek. I remember seeing the stone ovens that the cooks had built along the railroad.

The story isn't closed yet. All I know for sure is that the cross was there in the 1930s.

TULE FLAT

Tule Flat, or Tule Desert, if you prefer, is a large, open valley that lies east of the Meadow Valley Wash and drains generally to the south and southeast from the Clover Mountains. The outlet is through Toquop Wash and Beaver Dam Wash into the Virgin River near Littlefield, Arizona. Tule Spring is in the central part of the flat, close to a low, rounded hill that is part of the Tule Springs Hills.

Hafen & Frei Brothers and George Lytle were among the cattlemen who ran cattle on Tule Flat. Lytle, in "Memories", makes several references to Tule Flat when he ran cattle there.

The original road from Carp to U.S. Highway 91 on Mormon Mesa was the one mentioned earlier, going eastward up a dry wash from near present Lyman Crossing and entering Tule Flat. It joined a road that continued north to the Cherokee Mine, Sam's Camp, Garden Spring, and elsewhere. The road south through Tule Flat dropped into Toquop Wash, crossed a small divide at the east end of the Mormon Mountains, crossed Gourd Spring Wash, and joined Highway 91 (known as the Arrowhead Trail before about 1930).

A more direct route was built by the Civilian Conservation Corps. It went up the hill past the Carp store and post office then across the hills to connect with the old road in Tule Flat. When my wife and I went down the Meadow Valley Wash in 1972, we found that the "old" road to Tule Flat was the current road, and the one past the Carp store was apparently not passable.

In hot weather in June 1938, Elmer Breckinridge was driving to Carp, with 14-year-old Roy Burgess, when the car broke down on Tule Flat. He used up their water filling the radiator and trying to get the engine started. When he couldn't get going, they started on foot for Carp. Elmer was 71 years old, but the boy gave out first, after about 10 miles. Elmer missed the road fork that would have brought him in at the Carp store, and instead he came in at the Hulse ranch, which meant he walked about 14 miles after he left the boy.

Mr. Hulse rode an old grey mule that seldom moved faster than a walk. This time Mr. Hulse applied all the persuasion he could; he told us, "Mule must have thought there was a war on". Our place was the closest one that was inhabited, so he brought word to us. Ashley Rice, the representative for the W.T. Rawleigh Company, was at Carp, and he and my father left at once to find the boy. The *Caliente Herald* on June 18, 1936, said, "The boy had become delirous from the heat and lack of water and had wandered off the road. Mr. Rice tracked the boy afoot for some twenty miles before coming upon him at 3 p.m. Friday afternoon about a mile off the road and about six miles from where he had been left by Breckinridge. The boy was completely exhausted and had wandered around almost continuously, part of the time bare footed, believing he was on the road all the time."

My father and Ashley Rice said the boy had gone in circles sometimes, and finally his tracks went right through clumps of brush rather than around them. They found him lying dazed in the shade of some brush, and my father believed he would have died there.

Kids are not known for having good sense, and I was like the rest. When I was about 8 or 10 years old, my father decided to trail some cattle to Tule Flat, and he put all but one of the canteens of water on my saddle, because he would be doing a lot of riding but I would just keep the herd moving. While I was by myself, I concluded that if I drank all the water I could, I wouldn't need as much as the day went on.

It was a long, thirsty day, although not really dangerous. When we came back, he rode on ahead when the creek came in sight, filled a canteen, and came back with some of that delicious, warm creek water.

Tule Spring was the center of activity in Tule Flat. Bands of sheep grazed on the flat in some years, and I remember stopping at Tule Spring to watch the shearing in progress. I think Hafen & Frei Brothers filed on Tule Spring. For a year or two just before World War II, a Mr. Bush tried dry farming on Tule Flat. He had seen rye growing in other dry areas, and he thought it could be done there. Not a chance.

Toquop Wash had a road of sorts, and if it was passable, it made a shortcut to Beaver Dam Wash and Littlefield. Ed and Jed Terry had farms in Beaver Dam Wash, with an orchard. Jed brought a load of fruit to Carp every fall, and I think he used that road.

A family from the Littlefield area made a trip to Carp one year, traveling by covered wagon up Toquop Wash and across Tule Flat. I was a little kid, and I was fascinated by that wagon parked in our yard.

Where the county road crossed washes such as Gourd Spring Wash, we sometimes had to rebuild the road after a flash flood.

Toquop Wash had a nasty little pitch where the road went up the south side, and my father lost a truckload of steers there. He had hired Landon Frei to haul the steers from Carp, and as the truck started up that pitch, the steers surged to the back. The truck was overbalanced, and the front end went up in the air. The tailgate got low enough that the steers jumped out the back. My father had to climb out on the front bumper and bounce on it to get the front end of the truck back down.

THE RUCKERS

Headline on page 1 of the *Caliente Herald* on June 25, 1931: CATTLE RUSTLING BAND CAUGHT BY CULVERWELL.

The story begins in Colorado in 1907. Wilma Bankston sets the stage in "Where Eagles Winter", a history of the Disappointment Valley of Dolores County, Colorado. She tells of a Rucker family that included brothers Elbert, Frank, and Oscar, who were accused in July 1907 of horse thievery; Oscar and Elbert fled to Arizona. Her story ends there, and we shift to Lincoln County, Nevada, 18 years later, which brings us to the headline.

Charles Walsh remembers that when Oscar and Frank Rucker and their brother-in-law Jerry Seaman showed up at Carp about 1929, they had a contract with a pet-food company to ship horses to be killed for dog and cat food. They rounded up mustangs from the range and shipped them by rail from Carp. The loading chute was at the west end of the siding.

My father knew nothing about the episode in Disappointment Valley. He was favorably impressed by the Ruckers, and he loaned them some camp equipment and helped them out. Stories in the *Caliente Herald* on June 25, July 9, Aug. 27, and Sept. 3, 1931, and the minutes of the trial, tell the outcome.

According to the lead paragraph of the story on June 25, "A band of rustlers, which officers declare has operated successfully at intervals throughout the past two years, is believed to have been broken up during the past week as a result of the arrest of the alleged marauders by Sheriff Chas. Culverwell, veteran Lincoln county police officer". At least 50 head of cattle had been killed and butchered in that area during the previous 2 years. Meat was in great demand to feed the large number of men who were working on the construction of Hoover Dam.

William T. Stewart, Jr., of Pahranagat Valley, brought about the downfall of the Rucker gang. He was riding near Chalk Spring, in Sand Spring Valley, on the border between Lincoln and Nye Counties, about 145 miles north of Las Vegas, when he found where two calves and a heifer had been shot and butchered. He returned at once to Alamo and called Sheriff Culverwell. The two of them went to the scene to gather evidence.

An automobile with unusual tire tracks had left the scene, and they followed it all the way to Las Vegas. Along the way, they found where five other cattle had been killed.

When they got to Las Vegas, the sheriff and Stewart began checking the butcher shops. When they got to the Nevada Meat Market, Stewart found in the ice box two calves that he identified as his property. Mark Bleak, the owner of the meat market, said he had received the two animals from Oscar Rucker. Sheriff Culverwell waited at the market, and when Rucker came in to get his money, the sheriff arrested him. Rucker claimed he had killed the calves at their ranch, 27 miles from Las Vegas. Culverwell offered to let Rucker show him the exact spot, but Rucker allowed that he would talk to an attorney instead.

Culverwell soon arrested Jerry Seaman at the Bill Morgan ranch at the foot of Charleston Mountain. Seaman had gone there to hide when he heard of Oscar's arrest; he claimed he was in Los Angeles when the calves were killed.

Frank Rucker was arrested on June 24 at Willow Springs Wash, near the McGriff ranch (evidently near Las Vegas). With that, Sheriff Culverwell said he had broken up "the worst gang of rustlers that ever infested southern Nevada".

The Ruckers and Jerry Seaman were bound over to district court at the preliminary hearing in Caliente on July 7. They were charged with stealing two calves from Stewart and a heifer from John Wright, another rancher of the Pahranagat Valley. E.C.D. Marriage was the Justice of the Peace, Frank E. Wadsworth, the District Attorney, represented the State, and Julian Thruston presented the defense. Bail was set at $1000 for each defendant. My father helped put up the bail, but after the trial was over, he said, "I guess those boys did it, after all". Two of his Dutch ovens were in their car, and he never did get them back.

Besides Stewart and Wright, the prosecution called R.R. Smith, a mining man who was working at White Blotch Spring, near Chalk Spring. He said the Ruckers and Seaman visited him twice, at about the time of the alleged theft, and they camped overnight at his camp on June 11. He identified Seaman's Willys Knight roadster with the rumble seat; its Lee tires matched the tracks that the sheriff had followed to Las Vegas.

The case of the State of Nevada vs Oscar Rucker, Frank Rucker, and Jerry Seaman, Case No. 314-B, went to trial on Aug. 25, Hon. William E. Orr, District Judge, presiding. Wadsworth and Thruston were the attorneys. The jurors were L.C. Denton, proprietor of the Rex Theater in Caliente; Herbert Gerson, a carpenter from Pioche; S.A. Hollinger, a rancher from Ursine; Alva Ewing, a carpenter from Pioche; George W. Thiriot, a farmer from Hiko; Pete Sadovich, a miner from Pioche; Leo H. Hall, a miner from Pioche; H.M. Fieldson, a machinist from Caliente; Fernard Kuffer, a rancher from Hiko; Mell Mathews, a musician from Panaca; Amos Phillips, a farmer from Panaca; and William Hooper, a laborer from Alamo. Herbert Gerson was Foreman of the jury.

The witnesses for the prosecution were W.T. Stewart, Jr., Charles Culverwell, R.R. Smith, Mark Bleak, Alvin Bleak, E.C.D. Marriage, Roy Neagle, John Wright, Dan Stewart, Zeb Ray, and Raymond Bleak. The witnesses for the defense were Mrs. Ada Roe, Mrs. Laura Reyes, Clarence Wilson, William Brown, Ernest Nickols, Ed Imus, Wallace Ballor, Mrs. D.B. McKinney, George Tennille, and Richard Tennille.

The items entered as evidence were an automobile tire, one pair of shoes, the calf's hide, the calf's head, a strip of hide taken by the sheriff, a strip of hide taken by witness Stewart, the four feet and legs of the calf, and the hide of the brockle-faced calf.

William Stewart testified that he found where the animals had been butchered and that he went with Sheriff Culverwell to Las Vegas. He said also that three sets of footprints were found at the scene of the crime, and one set was made by narrow-toed English shoes with a worn hole in the sole; the tracks matched those of shoes taken from Frank Rucker.

The sheriff and the attorneys wanted to have the hide of one animal introduced into court, but according to the *Herald*, ". . . the Hattie T calf's hide with its far reaching message seldom managed to get into the court. . . "

Mark Bleak said he had found that Rucker had apparently cut some small strips of hide from a carcass in his ice box, presumably to prevent identification. Roy Neagle, Bleak's butcher, said the calves were in good condition when brought in, and they could have been brought from 200 miles away. He said also the Willys Knight had plenty of room for the animals.

Zeb Ray and Pat Gallagher testified that Oscar Rucker and Jerry Seaman had stayed at Smith's camp on June 11, but they believed the third man was Clarence Wilson. Eight other witnesses testified that Frank Rucker was in Las Vegas, not at White Blotch Spring, on June 11; they said Clarence Wilson was the third man.

Dick and George Tennille testified that they had lived at Wickieup, Arizona, and the Ruckers "bore a good character" there. The case went to the jury soon after 7:30 pm, Aug. 28. The jury announced at 1:15 am, Aug. 29, that they had reached a verdict. They found Oscar Rucker and Jerry Seaman guilty and Frank Rucker not guilty of the crime of Grand Larceny. They had been tried on the charge of killing two animals, evidently the two that belonged to Stewart; the second charge was the killing of one animal, evidently the one belonging to Wright, but the charge was dismissed on the basis of insufficient evidence.

Oscar Rucker and Jerry Seaman were sentenced to serve 1 to 14 years in the State Prison at Carson City. Sentencing had been ordered for Sept. 2., but the defendants agreed to allow the order to be vacated and the judgment pronounced as soon as the verdict was read.

As a boy, I knew something about the Rucker brothers, but not much. My impression was that they were acquitted. Finally, in 1958, I began trying to find out more about the case. The County Clerk of Lincoln County, in Pioche, said no transcript of the trial was available, but I could get a copy of the minutes. When the copy arrived, I realized that about all I remembered correctly was the names of the Ruckers. No other sources of information were available to me, and I let the subject ride.

In November 1988, my wife and I attended a book-signing party in Grand Junction, and I got a copy of "Where Eagles Winter". When I read the passage about the Ruckers in Disappointment Valley, I came alive. Could they be the same Ruckers?

I wrote to Wilma Bankston, and she gave me the address of Mr. & Mrs. Loren Rucker; he is a nephew of Oscar Rucker. Loren and Alice had been trying to find out more about the rustling episode in Nevada, and I had been trying to get access to the *Caliente Herald* for the 1920s and later years. Alice gave me the address of the Nevada State Archives, and they have the *Herald* on microfilm. I began borrowing reels of microfilm through our public library in Grand Junction, and that's how I found the articles about the case.

SHOOT-OUT AT GALT

"OFFICERS HAVE GUN DUEL WITH MEXICAN BANDITS NEAR GALT"; that was a headline in the *Pioche Record* on April 12, 1924. Here is the story as it appeared:

The last report of the two Mexicans who for several days have created a reign of terror along the Union Pacific right of way was turned in by a section boss near Galt, of whom they demanded food and, it is believed that they are still in this neighborhood.

The bandits' first holdup was reported by J.J. Grandin, lineman for the Union Pacific railroad who had stopped his motor car and was working in the signal box when two Mexicans approached him one of whom thrust a Luger pistol in his face and commanded him to hold up his hands. They then took his watch and chain and disappeared down the track. Mr. Grandin reported the robbery to a section foreman at Elgin who after inspecting the section house found that he also had been robbed. Sheriff Culverwell was notified and left immediately on a helper for Elgin with Deputy Sheriff Harrington, train No. 3 having been held at that place. Leaving the train near Rappelje, Sheriff Culverwell and Harrington separated. Harrington using the track motor and Culverwell on foot was searching for footprints in the likely places, after a short time Culverwell saw two men coming down a wash toward the tracks and on seeing him they started to run up the side of the canyon paying no attention to his shouts and when nearing the top of the rim of the canyon, Culverwell shot ahead of the men who immediately dropped in the brush and commenced shooting at the Sheriff, with bullets whistling around, Culverwell also dropped and fired about 15 shots at the hidden Mexicans, none of which apparently took effect.

After scouting around Sheriff Culverwell got a horse at a near by cattle station and again made after the Mexicans and within a few minutes was again under fire from the top of the canyon the bullets passing between the horse's head and his body as he rode up the draw, but by this time the sun was almost down in the west and Culverwell was forced to give up the hunt.

The next morning, after sleeping out in the brush, Sheriff Culverwell was forced to come back to Caliente on account of the special session of court in Pioche and a posse composed of Special Officer Hedges and Deputies Harrington and Tracy made every effort to pick up the trail of the bandits, however, they are still at large.

Here is another little episode that involved law-enforcement and Galt: The *Lincoln County Record* reported on Sept. 16, 1926, that Robert Alvarado broke into the section house at Galt on Sept. 8 and stole some clothes and money. He was caught by deputy sheriff A.L. Hilburn and railroad officer E.F. Sherwood. A later issue said he was tried in Pioche and received a sentence of 1 to 5 years.

THE STOLEN POWER LINE

Another law-enforcement story, about the theft of power line in Lincoln County, was in the *Herald* on April 21, 1938. The theft was uncovered when Dennis Moon, George Pickert, and Clarence Campbell delivered about 2 tons of 7-strand copper wire to a junk yard in Salt Lake City. The operators of the junk yard told the men the sale would have to be cleared through the sheriff's office, and the men left and were not seen in those parts again. Sheriff Tennille was notified, and during the week before April 21, Moon was arrested in Pioche and Pickert and Campbell were arrested in Las Vegas.

A power line had been built to the Gold Springs district, near the Nevada-Utah state line, but the power had not been turned on. The three men cut the line, hitched a truck to the wire, and pulled down about 3 miles of wire. They pulled down insulators and cross-arms, and even some poles came down. They cached about 500 pounds of wire near the scene, took 900 pounds to Las Vegas, and took the rest to Salt Lake City.

When my father told me about that episode, he laughed at the way it turned out, and now that I have read the newspaper story, I laugh at it, too.

"BUCK" TENNILLE

Some names from my years in Lincoln County are high on my list of names of people who are worthy role models, and the name "Buck" Tennille is one of them. My regard for Buck is derived largely from my father's regard, and in my interviewing people and digging in the archives, I have never found anything to lead me to question that opinion.

The following part of the story appeared in the *Caliente Herald* on May 14, 1931, and it is a good place to start:

The award of the distinguished service medal to J.B. Tennille of Caliente for "extraordinary heroism" recently announced by the War Department has a thrilling story back of it. On September 29th, 1918, Tennille then a corporal in the Ninety-First Division of the American army took part in an attack on a sector of the German front, the first advance in which Tennille took part was unsuccessful the Germans had planted a number of Machine gun nests on a small hill commanding the American advance and losses were so heavy that the retreat was ordered, but the Ninety First was determined to win that salient and the commanding officer again sent the boys forward in waves to take the strategic position from the Germans. Corporal Tennille, crouching low with the first wave to go over reached the German trenches, his buddies shot down on all sides, he jumped into an enemy trench and found to his surprise that the trench was deserted, following down the connecting trench system through a low ravine he was able to flank the system of machine gun nests and creeping upon the first nest completely surprised six Germans whom he took prisoners, the silencing of this nest led to the capture of the hill in a few minutes and the saving of hundreds of American soldiers from death. Corporal Tennille said, "it was just luck" but the United States Government thought otherwise and after the citations had been brought to the attention of the Department by Harley Woodworth, service officer of the Lincoln County Post No. 23 of The American Legion, the "extraordinary heroism" of "Buck" Tennille was suitably rewarded.

Another part was described in A.E. Cahlan's column "From Where I Sit", in the *Las Vegas Evening Review-Journal*, Feb. 1, 1938:

Back in the halcyon days of 1917, two young men left a Nevada mining town for Camp Lewis. They had been friends for years. They became buddies in training camp and that friendship deepened to an abiding love, built upon the association and comradeship of war time service.

Together these two men went across to face the enemy in France. Together they went into the front line trenches and together they went over the top into that No Man's Land from whence many an American soldier never returned. On one occasion, one of these two did NOT return and his buddy, true to the loyalty of deep friendship, went out into the darkness to determine his fate.

With shells screaming overhead, and the staccato notes of machine guns splitting the silence of the night, this doughboy searched the shell-holes for his buddy, finally found him lying there wounded, and brought him back to safety, thus saving his life that he might return once more to his home and the loved ones he left behind.

The other day in the little courtroom in the ancient courthouse at Pioche these two men stood side by side. The friendship of world war days had continued down through the years as both entered the ranks of public service and were honored by their fellows by election to important public office.

The scene was the conclusion of a grand jury session which resulted in the indictment of one on charges of embezzling the funds of his office. He was the one whose life had been saved on that dark night so many years ago, and it became the duty of the one who had willingly risked death to bring him back from that shell-hole in France to take him into custody as his prisoner.

It was a touching scene. Tears streamed down the cheeks of the officer, who was Sheriff Jas. B. "Buck" Tennille of Lincoln County, as he heard the judge commit his buddy, Earl L. Mathews, former assessor of the same county, to his care to be brought back in court when called to trial for the offense charged by the grand jury.

There were few dry eyes in the little courtroom as the full significance of the drama there being enacted dawned on those in attendance, and old-time court attaches, accustomed to usual court scenes through years of experience could be seen blowing their noses suspiciously.

As the two left the courtroom, a pin could have been heard had it dropped to the floor. There wasn't a sound.

The friendship continues—it isn't the kind that ever dies, no matter what the test. But the circumstances are materially altered from the night it reached magnificent heights on the battlefields of France.

As I recall, Earl Mathews had been gassed while he was in France, and his health was not good. The *Herald* said on May 19, 1938, that he had been released from prison on a conditional pardon so he could be admitted to the veteran's hospital in San Francisco; they would not accept a prisoner. A week later, on May 26, the paper said he had been admitted to the hospital and was near death; however, he survived until Nov. 23, 1941. A sad ending to a sad story.

THE WINTER OF '37

My personal experience with the winter weather in January 1937 has already been described. Here is how some other people were affected, as related in the *Caliente Herald* during that month.

The headline on Jan. 7 was "Sub-Zero Weather Broken By Heavy Snowfall Tuesday". Temperatures of -14° to -36° had been reported from Caliente to Spring Valley. However, a snow storm that started on the night of Jan. 5 had left 9 inches of snow at Caliente, and now the cold weather had abated.

On Jan. 14, the *Herald* ran a story under the headline "One Dead And Three Sick In Groom Party". The story was picked up from the *Las Vegas Review Journal*, dated Jan. 12. A search party had been looking for five people who had not been heard from since Dec. 19 and whose car had been found the day before, abandoned in the snow on "the old Wahmonie highway", southwest of Groom. A search plane had been directed by Lee Prettyman to the vicinity of the Prettyman Mine the day before, with no results. Then he realized that they had not looked at the Kelly Mine, the closest one to the stalled car, and when they flew over the mine, they saw in the snow on top of a building and on the ground in front of the building the message "Help! One Dead. Three Sick. Need Medical Aid. Prettyman Party."

The five missing people were Mrs. Lee Prettyman, Mr. and Mrs. James Poe, Fred Miller, and Doris Dunn. A Mr. and Mrs. Smith also lived at the Kelly Mine, about 15 miles southwest of Groom and 20 miles south of the Prettyman property.

As soon as the searchers got back to Las Vegas, they notified Deputy Sheriff Frank Wait; he sent Ray Griffith and Dr. Roy W. Martin to accompany the party led by Sheriff M.E. Ward. They left Las Vegas at 3:00 am, hoping to reach the stranded party by nightfall. Four CCC boys took a bulldozer to assist in the search.

Lee Prettyman had left the Prettyman Mine, and when he failed to return, the group started for Las Vegas on Dec. 27. Their car stalled about 20 miles from the Kelly Mine, and Fred Miller volunteered to walk to the Kelly Mine for help. If he did not return in 2 days, Poe was to go for help. Poe left on Jan. 2 and reached the mine after 22 hours. He and Mr. Smith returned to the car on Jan. 4 and brought the others to the mine.

Sheriff Ward's party reached the Kelly Mine and rescued Mrs. Prettyman, the Poes, and Doris Dunn. Fred Miller was not there.

Other search parties had left Caliente to look for Mrs. Charles Hannis and her daughter Helen, the Smiths, Bill Turpin, R.G. McCubrey, and Ed Lane. Lee Jennings and Rico Huerta had left to take food and supplies to Mrs. Hannis and her daughter at the Hannis Mine, but the rescue party was stranded; they were found by another rescue party about 25 miles west of Crystal Springs.

W.L. Keele and Marion Coyle had left for the Hannis Mine on Jan. 13, but when they were 7 miles from the mine, their car broke down. They walked to the mine, in sub-zero temperatures and through deep show, each man carrying 30 pounds of provisions. A party organized by Sheriff J.B. Tennille to search for Keele and Coyle found them at the Hannis Mine. The party went on to Groom to look for Ed Lane. He was safe and had fuel and supplies to last several weeks, so he stayed there.

But Fred Miller was not safe. The sheriff's party found his frozen body at Groom.

At that same time, Bill Horn and Wm. Fraser had left Delamar to reach Willow Spring, about 12 miles away, where Bill Ivy was operating the pump station for the Caliente Cyaniding Co. mill at Delamar. They got to within about 6 miles of the camp and walked the rest of the way, but they could not return with Ivy. They returned to Delamar and went to Elgin. They got a team and wagon there and bucked snow for 13 hours to reach the camp with the horses and the front wheels of the wagon. They made a platform on the two wheels, put Ivy on it, and returned to Elgin and put him on a train to Caliente.

When I hear people wishing for a return to the "good old days", I think of things like that from the good old days, and I'm glad not to go back.

Oose.

Delamar assay office.

NOTES

ACKNOWLEDGEMENTS & CREDITS

Permission to quote from or use material from the following published sources is gratefully acknowledged: Connie Simkins, many long and short quotations from the Caliente Herald, the Lincoln County Record, and the Pioche Record; Walker D. Wyman, the Harold Bryant cartoon from "The Wild Horse of the West", Caxton Printers, 1945; and Thomas Mitchell for material quoted from the Las Vegas Review-Journal, including these articles I wrote in 1959: "Days When Carp Was Busy RR Stop Recalled", Aug. 16; "Engineer's Fight With Flood Told", Nov. 15; "Famous 1910 Flood Taught Railroaders That Indians Knew More Than Surveyors", July 19; "It's Cloudburst Season Again — Writer Recalls Some Dillies in Other Years", July 26; "Old Meadow Valley Wash Cross Puzzles Nevada Man", Oct. 11.

Photographs are attributed if I know the source. The rest are from our family files, which includes photos from unknown sources.

One special credit is in order. The manuscript of this book was in progress when Marjorie and I were married, and for all those years, it was "Walter's book". Now the real world has caught up with us, and she has become involved in editing, checking, questioning, and writing, so it is "our book". Even though I am the author of record, I credit her with making it better than it would have been.

A book might be accurate, interesting, thorough, and expertly written, but if it isn't pleasant to see and to read, it's a failure. Years of work may go into the manuscript, and then sometimes it all comes to naught at the very end, in the production of the book. I have been fortunate in having Kitty Nicholason as a typesetter who is also a first-class designer and adviser in style, format, and layout, and is a friend besides.

The following people provided information by interview or by correspondence (some of the information dating from the 1950s).

Bill Acklin
Gene Anderson
Tom Anderson
Susan Atkinson
Clinton and Sylvia
    Averett
Ross Barclay
Harry Bennett
Don and Barbara
    Bradshaw
Jim Bradshaw
Lewis Bradshaw
John Bromley
Melvin Bunker
Anona Cavner
Paul Christensen
Frank Cornelius
Charles Culverwell
Eugene Cunningham

Geneve Conaway
    DeLauer
Thomas Dixon
Philip Dolan
Press and Katharine
    Duffin
Marion Earl
Robert O. Gibson
Tom Henrie
Dale V. Hunt
William Kratville
Nell Murbarger
Bill Newell
J.H. and Wanda
    Nicolaides
Frank and Vilate Pace
Stanley Paher
Earl Pampeyan
Fay Perkins

John Perkins
R.F. "Chick" Perkins
Don and Dorothy
    Phillips
Will Pratt
Dorothea Rowe
Mary Ellen Sadovich
Trent Shaskan
Rae Tennille Smalley
Helen Dula Smith
Willard and Florence
    Smith
Brad Stuart
Lavette Tennille
Leroy Thacker
Charles and Josephine
    Walsh
Art Wengert
Sam Wengert

POPULATION TRENDS

This table gives the numbers of registered voters as published in the Pioche or Caliente newspapers. Some years didn't have the list for the General Election, and generally (as shown for the two elections in 1926) some voters didn't register for the Primary Election. These numbers should be taken as reasonable estimates, because some duplication can occur. For example, some Henries were registered at both Carp and Elgin in 1930 through 1936, and Clarence Mabey was registered both places in 1920. The registration list for Carp apparently includes voters at Leith, and I don't know the names well enough to separate them. Anybody who lived above Elgin was registered in Caliente.

YEAR	ELECTION	PRECINCT		YEAR	ELECTION	PRECINCT	
		Carp	Elgin			Carp	Elgin
1920	Primary	11	21	1938	General	32	39
1922	Primary	26	29	1940	General	26	29
1924	Primary	28	26	1942	General	26	27
1926	Primary	19	23	1944	General	36	28
1926	General	29	27	1946	General	20	22
1928	General	24	28	1948	General	13	14
1930	General	40	54	1950	Primary	15	14
1932	General	54	47	1952	General	17	11
1934	General	46	41	1954	General	19	10
1936	General	42	29	1956	General	25	13

So many men were at work on the railroad tunnel concreting project that Tunnel Precinct was set up for 1928 and 1930; the lists of voters for the General Elections had 85 and 110 people, respectively. Some of the names would have been in other precincts in other years; for example, Frank and Ida Hardy lived at Carp, but they were registered in Tunnel Precinct.

The original Census records for 1920, which have recently become available, list Elgin precinct, but some of the names are Carp people. The Census includes everyone, adults and children, and for 1920 the count was 215 in the precinct; I recognize 29 names as having been Carp residents, which leaves possibly 186 at Elgin. The Census data for later years give only the total count for Lincoln County.

BIBLIOGRAPHY

Anonymous, "Nevada, A Guide to the Silver State", American Guide Series, Binfords & Mort, 1957.

Ashbaugh, Don, "Nevada's Turbulent Yesterday", Westernlore Press, 1963.

Averett, Walter R., "Directory of Southern Nevada Place-Names", published by the author, 1962.

Bankston, Wilma Crisp, "Where Eagles Winter", published by the author, 1987.

Bradshaw, Hazel, "Under Dixie Sun", Washington County Daughters of Utah Pioneers, 1950.

Brooks, Juanita, "The Mountain Meadows Massacre", University of Oklahoma Press, 1962.

_____, "John D. Lee", The Arthur H. Clark Co., 1973.

Brundy, Clyde M., "The Remote and the Remembered", *Nevada Highways and Parks*, Fall 1971. (Also personal communication.)

Callaghan, Eugene, "Alunite", *in* D.F. Hewett and others, "Mineral Resources of the Region Around Boulder Dam", U.S. Geological Survey Bulletin 871, 1936.

_____, "Clay", *in* D.F. Hewett and others, "Mineral Resources of the Region Around Boulder Dam", U.S. Geological Survey Bulletin 871, 1936.

——, "Geology of the Delamar District, Lincoln County, Nevada", Nevada State Bureau of Mines Bulletin 5, 1937.

Condie, Le Roy, "Little Mormon Cowboy Goes to Tuweep", published by the author, 1984.

Cox, Nellie, "The Arizona Strip - A Harsh Land and Proud", Cox Printing Co., 1982.

Denton, Hazel B., "Lincoln County's New Look", *Nevada Highways and Parks*, Vol. XVII, No. 1, 1957.

Denton, Hazel Baker, "Caliente Once Upon a Time", *Caliente Herald*, July 12 through Oct. 4, 1945.

Dougherty, Samuel A., "Call the Big Hook", Golden West Books, 1984.

Duffield, M.S., "The Outlook for Mining in the New Territory Opened Up by the San Pedro, Los Angeles & Salt Lake Railroad - II", Engineering and Mining Journal, Jan. 28, 1904.

Edwards, Elbert B., "Clover Valley", *in* Ruth Lee and Sylvia Wadsworth, "A Century in Meadow Valley, 1864-1964", Panaca Centennial Committee, 1966.

Escobar, Corinne, "Here to Stay; The Mexican Identity of Moapa Valley, Nevada", Nevada Historical Society Quarterly, Vol. 36, No. 2, Summer 1993, pp. 71-89.

Gamett, James, and Stanley W. Paher, "Nevada Post Offices, An Illustrated History", Nevada Publications, 1983.

Gilpin, Laura, "The Enduring Navaho", Univ. Texas Press, 1968.

Hadley, Diana, Richard V.N. Ahlstrom, and Scott Mills, "El Rio Bonito: An Ethnoecological Study of the Bonita Creek Watershed, Southeastern Arizona", Arizona State Office of the Bureau of Land Management, Cultural Resource Series No. 8, Sept. 1993.

Interstate Commerce Commission, "Investigation No. 2618, The Union Pacific Railroad Company Report *in re* Accident at Moapa, Nev., on August 20, 1942". Report dated Oct. 24, 1942.

Jaeger, Edmund C., "The California Deserts", Stanford Univ. Press, 4th ed, 1965.

Kratville, Wm. W., "Steam Steel & Limiteds", published by the author, 1962.

Kratville, William, and Harold E. Ranks, "Motive Power of the Union Pacific", Barnhart Press, 1960.

Lanner, Ronald M., "Trees of the Great Basin, A Natural History", University of Nevada Press, 1984.

Lingenfelter, Richard E., "Death Valley & The Amargosa, A Land of Illusion", University of California Press, 1986.

Lingenfelter, Richard E., and Karen Rix Gash, "The Newspapers of Nevada", University of Nevada Press, 1984.

Lytle, Geo. P., "Memories", Washington County News, St. George, Utah, 1981.

Martin, Lou, "Lost Freight Train", *Railroad Magazine*, Vol. 33, No. 1, Dec. 1942.

Mathews, Charles P., "Early Ranching and Old Time Dances", in Ruth Lee and Sylvia Wadsworth, "A Century in Meadow Valley, 1864-1964", Panaca Centennial Committee, 1966.

Minobras, "Nevada Industrial Minerals", 1973.

Mozingo, Hugh, "Shrubs of the Great Basin, A Natural History", University of Nevada Press, 1987.

Myrick, David F., "Railroads of Nevada and Eastern California", Howell-North Books, 1962, Vol. 2.

Papke, Keith G., "Fluorspar in Nevada", Nevada Bureau of Mines and Geology, Bulletin 93, 1979.

Perkins, George E., "Pioneers of the Western Desert", Wetzel Publishing Co., 1947.

Shriver, Anne, "Jackrabbit Missionary", Western Printing Publishing Co., 1968.

Signor, John R., "The Los Angeles and Salt Lake Railroad Company", Golden West Books, 1988.

Spurr, Josiah E., "Descriptive Geology of Nevada South of the Fortieth Parallel and Adjacent Portions of California", U.S. Geological Survey Bulletin 208, 1903.

State of Nevada, Eighth Judicial District Court of, In and For the County of Lincoln, minutes of trial, The State of Nevada, Plaintiff, vs. Oscar Rucker, Jerry Seaman, and Frank Rucker, Defendants, No. 314-B, convened August 25, 1931.

Stebbins, Robert C., "Western Reptiles and Amphibians", Peterson Field Guide, Houghton Mifflin, 2nd ed., 1985.

Teale, Edwin Way, "Wandering Through Winter", Dodd, Mead & Co., 1965.

"The Encyclopedia Americana", Americana Corporation, Vol. 20, p. 214, 1954

Tingley, Joseph V., "A Mineral Inventory of the Caliente Resource Area, Caliente District, Lincoln County, Nevada", Nevada Bureau of Mines and Geology, Open-File Report 84-1, 1984.

——, "Mining Districts of Nevada", Nevada Bureau of Mines and Geology, Report 47, 1992.

Truett, Velma Stevens, "On The Hoof In Nevada", Hall, 1950.

Tschanz, C.M., and Pampeyan, Earl H., "Geology and Mineral Deposits of Lincoln County, Nevada", Nevada Bureau of Mines Bulletin 73, 1970.

Union Pacific Railroad, track diagrams between Byron, Nevada, and Modena, Utah.

U.S. Census Bureau, 1920 Census report, including Lincoln County.

Walsh Charles H., "Historic Railroad Well", *Water Well Journal*, July 1992.

Wooten, H.H., "The Land Utilization Program, 1934 to 1964", U.S. Department of Agriculture, Economic Research Service, Agricultural Economic Report No. 85, n.d.

Wyman, Walker D., "The Wild Horse of the West", Caxton Printers, 1945.

Zwinger, Ann Haymond, "The Mysterious Lands", E.P. Dutton, 1989.

INDEX

Primrose (*Oenothera* species), birdcage, 81; evening, 81
Prince, Lillian, 94
Public Works Administration, 68
Pumping plant, Carp, 51,**54**,58,59,**59;** Dry Lake, 58; Elgin, 48; Moapa, 58
Pump Station, 104
Puncture vine (*Terrestris tribulus*), 77
Purple sage, 24,80; (*Salvia dorrii*), 80

Rabbit brush (*Chrysothamnus nauseosus*), 68
Rag dump, 16,51
Railroads: Atchison, Topeka & Santa Fe, 129; Caliente & Pioche, 36,37; Denver & Rio Grande Western, 107; Las Vegas & Tonopah, 102; Los Angeles & Salt Lake, 101; Los Angeles Terminal, 101; Oregon Short Line (OSL), 15,30,101,102,110; Pacific Electric, 129; Salt Lake & Ogden, 141; Salt Lake Route, 101,108; San Pedro, Los Angeles & Salt Lake (SPLA&SL), 2,5,30-32,34,101-125,129; Southern Pacific, 126; Tonopah & Tidewater (T&T), 129; Union Pacific (UP), 3,20,29,42,46,101,103,107,108,110, 112,156,157; Utah & California, 101
Railroad well (Carp), 51,59,60
Rainbow Canyon, 1,3,23,41,106,112,149
Rainbow Canyon Route, 15,66
Ramey, George, 128
Ranches: Acklin, 10; Averett, 70-77,**70-72,75**,85,95-97,**98,99;** Ballow, 11; Barnes, 29; Barnett, 16; Barnett-Farrier, 16; Barter, 11; Bar Z, 62,63; Black, 11,21,85; Bradshaw, 16,26,41,43,44,104; Caldwell, 17,104; Carden, 11,13,48; Carson, 11,12,22,26,27,104; Clark Reed, 12; Colburn, 12; Conaway, 7,8,104,136; Condiff, 18,96; Conk, 19,21,65,85,91; Crow, 16; Culverwell, 30-32,101; Dimmick, 19,62-64,98; Duffin, 7; Dula, 10,136,146; Elliott, 4,11,13,20,22,**21,**25, 26,38,44,67,68,75,78,91,128,129,147,149; Ferguson, 8; Hafen & Frei, 20,92; Hartey, 26; Henrie, 17,87; Hilburn, 19,70; Hulse, 19,152; Huntsman, 20; Huston, 19,65,66; Kiernan, 8,16,17, 26,49,71,83,102,104,131; Liston, 34; Lone Tree, 17,18; Lyman, 18,63,64,71; Mabey, 19,65,69,70,89; Mariger, 44; McGuffie

(McGuffey), 12,21,26,71,85; Montgomery, 65,68,70; Newman, 7; Pippin, 104,129; Red Rock, 11,26; Reese, 82; Ryan, 7,104; Schlarman, 16; Schmidt, 17,18; Sharp, 7; Swamp, 13; Tennille, 8-10,25,102,136; Walking X, 63; Yoacham, 29
Rapelje, 4,5,116,157
Rapelje, Sarah, 5
Rappelje, 5,15
Rappelje, Isaac, 5
Raven (*Corvus corax*), 82
Ray, Walter "Walt", 37; Zeb, 155
Reece, H.M., 43; Thomas, 87
Reed, Clark, 12; Eva, 12
Reese, Alfred, 87; Don, 87; Matt, 20,61,93; Mathew, 87
Reppelje, 15
Reyes, Mrs. Laura, 155
Rex Theatre, 33,39
Rice, Ashley, 152; Hyrum, 34; Marguerite, 86
Richard, A.J. "Andy", 147; John, 18
Riding, George K., 34
Riggs Spring, 139
Riggs Wash, 42,44,48,67
Road over the hill (over the summit), 15,67,68,97
Robber's Roost, 13-15,25
Roberts, Agnes R., 86; Charles H., 148; Leslie, 136
Rock fences, 106
Rock Springs Canyon, 1,11,103,139,140
Rock Springs station, 139,141
Roe, Mrs. Ada, 155
Roeden, Charles W., 145
Rose, L.L. "Pete", 65
Rowe, Lawrence A., 42,46; Mrs. Lawrence, 46; Mrs. W.F., 46
Rox, 1,3-5,15,20,43,44,51,107,125,129
Rucker, Alice, 156; Elbert, 153; Frank, 153-156; Loren, 156; Oscar, 153-156
Running extra, 108
Running light, 107
Russian thistle (*Salsola kali*), 77
Ryan, James "Jim", 7,27,62,145; Patrick "Pat", 145
Ryberg Brothers, 47

Sadovich, Pete, 155
Sagebrush (*Artemisia tridentata*), 24,25,78,79

Woods, Lyman, 18
Woodworth, Harley, 159
Wooten, H.H., 84
Workman, A.M., 94; Mrs. A.M., 94
Wright, Billy, 94,97; Dorolene, 93,94;
    Dorothy, 93,94; E.K. "Ernie",
    56,69,93,94; John, 154,155; Juanita, 97
Wyman, Walker D., 73

Yermo (Calif.), 106
Yoacham, Archie, 65

Zwinger, Ann, 78,79